To Wesley, Doris
Jim & Pat
With much appreciation
Best Wishes
Ted

Thanks for family
support to CAP!
Gymon

MW00896911

To Jim & Pat, a great
couple who became great
friends thru our CAP family.
God bless & keep you!
Dennis 1995-1999
2009 Dec 22

Jim & Pat
Superior Mentors
in so many areas
of my life.
Dave McClard

Enchanted Wings

The History of the
New Mexico Wing
Civil Air Patrol
1941-2010

Ted Spitzmiller
&
Gwen Sawyer

iUniverse, Inc.
New York Bloomington

Enchanted Wing
The History of the New Mexico Wing Civil Air Patrol

iUniverse books may be ordered through booksellers or by contacting:

iUniverse
1663 Liberty Drive
Bloomington, IN 47403
www.iuniverse.com
1-800-Authors (1-800-288-4677)

ISBN: 978-1-4401-8126-9 (sc)
ISBN: 978-1-4401-8127-6 (ebk)

Printed in the United States of America

iUniverse rev. date: 11/3/2009

Enchanted Wings

The History of the
New Mexico Wing
Civil Air Patrol
1941-2010

Ted Spitzmiller
&
Gwen Sawyer

Acknowledgement

I am grateful to Gwen Sawyer for her assistance in preparing this book. As the first female Spaatz cadet in the nation, Gwen brings historical insight that few others have.

I am also indebted to the NM Wing Historian James Norvell and his wife Pat and to those listed below who have directly contributed information in many forms. For some it was old photos and documents, while for others it was newspaper clippings. Still others scanned their logbooks and memories. The members themselves through their experiences tell much of this history. I am particularly appreciative of those who provided extensive narratives. Some of the photos reproduced here are of poor quality, but we are hopeful they will stir remembrances.

For those who contributed and are not acknowledged my apologies.

Frank Buethe
Dave Finley
Chuck and Corliss Grubert
Joe Gold
Larry Harrah
Richard & Roberta Himebrook
Kenneth Kietz
Bob Martin
Jim Morewood
Claude Luisada
Judy Licht
Robert & Jan McNicol
John Lorenz
Jerry Burton
Stan Roeske
Jon Daffer

Roland Dewing
Robert Gibson
Pat Patterson
Bill Chambers
Robert Haulenbeek
Pat & James Norvell
Charlene Reames
Dennis Manzanares
Allene & Ivar Lindstrom
Larry Zentner
Don Jakusz
Norm Reames
Pat Chochrell Balok
Beverly (Pepe) Vito
Carol (Sawyer) Roeske
Gordon Weimer

Anthony Torres
Ralph Meyerhein
Eugene McKim
Chuck Fairchild
Paul Ballmer
Harold Roberts
Andrew Selph
Richard Pryor
Jay Tourtel
Les Himebrook
Tony Sobol
Paul Kinzelman
Dwight Jennison
LuAnn Sallee
Paul Harbin
Kathy Courreges

To Jim — Thanks for such a great friendship — Roberta

To Jim, for years of friendship, may it continue Ric

Dedication

This book is dedicated to those who made the Civil Air Patrol a part of their family as exemplified by Ric, Roberta, and Leslie Himebrook and so many others

Table of Contents

Foreword

Enchanted Wings, the history of the New Mexico Wing of Civil Air Patrol is a valuable work, full of interesting facts and reminiscences of the past and present, a credit to the members of the wing. In this book, the reader will find recorded the achievements of men and women from all walks of life who have banded together and by their enterprise, industry, honesty and hard work have made significant accomplishments in all three areas of CAP—Emergency Services, Cadet Programs (youth leadership), and Aerospace Education.

In reading this book, the overwhelming emotion has been a sense of pride. Pride in a group of volunteers whose history centers on giving of themselves for the service of others and facing obstacles that require courage, determination, and persistence. The reviews of much of the work of our wing emphasize fostering local ties, supporting patriotism, helping humanity…just serving others. There are stories of stirring incidents and intense experiences, flavored with a strong human interest that will naturally provide to a large portion of the readers, its most attractive feature. It has been said, “We review the past, not in order that we may return to it, but that we may find in what direction, straight and clear, it points into the future.” This history shows our spirit of service to others and to our country is our key to the future. It is my hope that as this book is read, the reader will feel this spirit and carry it forward.

One definition for the author of a history book is “A historian is a prophet looking backwards.” Ted Spitzmiller, the lead author of this book is a perfect example of that. He is a published historian with scores of articles in major aviation magazines over the past 25 years and several books to his credit. However, more importantly for this work, he has lived the New Mexico Wing CAP History. He first joined the New Jersey Wing as a cadet in 1959 and, upon moving to New Mexico in 1973 joined the Los Alamos squadron. He is now an active pilot and aerospace instructor working with cadets and schoolteachers.

Indeed, as the author states, future generations will be able to benefit from the sense of perspective and their place in the organization as they catch the enchanted spirit of service from the past.

Richard F. Himebrook, Col
NM Wing Commander, Civil Air Patrol

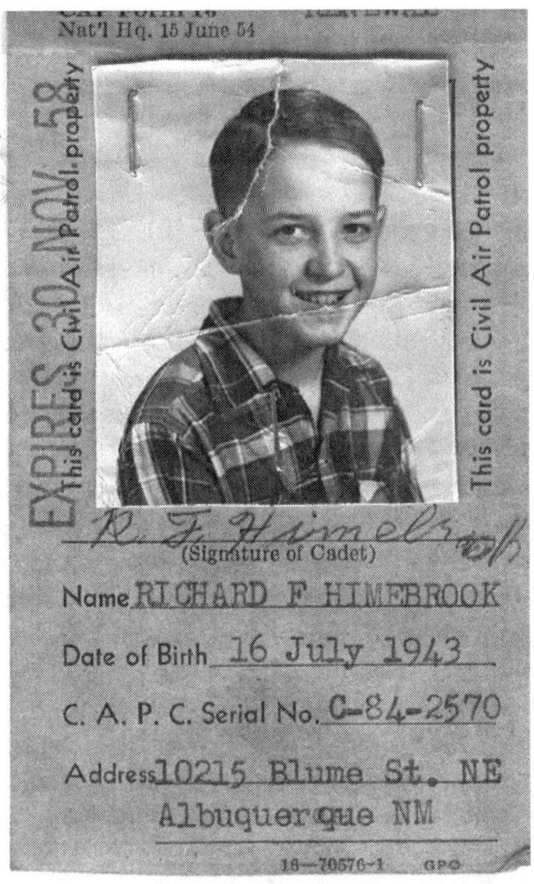

Nat'l Hq. 15 June 54

EXPIRES 30 NOV. 58

This card is Civil Air Patrol property

This card is Civil Air Patrol property

(Signature of Cadet)

Name RICHARD F HIMEBROOK

Date of Birth 16 July 1943

C. A. P. C. Serial No. C-84-2570

Address 10215 Blume St. NE
Albuquerque NM

16—70576-1 GPO

1 Ric Himebrook became a CAP cadet in New Mexico Wing on 27August 1957

1. Introduction

The history of the New Mexico Wing dates back to the origin of the Civil Air Patrol, almost 70 years ago from this writing. Over that period, thousands of men and women have devoted countless hours to the organization and its mission trilogy:

- providing emergency services—helping others in need,
- preparing our youth for the future, and
- educating America to the role of aerospace technology in our society.

It is unfortunate that a large amount of our history has not been recorded so that future generations can benefit from the sense of perspective and their contribution to the organization.

While his book attempts to capture as much of our history as possible it is not a comprehensive history. It relies heavily on past editions of Squadron and Wing newsletters, memos, and newspaper accounts and interviews with past and present CAP members. As such, some of the content is perhaps influenced by imperfect memory. However, we have endeavored to validate as much of the information as possible The book is presented as a series of chapters that highlight the various people, activities, events, and resources that have been melded together over the years. The rank noted for various members represents that which the person held at the time of the event.

Some information just did not seem to fit in a particular segment of the book. However, I did not want to lose anything that some readers might find of value. Therefore, you will see an occasional sub-chapter labeled 'Snapshot in Time' where this information is included.

While the emphasis has been to resurrect as much of the history from the ancient past as possible, we must also recognize that contemporary activities represent history for future generations of CAP members. Thus, with respect to the squadron history, where much has been lost, we have documented the recent activities and events that will be tomorrow's history. There are almost 600 past and present CAP members mentioned in the following pages and listed in the index.

As New Mexico is known as the Land of Enchantment... thus the title of this book.

2 A Curtiss Robin from the 1930s is the type that Douglas 'Wrong Way' Corrigan flew to Ireland from New York in 1938. Sydney Gottlieb is reported to have operated one for the CAP in New Mexico during the war years.

2. CAP Overview

The Civil Air Patrol (CAP) formed on December 1, 1941 just one week before the attack on Pearl Harbor. It was an effort to organize what we now call 'General Aviation' (GA)—small civilian aircraft, into a part of the civil defense initiative. At the time, CAP pilots who owned their own aircraft wanted to contribute to the security of the United States. They also wanted to make sure that they were not shut-out of flying should war come. The organization was structured similar to the Army Air Corp of the time. Each state was represented as a 'Wing,' with further subdivision into 'squadrons' based on geographical locations. The individuals were given military rank commensurate with their abilities and some received pay—$6 per day. (While CAP members today serve without pay, many of their employers provide paid leave for the time spent on search missions).

Almost immediately, with America's entry into World War II the following week, it became apparent that the military did not have enough aircraft to patrol out over the Atlantic coast where German submarines were taking a high toll of merchant shipping. Despite criticism of their 'civilian' status and lack of military training, experiments in Atlantic City, NJ and Rehoboth, Delaware in early 1942, soon proved that a valuable contribution could be made.

Just days into the trial period, two small CAP Fairchild F-24 high wing monoplanes flying off the coast of Cape May NJ were accompanying a group of ships northbound. The pilots spotted a submarine and the presence of these airplanes convinced the sub commander that he was being attacked—forcing him to break off his planned torpedo assault. These simple efforts allowed the tankers to make port safely in New York and proved the viability of the plan.

It was not long before the small planes were granted authority to carry bombs and in July of 1942 an unarmed CAP plane reported sighting a submarine 40 miles off the coast of New Jersey. A twin engine CAP Grumman Widgeon armed with two 325-pound depth charges heard the call over thc radio and went to the scene. Dropping both bombs in the area of the periscope wake, oil and debris were subsequently sighted—giving the crew credit for the destruction of the sub.

To the Coastal Patrol mission was added a Mexican Border Watch to guard against illegal entry into the US from the south. The Coastal Patrol ended in August of 1943 when the Navy finally had sufficient aircraft to provide for the mission. However, 26 CAP members lost their lives— not to enemy action, but simply the result of the demanding flying environment of poor weather, occasional pilot error, and aircraft maintenance issues. The wide-ranging activities of CAP during the period are well document in the book *Minutemen of the Air* by Carroll V. Glines and Gene Gurney. Another good history of the CAP is *Hero Next Door*, by Frank A. Burnham, 1974 (Aero Publishers).

3 Silvis Minoli (r) -- An early member of NM Wing and his Taylorcraft.

3. Origins of NM Wing

When its Coastal Patrol mission ended in 1943, CAP continued other activities, specifically addressing the need to provide for domestic search and rescue (SAR) within the boundaries of the continental US for aircraft that were 'overdue' on their flights. While the New Mexico Wing missed the Coastal Patrol action, it has played a major role in SAR activities since its inception.

Little is known of the origins of the New Mexico Wing except for what may be gleaned from personal archives and from the 'Clippings Book 1944-1945.' This scrapbook, kept at Wing headquarters, has newspaper items from as far back as 1942. The essence of many of these clipping have been included in various parts of this history. These news items tell us that membership in CAP was very popular in New Mexico during the war with most communities participating in the Cadet and Senior programs.

One article, tucked away for more than 65 years by the Earl Livingston family, dates from January 6, 1943. It notes, *"Two members of the New Mexico Civil Air Patrol have been called into service, Capt. Walter Biddle, in charge of the local CAP squadron, said yesterday. They are Howard Livingston and Henry Mares. Others will be sent into service as fast as they complete their training courses, Capt. Biddle said. Squadrons in Santa Fe, Albuquerque, and Roswell have been ordered into courier duty for the Army according to a dispatch of the Associated Press from Santa Fe."*

An accompanying article from a few months later shows 2Lt H.E. Livingston on the wing of an Ercoupe—a small airplane popular during that time. The caption reads, *"This is H.E. Livingston, second lieutenant in the Civil Air Patrol, stepping from his plane which carries mail and equipment between isolated Army bases in this area. Carrying the mail via air for Uncle Sam is Mr. Livingston's military job. In private life he is president of a supply company in Albuquerque.*" Howard Livingston would go on to become the Wing Commander in 1950 and his son Earl, would assume command from 1975 to 1979.

4 "2Lt H.E. Livingston, stepping from his plane which carries mail and equipment between isolated Army bases in this area" (January 1943).

Another article from a Santa Fe paper of February 4, 1945 provides the following:

> **Loretto Civil Air Patrol Squadron Given Uniforms**— Excitement among the members of the Loretto squadron of the Civil Air Patrol reached its zenith on January 23, when the girls received their uniforms and donned them for the first time. The girls are now looking forward to their actual admission into the patrol through their oath.
>
> At present, the squadron is studying Morse code under the direction of Lt. Showman. Many activities have been enjoyed by the group. 'Talkies' depicting the necessity of military discretion among all people, military and civilian alike have been a special feature.
>
> The highlight of all was the participation of the squadron in the joint meetings of the Civil Air Patrol units of the city preparatory to their review by Col. James Breese, which took place January 8."

5 Loretto Squadron February 1944
(L to R 1st row) Doris Briggs, Elaine Nelson, Lt. Showman, Pearl Miller, Betty Gianero (2nd row) Betty Ferran, Lucy Santistevan, Mildred Rivera, Lucia Cardena, Sheilagh Flynn (3rd row) Connie Jean Hendricks, Maria Mourer, Betty Jean Scofield, Mary Lucero

A picture accompanied the article that shows fourteen young ladies in uniform along with their names. In recognition of the contribution of women, and the transition into non-traditional roles, co-author Gwen Sawyer has prepared a segment of this book dedicated to that aspect of CAP.

We are indebted to those who had the foresight to save these news clippings to allow us, many years later—a glimpse into the past.

6 The Stinson L-5 served in NM Wing for many years.

With the growth of general aviation for travel following the war, central New Mexico was a funnel for air traffic from the east to California. The expansive mountains to the north of Santa Fe that continue into Colorado, and the large restricted airspace of White Sands Missile Range to the south, dictated that flow.

By the early 1960s, the old low frequency airways were giving way to the much more precise VOR navigation and the corridor through the center of New Mexico became the Victor-12 airway that stretched from Harrisburg, Pennsylvania to Santa Barbara, California—a Route 66 of the skies.

7 1948-50 Wing Commander Col. Kilbourne House, 2nd from Left, with Capt. Joe Bridges, USAF, Wing LO in center. The Sikorsky S-51 helicopter in the background was operated by the USAF.

However, central New Mexico is also filled with risks that many pilots coming from the low lands of the east are ill prepared for. The terrain gradually and deceptively rises from the almost sea level elevations of the Mississippi basin (800 miles to the east) to the 6,000 feet of the still flat prairie of eastern New Mexico. Here, the upslope topography makes weather conditions volatile during the winter months. Then, the sudden rise of the Sangre De Christo and Sandia mountains, presents the flat lander with an entirely new paradigm of flight with high density altitudes, mountain wave conditions with treacherous rotor clouds and downdrafts. Summer thunderstorms can appear rapidly, move quickly and block mountain passes. Night flying is likewise more arduous with few towns or highways to mark progress or provide for emergency landings. The horizon on a moonless night is non-existent.

8 Presidential Dinner May 1949, Howard Livingston (2nd fm rt), and Senator Clinton P. Anderson, (4th fm rt), Capt. Joe Bridges, USAF LO.

Likewise, the northern portion of the state is populated with a series of mountainous areas leading into southern Colorado. North-south traffic virtually demands the use of mountain passes because of the limited ceiling of many light aircraft.

With the rise in air travel in the 1950s and the proximity and environment of central New Mexico, it was a foregone conclusion that there would be many accidents. As radar was yet to be a major player in observing air traffic (and weather) and with the ELT still more than a decade into the future, a downed plane required a rapid response from the aviation community if any survivors were to make it back to civilization. Even summer nights in the mountains can present below freezing temperatures and survivors, who may be experiencing shock, may not make it through but a few days.

Compared to the rest of the nation, New Mexico had few pilots in the early years—an October 17, 1945 newspaper article reported there were 542 licensed pilots in New Mexico and 70 airfields. The 2009 FAA database lists New Mexico as having 3928 pilots and 170 airports of which 61 are public use.

9 Col. Howard Livingston (3rd fm rt), at the Wing Commanders annual Conference May 25, 1950, Washington, D.C. Senator Clinton P. Anderson to his right and Capt Joe Bridges. Note the spelling of New Mexiko on the table placard.

4. NM Wing Flight Operations

The Search and Rescue Scenario

The difficulty in locating an aircraft in rugged terrain cannot be over emphasized. As has been repeatedly demonstrated over the years (and most recently with the Steve Fossett search), the wreckage of small aircraft can easily be missed even by the most trained observer. This is especially true if the aircraft no longer resembles its former shape. Foliage, snow cover and even the angle of the sun all work to obscure telltale evidence of its presence.

The increased use of small light aircraft (General Aviation—GA) for transport and recreation following World War II, coupled with enhanced range, speed and weight carrying ability, have made GA an important link in America's transportation system. With this capability came the inevitable errors of judgment and occasional mechanical failures that put flyers down in the most inaccessible places. The 1950s and 60s presented CAP with a significant challenge to respond rapidly and to coordinate search activities.

By the early 1970s, the FAA required all civil aircraft registered in the United States to carry an Emergency Locator Transmitter (ELT). These small devices (weighing about 4 pounds) are fastened to the aircraft and provide a radio tone on the emergency frequency of 121.5 should the unit (and the aircraft in which it is mounted) experience a high G force—as in the impact of a crash. This 'radio beacon' can then be detected and homed on (using Direction Finding equipment—DF) to quickly locate the downed plane. Aircraft are encouraged to regularly tune and monitor the frequency although beginning in 1982, a system of earth satellites became available to help perform that task.

While the ELT idea was sound, 97% of all activations are false signals. Most of these are easily detected as they occur as the result of a 'hard' landing or inadvertent manual activation. Pilots are encouraged to monitor 121.5 before engine shutdown following each flight to verify that they are not transmitting the signal. In one situation, a young man broke into a CAP facility and stole an ELT. He apparently did not know what it was, but it looked like it might be worth something. On the way home, he accidentally dropped it. A SAR mission was started when an over-flying aircraft picked up the signal. It did not take but a few hours before a CAP plane was circling his house and a State Trooper was knocking on the door.

Assuming that an ELT was not activated for some reason, two types of searches are typically flown for 'over-due' aircraft. First is the "route search" for the obvious reason. If the plane was on its intended route when a problem occurred, then it is probable that flying that route will result in finding the aircraft. However, until VOR navigation became prevalent in the 1970s, the accuracy of the low-frequency navigation systems then in use, were such that being within a few miles of your intended course was considered good navigation over long distances. The same is true for ded-reckoning techniques. The second type of search is the 'grid' in which a CAP plane is assigned a 10 X 10 mile square to search in one of numerous grids that overlie the probable area in which the plane went down. A third type used in rugged terrain is the contour search.

Pilots who fly long cross-country trips of several hundred miles or more are putting themselves at risk if they do not file a flight plan and make regular position reports to FAA facilities so that searchers can narrow the scope of their efforts should the plane fail to arrive at its intended destination. Experience has shown that if there are survivors, the first 24 hours are critical to finding them alive.

The Civil Air Patrol's role in Emergency Services (that include search and rescue as well as disaster relief and homeland security) requires that it not only maintain the appropriate assets, but that there is a cadre of people who are trained and skilled to execute the various roles to accomplish those services. As CAP's membership is voluntary, and the majority of its senior members are gainfully employed in the working world, this can present a considerable challenge.

Allene Lindstrom of Los Alamos was a CAP member for over 30 years. A Flight Instructor, she has held most of the positions at the squadron level and several at wing.

Allene's early recollections of Search and Rescue operations are that *"they would commence with the first storm of the season, usually around Labor Day, when we could expect to search for an aircraft on an East-West route. As winter arrived, another main trap was Palo Flechado Canyon near Taos for skiers coming in from the East. Over the years the number of aircraft searches diminished, probably due to better weather reporting."*

"We trained to stay in our assigned grids, fly the pattern and not stray. The MC [Mission Commander] *needed to insure the safety of the mission and therefore keep only one search plane in a specific grid at a time. Pilots were charged 'airtime' to fly missions when I first joined CAP. It was $5.00 per hour with the cost divided by all on board. Fuel may have been provided by Wing."*

"Ground teams were Cadets with Seniors assigned for ground interrogation and possible security of wreckage. Over time, more organizations participated in Search and Rescue. Many hours were flown as 'High Bird' for air/ground and air/air communication. Local cadets worked the CAP radio frequencies and provided critical communications—in many cases with the assistance of Ham Radio operators, in particular, W5PDO in Los Alamo.".

As a mission pilot/observer she remembers, *"I became intimately acquainted with many parts of New Mexico. This included the Malpais around Grants* [a Spanish word for 'Badlands'— the ancient lava flow that produced extremely rough terrain]. *I flew many of these missions with Tom Cordell or John Sutton in a Cessna 150. In the days before LORAN or GPS it was vital that the Mission Pilot know the prominent areas as we often flew too low to be able to receive any VOR positional information. The mountainous areas of Northern New Mexico from Farmington to Dulce to Taos were challenging locals."*

http://www.caphistory.org/images/ConductingSearchGraphics.jpg

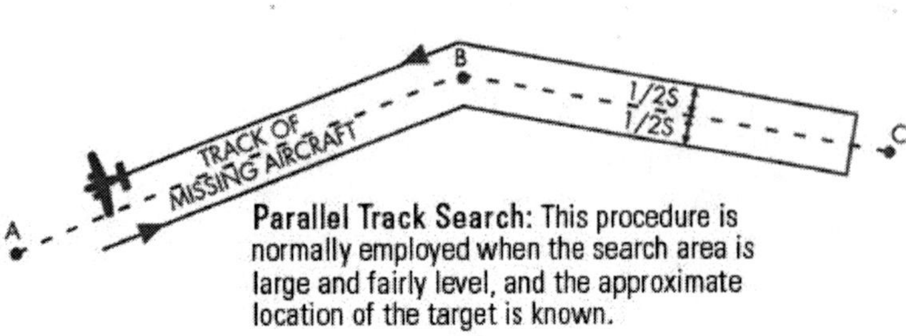

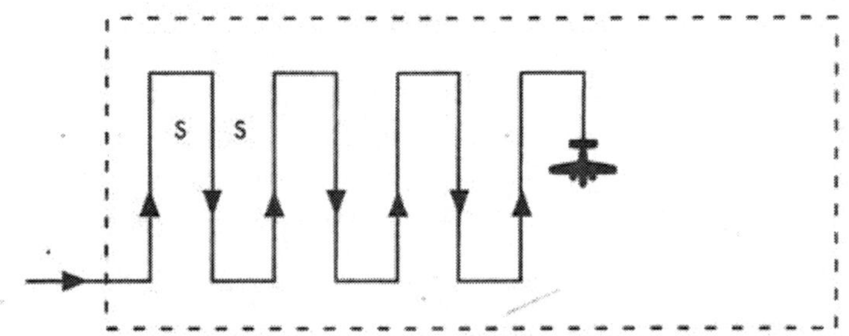

Creeping Line Search: This procedure is normally employed when the search area is narrow, long, and fairly level.

Contour Search: Extremely dangerous and the crew must be experienced, well-briefed, and (before takeoff) have studied large scale maps indicating terrain elevations and contour.

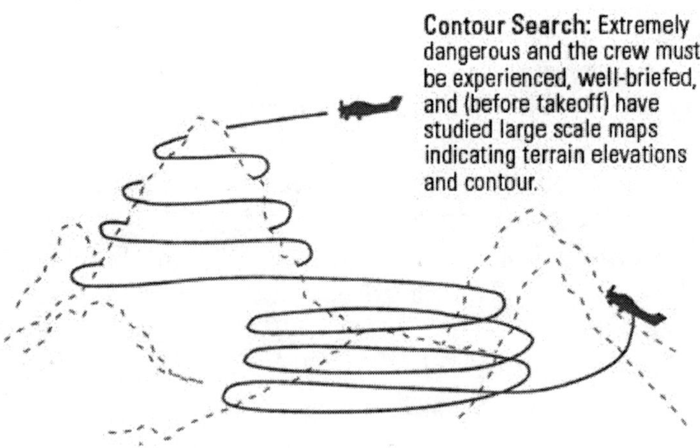

10 Common search patterns

Not only must the aircrews be certified and current to FAA and CAP standards, but they must be prepared and organized to operate the assets—aircraft, communications equipment and specialized detection gear. To accomplish this, each CAP wing provides its members with a wide variety of training programs that covers the entire spectrum of emergency services. This training culminates in periodic real-life scenarios that afford the members the requisite experience—these practice sessions are called Search And Rescue EXercises (SAREX).

It is interesting to see how the newspapers of the era reported CAP events such as this SAREX from May 1958.

> **Sandians, Youngsters Participate in Civil Air Patrol Rescue Test—** Several Sandian's and many Sandia youngsters are sporting sunburns acquired on the annual Civil Air Patrol Simulator Air Rescue mission held at Truth or Consequences, NM, last week. The target for the training mission was a simulated wrecked airplane with survivors planted in the area in the early morning hours to wait 'rescue.' The CAP units on hand for the exercise included 24 aircraft, 99 adults, and 182 cadets.
>
> After the 'wreckage' was sighted, Mel Pliner (1222) was among those dispatched to the area with a ground to rescue party. He covered the accident for the CAP Public Information Office.
>
> A communications network was set up and Virginia Simms (2232) operated the message center at T or C. E.H. Morterud (5523) established radio facilities at CAA offices at the Airport to file flight plans for the CAP pilots in the 'search'. Robert Higley (2111) stayed behind in Albuquerque to act as a relay station if one was needed.
>
> The communications department of the New Mexico Wing is under the direction of J. L. "Whitey" T. Hollenbeck (1614). The Air Rescue Section for the state is under the direction of William T. Ward (5211) and it is his responsibility to organize a search for any aircraft reported overdue.
>
> Others taking part in the SARCAP included Roma Coats (5512) and Howard F. Burgess (1652).

SAREX missions are planned to be as close to actual situations as possible and often involve the complete spectrum of positions that must be manned to accomplish the task. One such exercise held in Santa Fe in September of 1989 involved 120 senior members and 36 cadets. Thirty pilots flew 22 aircraft in missions that practiced locating ELTs placed at old aircraft crash sites. This particular SAREX involved members of seven squadrons.

When a Real Emergency Deployment of Civil Air Patrol assets is required, the mission is referred to as a REDCAP although in more recent times the mission is called a SARCAP. While the author was unable to locate information relative to the number of REDCAPS over the years, one report indicated that CAP conducted 134 REDCAPS across the nation in 1953.

In 1992, NM Wing had 16 REDCAPS that resulted in eight SAVES and three FINDS. Five of those saves came from one mission in which an aircraft went down in bad weather just a few miles from Taos. A SAVE is where the mission results in a life saving situation, whereas a FIND means the objective was located. There were also two SAREX training missions during 1992.

In 1993 NM Wing was ranked Number One for its SAR capabilities in the Southwest Region which includes five other wings—Arizona, Texas, Oklahoma, Arkansas and Louisiana.

Notable SAR Missions

Perhaps one of the most notable search efforts was for the renowned Dr. Randall Lovelace, founder of the Lovelace Clinic in Albuquerque. Lovelace, a former NM Wing Commander, was lost on a Flight from Aspen, Colorado to Albuquerque with his wife Mary and Cutter Flying Service pilot Milton Brown in December 1965. The twin Beech Travelair (N9975R) was not reported missing until the following day, as the pilot had not filed a flight plan. The 282-mile flight path was the focus of the search but bad weather had moved into the area. The effort involved more than 30 aircraft of which a dozen were CAP planes from both states.

The wreckage was spotted on the 11,000-foot level of Independence Pass a few miles east of Aspen by a helicopter who reported the Lovelace plane had *"hit hard against the mountainside."* Apparently, the pilot had survived the crash and had placed Lovelace and his wife together under a blanket before he too succumbed to his injuries and the weather. A rescuer conjectured that *"It appeared the plane got too low in the canyon and tried to make a quick turn to get out and lost altitude. It looks like the wing caught in the snow and cart wheeled, broke in half and all the occupants were thrown out in their seats."*

***

A search and rescue operation is never an easy part of the CAP mission. For the friends and relatives of those who are lost, it is an agonizing period. For those who are searching, it can be an emotional rollercoaster. The early stages are filled with anticipation and hope that the downed plane will be found and those aboard will be rescued. If the plane is not found in the first few days, frustration begins to build as the searchers may feel they have missed some tell tale evidence that could have led to the crash site. Not finding the plane at all is despairing.

Such was the case with a Cessna 172 N2587Y that was lost on a flight from Page, Arizona to Addison Texas in April of 1995. Four people who had gone to Lake Powell on a fishing trip had started their return flight but never arrived home. It was uncharacteristic of the 2000 hour Private Pilot not to have filed a flight plan, but it was expected that he would probably have refueled in Santa Fe, and Plainview Texas. While this route would normally have brought in the CAP resources of three states (AZ, NM, TX), it was also considered that the pilot may have elected to do some sightseeing in the south of Utah (Monument Valley) and Colorado on the return flight. Thus, Utah and Colorado Wings were also involved.

After 12 days of intensive efforts, more than 800 volunteers had flown 398 sorties totaling 1075 hours. The Incident Command had initially been set up in Farmington under the direction of LtCol Ruth Roberts of the Farmington Squadron with Capt. Sharon Lane as the Public Affairs Officer.

Although VFR conditions prevailed for most of the search period, the spring winds of the southwest often kept the search aircraft higher than they otherwise might have flown.

After the search was suspended following 12 days of fruitless effort, the husband of one of the passengers was quoted as saying, *"It was a major effort to keep them looking that long... I feel defeated... we can put a man on the moon but we can't find a plane that crashed in our own country."* He echoed the frustration of the search team.

Because the plane's occupants were well known and respected in their community, there was even *"congressional pressure to prolong the search,"* acknowledged CAP Capt. Nena Wiley, Arizona Wing PAO. *"We exhausted every viable lead."*

As is often the case when a plane is not found by the initial search, someone who happens to be in the area for another reason eventually discovers it. Thus, it was four months later, on August 19, 1995 that a Navaho Sheepherder came across the wreckage at the 9000-foot level in rugged forested terrain. It was resting nose down and virtually hidden from the air by the trees. Apparently, no one had survived the crash.

An investigation by the NTSB revealed that there apparently had been no malfunction of the plane. The 'Probable Cause' listed was

11 During the Search for N2787Y in April 1995, Michael Daly reviews his search effort with Art Olson.

"the pilot's failure to maintain terrain clearance." Contributing was the "*pilot's lack of mountain flying experience and the rising terrain.*" The NTSB is noted for its ability to state the obvious. That the pilot was flying over-gross and did not have a current medical nor biennial flight review are additional factors to consider.

Sharon Lane recalls, *"Once the plane was found, the Farmington Composite Squadron was asked to send a plane out to photograph the crash site to determine how visible the wreckage was from the air. Although having the exact coordinates, the pilot had to circle the area several times before they were able to spot even a small piece of the wreckage."* It is ironic that the crash site was within four miles of a direct course between Page and Santa Fe.

***

Sometimes the searcher becomes a casualty. A low-level accident occurred May 9, 1965 that involved a T-34 (N423NM). It was being operated with only the pilot, M.L. Perry, the Wing Operations Officer aboard. During a search for a lost child along the Rio Grande near Los Lunas, the plane hit a cable suspended across the river, killing the pilot and destroying the aircraft.

***

On rare occasions, a search can be initiated and completed with just one flight. In November 1973, two hunters were reported missing in the Bear Creek canyon area of the Pecos Wilderness, east of Santa Fe. With nighttime temperatures below freezing and knowledge that these 'Day' hunters were without food or overnight provisions made the search critical. A mission was authorized and the first responders were pilot Tom Adams and Observer Al Manthei from the Los Alamos Squadron flying the C150 N5870E. Just four hours into the mission and one hour and 20 minutes after departure, the hunters were spotted.

***

The power of a thunderstorm was evident in the crash of a Cessna 170 enroute from Las Cruces to Los Alamos in August of 1974. The plane was reported missing when the husband and wife failed to arrive on what had been a routine night flight for them on numerous occasions. The experienced IFR rated pilot reported to the T or C Flight Service at 8:30 PM that he was deviating for thunderstorms but that was the last communication with the plane. Fifteen CAP and State Police planes were mobilized early the next morning and the remains of the remains of the aircraft were found after a short search at 3:45 PM that afternoon just 20 miles south of Belen.

***

Mission 43-005 in February 1974 was a search for N4980T, a PA-34 Seneca overdue on a flight from Texas to Taos with only the pilot aboard. He had reported to the Santa Fe tower that he was pressing on to Taos (50 miles to the north) despite encountering a significant snowstorm. The search began the next day and continued for several days thereafter. It was concentrated in the Espanola Valley with the following aircraft participating.

12 Some Crash sites are well hidden by dense forest.

Participating Aircraft Mission 43-005 February 1974			
N5265F	T-41	N3817Y	C-210
N5870E	C-150 (Los Alamos)	N3479R	C-182 (Taos)
N2913F	C-182	N9561S	7KCAB
N422NM	T-34A (SQ II)	N6122W	PA-28
N5949M	C-421B	N2676Q	C-182

Snow cover obscured efforts to locate the plane and it was not until the plane's owner flew in to Taos several days later that he spotted the plane, virtually intact just short of the threshold of runway 4. Prior to that morning, the snow had covered the aircraft and it was essentially invisible. The fact that it was so close to the airport may have also been a contributing factor to its not being noticed. The pilot had died when the seat had come lose and he hit his head on the instrument panel

***

Night searches are rare, but on one occasion, the ability of the aircraft and the downed survivors to communicate with lights made the effort worthwhile. On March 2, 1974, a pilot, his wife, and 15-year-old daughter departed Mound Ridge Kansas, for a VFR flight to Santa Fe. The pilot last reported to Las Vegas Flight Service but failed to arrive in Santa Fe that afternoon. With activation of an ELT, a search was started with the launch of a CAP T-34 and C206.

The pilot had attempted to cross the Sangre De Christo Mountains to observe the beauty of the snow covered terrain rather than divert around to the lower elevations to the south. The winds aloft at 12,000 feet were reported to be 40 knots and the inability of the Cessna C177 Cardinal (N30046) to climb out of a mountain wave forced the aircraft into the 11,500-foot summit. Fortunately, there were no significant injuries and the three donned their ski clothing for warmth, built a fire, and waited for rescue in 4-foot deep snow.

The T-34 (N422NM) arrived in the vicinity shortly before midnight and proceeded to perform a DF on the ELT signal. The dramatic find was relayed real-time by air-ground communications and telephone, as the pilot of the T-34, Harold Roberts, fighting the high winds and turbulence, reported that he and observer Ron 'Jake' Jacobson were able to locate the position of the ELT and were circling what appeared to be a campfire. The survivors used a flashlight to signal and Roberts used his landing light to acknowledge that they had indeed sighted them. Roberts noted some 35 years later, *"This was the most severe turbulence that I ever flew into deliberately. Jake and I both made frequent contact on the canopy with our heads, and were truly exhausted by the time we returned home."*

Roberts recalls some of the details a bit differently from other reports, *"I do not remember that there was a fire at the crash site. I do remember that as we circled the area a single flare was fired. Jake spotted the flare. I never saw it. We did flash our landing lights several times, but to my recollection, we saw no further signals from the ground. With the fairly recently installed DME, we took several bearings and reported the results. We then flew to Santa Fe and spent the night in the pilots lounge. The following morning we departed Santa Fe to return to the crash site in order to help guide rescuers. The ELT was no longer operating. If we had not located the crash site the previous night, finding survivors might have been very difficult."*

The next morning with the winds at 12,000 feet reported at 50 knots, a rescue party from the St. John's Search and Rescue as well as CAP personnel, began working their way towards the site from the nearest snow packed dirt road more than 5 miles distant. However, a military helicopter from Ft. Carson, Colorado arrived and made a daring landing just ½ mile from the crash site. However, the deep snow made travel for the crew difficult and it took them over an hour to reach the survivors. Had the survivors not had a relatively 'soft' crash in the deep snow, or if they had not had warm clothing and the ability to make a campfire, or if the CAP crew had not been able to fly a night ELT search, the outcome might have been tragically different.

***

In March of 1974, an Aero Commander twin left Albuquerque for Las Vegas, Nevada on a VFR flight plan with six persons aboard but apparently failed to arrive at their destination. With 5 hours of fuel, the possible search area was considerable. The CAP response to Mission 43-014 was immediate and significant, as more than 50 persons and a dozen aircraft were mobilized. A report that another pilot had heard what he believed may have been the missing aircraft asking Flight Service for a weather update and that the pilot appeared 'confused' added to the heightened awareness that the plane had encountered significant problems.

As the search was still in its early stages, a re-check of the ramp at Albuquerque 'found' the airplane. The pilot decided the weather was too bad to continue and he returned—but forgot to close his flight plan. Of course, a more thorough ramp search might have prevented the false alarm—if the thoughtful FBO had not placed the plane in the hanger to keep it warm.

***

13 T-34 over the Rio Grande Valley just north of Albuquerque looking towards the Jemez Mountains

***

The wording on a citation presented to John Brolley and Chuck Fairchild of the Los Alamos Squadron tells the next story:

> AFRCC MISSION NUMBER 6—084, 11 February, 1975
> On 9 February 1975 a Piper Cherokee 140 crashed somewhere in the large bowl of Cimarron Canyon between Cimarron and Eagle Nest, New Mexico. Two men and their wives from Oklahoma City had planned a skiing vacation at Angel Fire, New Mexico, just 10 miles south of Eagle Nest. As a result of the crash, the ELT was activated and localized to the Cimarron Canyon area by high flying aircraft. However, search by low flying CAP aircraft was not possible for two days because of high winds and blowing snow. Drifts were up to 20 feet deep to the search area. The bowl is ringed by high ridges of 12,000 to 12,500 feet on the north rim and by high ridges of about 11,500 feet on the south rim. Minor peaks are inside the bowl and the highway runs roughly east west at the bottom of the bowl at about 9,509 feet elevation. Many ground teams (some 80 to 100 people in all) operated along the highway with hand—held ELT direction finding equipment. They concentrated their search on the north side of the highway and along the lower ports of the north rim. They

were misled because of the multiple reflections of the ELT signal by the snow-covered mountains of the bowl.

On the second day, 11 February, the winds subsided enough to allow search aircraft inside the bowl of Cimarron Canyon. CPT John Brolley and 2LT Charles Fairchild of the Los Alamos, Composite Squadron flew the Squadron's Cessna 172 on the second sortie of the day for more than two hours in the afternoon in the rough turbulence of the bowl. The ELT direction finding equipment in the aircraft proved to be useless because of the multiple reflections of the signal. Finally, they resorted to signal strength estimates which led them to concentrate their search near the south rim of the bowl. Near the south rim plateau to the south of a minor peak within the bow, Fairchild saw something red in the snow. Circling many times, they could pick out the outline of the aircraft, which was partly covered with snow.

They directed an Army helicopter that had come down from Fort Carson, CO to the scene. A paramedic repelled down from the hovering helicopter to the crash site. He found the two women alive but both-were suffering from hypothermia and frost bite. Their two husbands had perished, one from hypothermia and the other from injuries received in the crash. Subsequently, The St. Johns College Rescue Ground team was directed to the scene and accomplished the evacuation of the victims the following day. Meanwhile the ELT quit in the early evening.

The persistence of Brolley and Fairchild in their visual and electronic search in extremely difficult terrain and flying conditions lead to their find and the subsequent saving of the lives of the two women.

***

The search mission itself can be hazardous in that it must be flown low enough for the observers to have a reasonable chance of locating wreckage, yet high enough to avoid unnecessary risks. In March 1977, a C-172 with four men aboard was reported missing on a flight from Pueblo, Colorado to Tucson, Arizona. The search centered on an area just west of Las Vegas, New Mexico at the southern end of the Sangre De Christo Mountains.

Chuck Fairchild took part in many SAR activities over the 25 years he was a CAP member. He recalls the search: *"Four postal employees started from Denver to ABQ for a weekend of golf, leaving after work on a Fri evening in a Cessna 182 'Skylane'.*

Unfortunately, an upper level storm was moving into the Rockies from the southwest at the same time. As they proceeded south along the east slope of the Rockies, they encountered increasing winds, turbulence, and some clouds, particularly as they approached Las Vegas. Their last contact was with Las Vegas Flight Service as they were some 20 miles north, so it was surmised that they continued on their flight plan route to ABQ.

A search started the next morning but the planes were hampered by the storm and didn't accomplish much. HQ was set up in Las Vegas by mission coordinator, Major Jules Gandelman, of Los Alamos. Two days passed with extensive search of the flatland north of and around Las Vegas and some search of the mountains SW of there. From Las Vegas, the plane's planned course was southwest across the southern tip of the Sangre de Christo Mountains where the airway had a minimum crossing altitude of 13,000 ft—fairly high for a Skylane. After thoroughly searching the flats, the mountains became the primary search area.

Since the CAP planes were already at Las Vegas, I flew over with Allene Lindstrom in her plane. All aircraft were already crewed when we arrived, so I sat around most of the morning listening to reports, and studying charts. That afternoon I was assigned to be "High Bird" (radio relay) in the C150. It took a while to climb to a comfortable altitude to head into the mountainous terrain, but I was stationed at about 11,000 ft over the southern tip of the Sangres where I could talk to both ground HQ and search planes. The planes were returning to the search from refueling and re-crewing so there wasn't much for me to do for awhile. Soon everyone was reporting in and getting back to the tedious task of searching.

In a short time came an urgent call, '541 going in—Mitre canyon'. I wasn't sure I had heard right so I called, '541 are you in trouble?' There was something in reply like 'going down', but not very clear because it was cut off by another plane calling me to report his position 'on station'.

Bob Haulenbeek was flying PA-28-180 N5122G during the SAR operation when he encountered unexpected winds over a ridgeline. The plane rapidly lost altitude and Haulenbeek (a future NM Wing commander) found himself inadvertently flying up a box canyon. With the terrain rapidly rising in front of him and no room to turn around, Haulenbeek had made a quick 'Mayday' transmission to the 'High Bird' that Fairchild was flying, indicating that he was going to have to put the plane into the trees.

Fairchild continues; *"I immediately broadcast, 'all aircraft stay off the air, we may have an emergency in progress'. After 30 seconds of silence, I called, '541, 541 report your situation'--no answer. After calling again, with no response, I reported to ground that we might have a plane down. For the next 30 minutes, there was much radio activity to try to account for where 541 was, and whether he was down. A plane was sent into the area that 541 was to search, and before long reported that he had spotted the plane down in a canyon, torn up some and mostly hidden by tall trees, but with one person outside the plane waving.*

The next 3 hours were devoted to getting a National Guard helicopter and rescue team into a clearing about a half mile from the downed plane, guiding the ground team there, and rescuing the two crew. My job, in addition to continuing to relay messages to and from the other search planes maintaining the search for the postal workers' plane, was to relay the messages back and forth between helicopter, state police, and CAP ground mission coordinator. It was a busy 3 hours, but the two CAP crew were out and into the SAF hospital before sunset.

One of the crew of the downed CAP Piper, a major from Farmington, had serious injuries and he required a long period of healing after some surgery. The next time I saw him at an exercise in ABQ he thanked me profusely for my part in the rescue. He confirmed what I had heard, that they had been caught in a downdraft above the canyon, due to the wind blowing over the ridges, and since they were headed up canyon they couldn't do anything except put it into the trees."

Haulenbeek, recently recalled the incident with clarity. *"I never knew that there were pines that tall in these mountains."* Once he recognized that he had been trapped in the canyon, he proceeded to 'fly' the plane into the treetops, unfortunately catching the left wing first. *"That spun us around 180 degrees so fast that my left arm and the yoke contacted my side with such force that I broke five ribs. My head came forward (these are the days before shoulder harnesses) and my head hit the right horn of the yoke—giving me a long, but not serious, gash.* The observer, Mark Sanchez suffered from a few cracked vertebras.

They were quickly located and medi-vaced by an Air Guard helicopter to Santa Fe. The lost aircraft was found within a mile of Haulenbeek's crash site by woodcutters almost a year later—there had been no survivors.

***

Chuck Grubert, a veteran of more than 35 years of CAP service, has vivid memories of many events and missions. His recall of the search involving a doctor in an A36 Bonanza going to Angel Fire for Skiing in February 1980 is particularly revealing. *"The pilot took off from Dallas at sunset headed for the mountains at night with bad weather approaching his destination. Apparently, he iced up. No ELT [signal]; probably destroyed in the crash. The search was shut down after about eleven days—just too much snow in the mountains. We wanted to find him when the snow left the high country but you can't reopen an Air Force mission. So, we had decided to schedule our first SAREX to resume the search. That didn't happen until August. Corliss and I drove up to Taos in our yellow camper so we had a place to live in."* Corliss, Grubert's wife, and longtime Wing Secretary (28 years) and now the CAP Wing Administrator, was the Mission Coordinator.

"I was running the flight line on this one particular day when one of the cadets came running out to me to say that Major Jennison was returning [from a search sortie] *and he (Jennison) wanted me to be*

ready to go as soon as he got back. As he taxied in I had my helmet, (this was a 'nice-to-have' item when you flew in the T-34; especially in bumpy weather) and immediately got up on the wing. The observer appeared from the back seat with two bags of vomit and an interesting shade of green on his face. I knew then why Dwight had returned so abruptly but I didn't yet know why he was so insistent on me being ready to fly."

"As I was getting buckled in, he had the engine turning already and we were airborne almost before I could get my helmet plugged in. As I came up on the intercom (the only way you could communicate in the T-34), he said 'I found it' and in the next breath, 'I lost it'.

Dwight had taken the last known radar position and used the 'expanding square technique' to search that area. When, due to terrain, that became unworkable, he began a contour search. (This area had been covered at least twice before in the original search the preceding winter.) He had been doing a contour search in the high terrain and fighting moderate turbulence when the previous observer became airsick. Since Dwight and Chuck had flown many times on past missions, he knew that Grubert was someone who could hang-in on the tight maneuvers without losing his lunch even in the turbulence they faced.

"Now Dwight Jennison was always a calm, cool, collected person... the epitome of the professional search pilot. But this time," Chuck recalls, *"Dwight was really animated. He had tried searching several fingers of land but because of the terrain, he couldn't use the spiral pattern to look into the trees. He had made multiple passes down a canyon going a bit lower each time. The T-34A with its 285 hp engine had the power to do that type of demanding search. Dwight said that as he was making one pass he saw something, but just then, the observer got very sick. He had tried to mark his spot in his mind but he was unsure so we would have to make a guess at where he was at the time."*

As we came down this one canyon, I was looking off the wing through the trees. I saw a flash of 'something else' go by. I told

Dwight 'I have the aircraft and took the controls in the back seat.' Dwight put his hands up [acknowledging transfer of the controls] saying 'what do you see'. I could not describe what I saw or even exactly where I had seen it, but I knew it was an airplane component. Bringing the airplane around tightly to that spot, I looked down and there was the top engine cowling of a Bonanza. After a couple more passes, we finally saw the rest of the wreckage. It had apparently rolled down the mountainside and was wedged up against the bottom of two pine trees. It looked similar to a cigar it was rolled up so perfectly.

A news article of the day provides the grim end of this story:

> Plane Missing Six Months Found in New Mexico's Taos Mountains—Rescue crews were making a four-hour journey on foot into sacred Indian land today to recover the bodies of a Texas family apparently killed in a small plane crash in February. Col. Lloyd Sallee of the New Mexico Civil Air Patrol confirmed that the single engine Beechcraft piloted by Dr. Richard Russell of Mesquite, Texas was spotted during a regular CAP training exercise late Saturday.
>
> About 25-30 searchers from Northern new Mexico rescue groups were making the trek today into the mountains of Taos Pueblo. "It's real rugged country," said Ray Piper of the Taos rescue unit. "There's nothing up there but sacred ground and three Indians have lead us in because they won't let us off the trails."
>
> The plane,—with Russell, his wife Bertha, and their children Brian, 13, Chris, 7, and Gina, a student at SMU—disappeared Feb. 21.

It was during the original REDCAP search for the Bonanza, that a CAP T-34 (N421NM) was lost near Taos on February 25, 1980. The pilot, who was also an active duty Air Force Major, apparently lost his depth perception as he was flying in the vicinity of Pecos Baldy—one of several mountains that reach well beyond 12,000 feet MSL. These higher peaks can be deceptive because, being above the tree line they present no objects that allow the pilot to determine accurately the distance to the surface. The pilot apparently misjudged his terrain clearance and was unable to power himself out of the situation. The T-34 hit hard and both the pilot and his observer were severely injured but were rapidly recovered.

The remains of the airplane were purchased by a third party who tried to use a helicopter to retrieve it several months later. However, during the airlift the downwash of the rotor set the suspended aircraft spinning and it had to be cut lose. Amazingly enough, the battered remains were eventually recovered and the plane was rebuilt.

***

A late winter storm in March of 1981 trapped two hikers on Santa Fe Baldy. SAR pilot Terry Bass and Observer Don Smith launched in T-34 N422NM as soon as the weather had cleared to permit an aerial search of the area. The sound of the low flying plane roused one of the hikers who was suffering from exhaustion and exposure, the other had already succumbed to hypothermia. The survivor began to walk and Bass and Smith were actually able to spot his tracks in the deep snow thanks to the T-34's ability to handle the high altitude and turbulent wind conditions. A helicopter was called to the scene and the hiker was saved.

14 In some instances, the wreckage still resembles the aircraft—well, parts of it.

***

Just six months later, a Navy OV-10 Bronco was reported missing on a flight from White Sands Missile Range to Albuquerque. Squadron II launched the T-34 at 1730 hours and by 1910, Capt. Dwight Jennison and 1st Lt. Chuck Grubert were over Elephant Butte reservoir picking up the very weak signal of a military ELT. As darkness started to settle, the crew determined that the most likely origin of the signal was 13.5 miles from the Truth Or Consequences VOR on the 020 radial. A helicopter arrived from Albuquerque and found the crash site using floodlights just 500 feet from the provided reference point. Unfortunately, the pilot did not survive the crash

***

Then there is the occasional serendipitous find. Four men in a Cessna 172 had departed Santa Fe in May of 1982 enroute to Durango when they crashed not far from the departure airport apparently the victims of density altitude. LtCol Bill Overton was on his way from Los Alamos to Santa Fe to participate in a SAREX later that day when he saw the remains of the aircraft. Unfortunately all four of the occupants were fatally injured.

***

During the last week of March in 1982, 52 CAP members took part in a search for a twin-engine Beech Baron carrying six Utah residents. The aircraft was sighted near the 10,000-foot level of Mount Whittington, 27 miles southwest of Magdalene. There were no survivors. The pilot had flown into known icing with an aircraft that was 392 pounds over-gross when he departed.

***

Of course, CAP pilots are always ready to lend a helping hand whenever the occasion arises. In 1982, Capt. Dwight Jennison and SM Tom Mueller had just landed at Albuquerque International in a T-34 when the tower asked if they might assist another aircraft that was having landing gear problems. The other plane, a Piper Arrow had experienced an electrical failure and, in addition not being able to communicate with their radio, the landing gear was not locked down—the reason the tower was issuing a red light—refusing permission to land. The CAP plane took off and rendezvoused with the other aircraft. Using hand signals they were able to inform the Arrow pilot of the situation. Then, again with hand signals, they suggested the Arrow induce some G-loading to see if the gear might move into place. The effort was successful that the plane landed without incident.

Jennison became one of the most experienced mountain flying pilots in the region. He developed and presented courses on Mountain Search Flying techniques.

***

Chuck Fairchild recalls another mission in February 1983 with Norm Elliott and Mark Peters in a Cessna 172 (N5098R). *"This mission was an efficient one, although it had an unhappy ending. An ELT had been heard on Friday afternoon in the Sangre de Christos, northwest of Las Vegas. A T-34 from ABQ searched some before dark but couldn't find anything, and 2 or 3 ground parties deployed that night to search. The next morning we launched 98R about 0730 to give it a try. There were clouds over the Sangres, but they didn't look to be impenetrable. They were bad enough that we had to maneuver through them and climb to >13,000 ft to be sure we were clear of any peaks hidden in them. After we reached the east side of the Pecos Wilderness the clouds diminished considerably so that we could see most of the search area. We contacted one of the ground parties, who directed us to identify a white spot on a mountainside about 5 miles from them. The spot turned out to be the target, a high-wing Cessna scrunched into a very small semi-clearing. There was no activity around the wreckage, but from what we could see from about 100 ft away during our slow passes the plane wasn't broken up badly, although the engine had been pushed back into the cockpit.*

A hiking party was on the way toward the peak as we spotted the wreckage, and news of the occupants' fate would be found by them. That was one thing I liked about searching from the air. When a wreck was found, the hard, grisly work was done by someone else--on the ground. We decided to tool off to Angel Fire airport to wait until the ground party reached the wreckage. After an hour on the ground, we flew back to the crash area where we could see one person of a ground search party walking around the plane. Soon, we received word indirectly that two persons, a man and a woman--both dead--were aboard the plane. After taking photos of the site, we flew back to LAM."

***

In December 1984, Fairchild relates yet another mission he flew solo in the C150 N50929. *"On Christmas morning, mind you, I was awakened by a 0630 call from Walt Hatch that we had an A/C missing in northern NM near Canjillon Mountain. Walt had to leave town immediately, so the duty fell to me to call for crews and get the mission started. After numerous calls to scramble crews, I ran out of possibilities and assigned myself to 'Hi Bird.'*

The search was for a family that disappeared on a flight inbound to Taos, almost on the same route that a plane had crashed a year before in northern NM (the search involving the F-111s}. High Bird is the call for a plane that flies fairly high in the search area and acts as a communication relay for the low altitude search planes that can't call directly to the distant mission HQ. Only one other plane was to be in the search area because the weather, while not too bad initially, was not conducive to having numerous planes in the mountainous terrain.

15 T-34 over the Sandia Mountains

The primary search aircraft, N5098R, piloted by Robert Gibson, who was an experienced search pilot by then, IFR rated and an instrument instructor, took off from Los Alamos at the same time I did. We proceeded to the search area about 40 miles north with the 172 pulling out in front. As 98R went on to their search grid near Canjillon, I established a circular pattern over the Abiqui area, between them and Santa Fe, the HQ. Due to the cloud cover, which seemed to be increasing, I was unable to get above 8500 ft but it was high enough initially to communicate with both.

Things went normally for a few minutes, and then 98R gave a call to say that the weather was worsening in the search area and that they might have to leave that area before long. He called shortly after that to say they had to get out, were going to climb above the clouds, file IFR, and go into Santa Fe. He also asked me to call SAF FSS to get the weather there and relay it to him. By this time, I had been forced down to about 7500 by clouds and was unable to contact SAF. After relaying this to 98R, I started looking for a way out of my area because the weather was lowering there also. In fact, because it had taken some time to determine that I couldn't contact SAF, and more time to re-contact 98R, a pocket with low clouds blocking all escape directions had formed.

The entire time orbiting the area I had made sure that Highway 84 between Abiqui and El Rito was nearby. It had little vehicular traffic and a couple of straight sections without any major obstacles. Descending more to set up an approach, I could see that there was still room to escape to the SE under clouds about 600 ft. above the surface. However, because the weather beyond those low clouds was uncertain, the better part of valor seemed to be to land on the highway, so I proceeded to do so. I then couldn't reach 98R to inform him that I was on the deck.

The weather continued to get worse for a while and some snow even fell, but then in a couple of hours it started to improve. Some vehicles came by and offered to give me a ride into town, and one family offered to get me some gas or food, but I explained that I had my lunch with me. Still unable to contact anyone an hour or so later, I became antsy and began eyeing the weather. When it improved slightly I took-off, intending to follow the road to Espanola, land there, and call for a ride back to LAM until the weather permitted retrieving the plane. To my surprise, as I approached Espanola under the low overcast the weather improved considerably. After clearing the low clouds, I called HQ to let them know my situation. Although still overcast, it improved to the extent that I could easily get into LAM and did. Fortunately, although HQ was concerned about me, they had not started a search, because of the weather."

***

Fairchild continues his narrative about the last CAP search that he participated near Roswell for a Cessna 210 that had been going from ABQ to ROW at night. *"I went down in the C150 to act as 'High Bird'. Of course, as in all missions, I searched the terrain for the missing A/C while I cruised down there. After landing, I learned that the plane must be close to Roswell because he had called in that he had the airport in sight. About the same time a pilot who was not associated with the CAP called in that he had spotted the plane in the desert about 10 miles NW of the airport and was going to land. Immediately the mission coordinator launched an observer and myself in the C-150 to scoot out there to relay messages and guide rescue vehicles to the spot. This we did for the next couple of hours. The C-210 didn't look as though it was damaged much at all and was on a very smooth strip of desert, but the pilot had been killed on impact, the landed pilot reported. We stuck around until the police cars, ambulance, etc. found their way to the site with our help, then we headed home--our part was finished."*

***

A Mooney Mark 20 was reported missing in December 1990 on a flight from Carlsbad California, to Santa Fe, New Mexico. It was a typical SAR mission—if there is ever a typical one when two people's lives may hang in the balance. The last known position was 15 miles south of Gallup—just an hour from their destination—when the pilot called Albuquerque Flight Service to extend his flight plan. The weather had not been good.

The REDCAP was headquartered at the Santa Fe airport and two CAP squadrons (Santa Fe and Los Alamos) began their efforts at 6:15 the following morning as the clouds from the storm began to dissipate and flyable conditions returned. ATC was able to provide a radar track of the VFR flight, which was critical, as there was no ELT signal.

Five CAP aircraft and a State Police helicopter launched. Four hours later the wreckage was spotted on the southern edge of the Jemez Mountains and the tail number was plainly visible. There were no survivors.

***

The NTSB report tells an all-too-often tale in the following accident of a home-built Long-Eze that occurred on May 29, 1995:

> WHILE ON A VFR CROSS COUNTRY FLIGHT WITH NO FLIGHT PLAN, THE AIRCRAFT FAILED TO REACH ITS DESTINATION. THE PILOT HAD MADE A POSITION REPORT WHICH PLACED THE FLIGHT IN THE VICINITY OF THE ACCIDENT SITE AT 7,500 FEET MSL. A GROUND WITNESS ON A ROAD AT 7,000 FEET MSL, OBSERVED THE AIRCRAFT PASS AT ABOUT 100 FEET AGL. AT THE TIME OF THE OBSERVATION, THE AIRCRAFT WAS PASSING IN AND OUT OF LOW CLOUDS AND FOG. DURING HIS WEATHER BRIEF FROM FLIGHT SERVICE, THE PILOT HAD BEEN INFORMED THAT VFR FLIGHT WAS NOT RECOMMENDED DUE TO LOW CEILINGS AND FOG ALONG HIS INTENDED ROUTE.

It was not until four days after the flight that a search was initiated. Using the information from the FAA, and the witness who had observed the aircraft, the remains were quickly found not far from I-40 by the first aircraft dispatched. They noted a highway sign as a landmark and flew back to Moriarity Airport and drove out to the scene. The Long-Eze pilot, who flew 737s for US Air, and his passenger did not survive. The NTSB report continues:

> IMPACT WAS INTO RISING TERRAIN AND TREES AND ALTHOUGH THE AIRCRAFT GENERALLY DISINTEGRATED ON IMPACT, THE WRECKAGE WAS CONTAINED IN THE IMPACT AREA... PROBABLE CAUSE: THE PILOT FLYING THE AIRCRAFT INTO IMC CONDITIONS AT AN ALTITUDE WHICH WAS INADEQUATE TO CLEAR SURROUNDING TERRAIN. FACTORS WERE LOW CEILING AND FOG.

***

16 This Long-Eze crashed on April 29, 1995 with two fatalities only a few hundred feet from I-40 and was found after a short search.

***

The Las Cruces Squadron was notified during the afternoon of 28 September, 1998, that a search was in progress south of Hope, NM. At 7:00 PM, a Cessna 182 piloted by LtCol Gary Martin and Captain Ansel Austin was launched from Crawford Municipal Airport (Las Cruces, NM) in support of this search.

The search was for a husband and wife hunting party who had been able to contact New Mexico State Police by cell phone. The couple could not give a definite location and because of vehicle problems, they could not get back to the roadway.

At 8:30 PM, the air search crew located a campfire within the search area. When the crew started circling the area, the subjects near the fire started signaling the aircraft with flashlights. Ground Team 2 from Alamogordo Search and Rescue was contacted by the aircrew and was directed to the scene. Due to the rough terrain in the area, it took the ground team 2.5 hours to reach the hunters. The Las Cruces aircrew landed safety at the Las Cruces Airport at midnight. It was later learned that the male subject was diabetic and had not had his medication. On 29 September 1998, the aircrew was advised that the Air Force Rescue Coordination Center had approved two assists and one save for this mission.

***

It is not just small civilian aircraft that CAP is called upon to search for. On February 26, 1961, an Air Force T-29 was reported missing on a flight from Farmington to Belen. In December 1965, a Lockheed Super Connie of Flying Tigers Airlines was lost over southern Colorado enroute From LA to Chicago with three aboard.

17 Night flight operations bring special considerations for safety. This aircraft was lost on take-off from Los Alamos.

***

Night operations require special thought and judgment. On the night of June 9, 2004, a CAP C172P, N9474L, was destroyed when the pilot attempted to make a 360 degree turn while on final approach at Las Cruces International Airport (LRU), Las Cruces, New Mexico.

VFR conditions prevailed for a planned flight to Albuquerque, at the time of the accident.

The airplane had just departed LRU when the low voltage light illuminated and the pilot decided to return to LRU. The pilot transmitted on the Unicom frequency that he was "turning base to final for runway 26" but was actually turning base to final for runway 22. The pilot of another airplane heard this report and elected to take off on runway 22. The pilot of N9474L sighted the other aircraft on the runway and started a 360-degree turn for spacing purposes. During the low altitude turn, the pilot lost track of the horizon in the pitch-blackness of the night, and the airplane struck large mesquite bushes and collided with terrain. The pilot sustained serious injuries, but the observer had only minor injuries. The pilot had flown for 6.9 hours on the day of the accident.

***

Persistence is often a determining factor in finding a missing aircraft. In September 1991, a Cessna 172 from a Texas flight school was reported missing. The experienced pilot, an Italian national who was enrolled in an advanced flight-training program, had not filed a flight plan. Nevertheless, when investigators looked through the pilots belongings at the school they discovered notes that indicated a possible route of flight into northern New Mexico.

The search had consumed almost a week because of poor weather conditions when Mission Pilot Allene Lindstrom and Observers Mark Peters and Eddie Esquibel, flew their search pattern. The crew noticed 'something white' among the trees in an area where five other aircraft had gone down in previous years. A ground party confirmed it was the missing aircraft. As is the case with many crashes where there are no survivors, the cause is often an educated guess and for this particular area, density altitude and adverse winds are often contributing factors.

***

With the modern navigational aids, radar coverage, improved weather prediction and reporting, as well communications, aircraft do not encounter near the problems as they did 30-40 years ago.

Thus, the number of search missions in recent times is relatively small.

One rather odd mission (94-M-1568A) developed during July of 1994. A 14 year-old Boy Scout, Robert Graham from Illinois, had become separated from his group on Tuesday the 12th, while on an outing in the Santa Fe National Forrest. A search was initiated with the Los Alamos Squadron launching two aircraft (one to serve as High Bird) and a State Police helicopter N606SP that spotted the boy at 1430 hours on Thursday. The helicopter requested permission from the Forrest Service (FS) to land and pick-up the scout.

Permission was denied on the basis that the '1964 Wilderness Act' which allows mechanized equipment in the National Forrest only under life and death circumstances. The Forrest Service indicated that their ground team was about 45 minutes from the place where the boy had been spotted. The helicopter dropped a note to the boy and requested him to remain at that location so the ground teams could find him. However, the ground teams failed to make contact and the boy spent his third night in the Pecos Wilderness. He did have a sleeping bag and had survived on Ginger Snaps and water.

The next day Maurice Sheppard and Gene McCall were again launched in Cessna N6319H to perform the search and then to function as High Bird when the helicopter arrived. A Customs Helicopter spotted the scout and permission was finally granted to an Air Force HH-53 helicopter to make the pick-up at 1545 hours on Friday.

The incident highlighted the need for better communication between federal agencies and a determination of what constitutes a 'life or death' situation.

***

The following, reprinted from The Cactus Courier of May 2007, describes a FIND awarded to the NM Wing as described by Maj Jim Talbert, of the Alamogordo Squadron.

On 19 Feb. 2007, a 78-year-old Australian tourist left his motor home at White Sands National Monument (WSNM) to photograph one of New Mexico's gorgeous sunsets, taking neither flash light nor matches. About sunset, the tourist's wife became concerned that he had not returned. She contacted the park rangers, after which put into motion the search and rescue actions for the evening. The Park rangers initiated a ground search that was expanded to include the NM State Police SAR lead by Ric Himebrook, the Incident Commander (and a CAP member). The Alamogordo CAP Squadron was notified, and the local commander, Capt Shirley Kay, began rounding up a flight team around midnight to search from the air. It was a high overcast moonless night. The Border Patrol offered an agent equipped with Night Vision Goggles (NVGs) and an Infrared (IR) Sensor. The observer, CAP LtC. Stephen Curtis, was trained on the spot how to use the IR sensor. Due to limitations of the sensor, LtC. Curtis had to keep the window open and hold the unit outside for maximum effectiveness. WSNM lies under restricted area 5107B that is hot 24/7 to an unlimited altitude. While the flight team prepared for the mission, Capt Kay coordinated with Range Control for the special clearance that was necessary to fly into the restricted area. At 0230 hours, the search team became airborne heading for the command post set up at the motor home belonging to the subject of the search.

The previous month, the NM wing had sponsored a night flying clinic, using a night such as this moonless, horizonless and with no ground lights as an example of what we could have to deal with on a night search. We were able to put the training to good use! The search began over the command post with a parallel search moving to the west. At the first course reversal, it became obvious to the pilot that there was a lot more wind at search altitude than on the surface. Using the onboard GPS to maintain the track, the pilot adjusted for the 25 knots of wind.

After 2 hours of searching to the west with the NVG's in the back seat operated by a US Border Patrol member and the IR sensor out the window in the front seat, the pilot elected to fly the search in the vicinity of the highway on the southern border of the park. Since there was no traffic on the road, tracking it became a real challenge. The only light visible was the Border Patrol check station at the opposite end of the park. On the inverse track, the pilot saw what appeared to be a camera flash at his 10 o'clock position. (The camera flash was part of the search briefing because the subject had left to take pictures.) A second flash appeared then a third one, just at the strut.

The pilot went into a turn about a point (I'll bet you private pilots thought you would never do that maneuver again after passing your check ride!), and called for the coordinates. With no ground lights and 25 KTS of wind, we were not sure of our exact location. Fortunately, the observer had a personnel GPS with a 'man overboard' selection which freezes the coordinates when selected. This information was passed to ground crews and NMSP Coordinator used his rescue software to obtain a satellite picture and mile markers on the highway to give the SAR Teams an entry point, however they did not have a GPS and did not know if they made it to our coordinates. Since we had no hits on either sensor, we were not sure if we had the subject or not. Therefore, we again expanded the search area, but returned to this point hoping for another flash.

18 Los Alamos Members David Watkins and Allene Lindstrom confer over last minute details before launching on a late afternoon flight in the U206.

The search continued until daylight, and the subject was not located. The CAP crew returned to the airport to change crews. The Border Patrol picked up the subject about 3 hours later, cold, thirsty, but in very good condition. The following day was Ash Wednesday, and the survivor and his wife were invited to attend a local church service, which happened to be the church of many of the search team members. So not only did we get to meet the man, but we also got "the rest of the story."

The first interesting point was the survivor had no idea anyone was looking for him. To him, the plane overhead seemed to be just a "military reconnaissance plane" that forgot to turn off its landing light. He had collected brush and grass to cover with and made a makeshift lining for his straw hat out of handkerchiefs to try to keep warm. He also covered himself with a plastic bag to keep himself warm. He stayed at the bottom of the dunes (which limited our sensor reception) and stayed awake. At sunrise, he heard traffic noises from the highway and traveled in that direction. He climbed the fence, crossed the 4-lane road, and walked to the lights, which was the Border Patrol station. All toll, he wandered about 11 miles.

Lessons we learned from this mission. No kidding, it is dark out there, and night is an instrument procedure! Night training is invaluable. Not everyone realizes that someone is out there looking for them, so they might not signal as we would wish they would. The pilot did not think to look at the radial and DME to back up the GPS coordinates, as he was busy flying the plane. It was very handy to have the Man Overboard selection on the GPS. It would be a great addition to all CAP planes to have a rapid (ONE BUTTON) means of freezing coordinates to pass on to the ground crews. Actually, the radios worked as they should have and we were able to talk to everyone we needed to. The best lesson is that it is great to meet the survivor and shake his hand.

With respect to the desire for the searchers to have *"a rapid (ONE BUTTON) means of freezing coordinates,"* The new G1000 equipped CAP aircraft that NM Wing received in 2006 has that capability… and much more.

***

On the night of 9 June 2009, NM State Police helicopter NM606SP crashed while conducting a rescue in the Sangre de Christo Mountains just east of Santa Fe. NM Wing was notified and a mission activated at approximately 10:30 PM Tuesday night to support the search. CAP was tasked for Visual and ELT/DF search, and High Bird communication relay. NM Wing also provided an

Air Operations Branch Director and Operations Section Chief for the Incident Command Staff at the Incident Base.

The Wing's Mobile Operations Center (MOC) was deployed (and used throughout the entire search) to run all air operations for the search. Assets involved included: two CAP C182s (N374CP, N2939E), 2 Army National Guard H-60 helicopters, the Bernalillo County Sheriff Dept helicopter, an MC-130H from Kirtland AFB, and news helicopters from Channel 13, Channel 7 and Channel 4. All air assets were controlled by CAP during the search.

19 Rugged terrain and inhospitable weather often define the search environment of New Mexico.

Squadron II flew sorties on Wednesday and Thursday supporting the search. Jim Steele and Dane Van Pelt organized crews, while Tom Godman, Dan Fernandez, Gene Johnson, David Simonson, Ernie Braunschweig and Ralph Meyerhein crewed the airplanes. They flew sorties up to 14,000 feet to provide the High Bird coverage, which was invaluable during the search. There was only one survivor and two fatalities (pilot and medi-evaced passenger)

Personal Reflections

Charles 'Chuck' Fairchild, a former naval aviator, joined the Los Alamos Squadron back in the 1960s. He shares with us his remembrances of flying SAREX missions.

"For 25 years I was a member of the CAP, primarily flying SAR missions. When the Los Alamos squadron upgraded to a T-34 from their old beat up Stinson in 1963, a few of us opportunists joined CAP just to get to fly the T-34. We attended ground school for a few weeks before checking out in the 2-place, retractable gear zipper.

Searching for downed A/C or missing vehicles and persons on the ground was usually an interesting escape from the humdrum. On some missions everything was low key and seemed to go well, although, it seemed, on many missions the objective wasn't found. In those early years search efficiency is low due to crew fatigue, or amateurish technique. However, the NM terrain that we usually searched was high mountainous--rugged, and forested--difficult for the observers as well as the pilot. Most of the searches occurred in nasty terrain because that was the mostly likely place for people to get into trouble. Turbulence was often present and weather frequently hampered getting into search areas. Observers (often non-pilots) were hard to come by because it was a fairly thankless, tedious, and occasionally scary task. First of all, not all the pilots were top notch, and secondly, sometimes the search area weather included clouds and/or turbulence that wasn't much fun for the crew.

I wasn't enthusiastic about the military part of the CAP—I had had enough of that in the Navy, but I went along with it. Halfheartedly, I completed several of the classes and training courses.

Most of the searches were dreary, weary things that lasted from a day to a few weeks. And, with most, the target aircraft, or truck, or hunting party, or whatever, wasn't found. Probably, during my 25 years I flew 1,000 hrs just looking.

***

The first I recall was a search in about 1965 for four lost hunters who were doing preliminary elk spotting in a Cessna 182 in the Pecos Wilderness--very high, rugged terrain. The mission coordinator was reluctant to send me out into high mountains with my 65 hp Mooney Mite, but did when I explained that it could out-climb most C-182s.

We searched 2 weeks, during which I flew 4 days, but didn't ever find the downed plane. It was found almost 10 years later by a hiker in the very area we had searched several times.

***

Another search in the Mite was in the TorC and Elephant Butte area. That was the first time Phil Ehart joined me in his Mite. We had fun flying together and felt a little safer by seeing another plane only a half mile away, but we didn't find anything.

***

Phil and I also flew search along the Rio Grande when the well-known physician, Randolph Lovelace III (founder of Lovelace Clinic in ABQ), his family, and charter pilot disappeared returning from an Aspen ski trip. The search extended from Aspen to ABQ with both military and CAP involved. Our search area was along and near the Rio Grande from LAM to the Colorado border. Phil and I flew several sorties, but weather was always a factor. So were other aircraft. The military was also searching the Rio, and once we were passed closely in the opposite direction by a T-37 whizzing by, and once by a huge C-130 cargo plane. On one sortie, we were separated by snow showers on the north side of the Valle. I made it home by scooting between and under a couple snow showers and Phil came in about 30 minutes later, after he had landed at Espanola until the weather improved. The Lovelace plane was found about 3 days after the search started—only 15 miles from Aspen."

***

Chuck Fairchild recalls a SAR in November 1982 with Walt Hatch as his Observer in C172 N5098R. *"One early winter search in November 1982 was for a Piper Navajo twin with a Taos artist, his wife and child, and a friend aboard, who were returning to Taos. They had disappeared at night within 100 mi of Taos in mountainous terrain (Brazos peak area) where snow showers were apparently in progress. They were on a flight plan, so the search started fairly quickly. Our search for them was fruitless. They were found the following August during a SAREX, near Canjillon Peak, not far from where this incident occurred. Strangely, there was a lot of money and a couple of valuable paintings aboard. But, this tale is not about the search itself, but just about an interesting happening during one of the sorties.*

We were assigned to a search area southwest of Dulce, a high probability area in the vicinity where radar lost the missing A/C. Enroute to the area on a NW heading, as we were passing the high country just south of the Brazos breaks, I caught a glimpse of a jet crossing below and about a half-mile in front of us. He wasn't moving at top speed, but neither was he going slow. I watched him move away from us to the right and start climbing to top Brazos peak. Just as I looked away from him to the front again I caught some motion to the left and looked to see another camouflage color F-111 disappear under our nose. Fortunately, he reappeared almost immediately on the right side low, close, but slightly in front of us. He had passed 50-100 ft beneath us, and just as he passed under us started his climb over Brazos peak. I'm not sure whether he saw us or whether his terrain following radar just delayed the climb until the A/C passed us, but I'm glad he didn't start climbing a few seconds earlier. Of course, I pointed out the planes to my observers and there was some degree of excitement and comment for a short while.

We immediately called a message to CAP ground HQ, through High Bird, that F-111s were in the vicinity, and for other search planes to watch for them. We continued to our search area, performed the search with negative results, and started back to base. As we crossed over the same mountains, slightly farther north, and headed easterly, it was déjà vu all over again.

This time the lead F-111 flew directly underneath us, right to left, about 100 ft below, and I didn't see him until he flashed into view, going away, as I was looking out the left side studying a lake almost directly below. We were only about 300 ft AGL, so he was really close to the ground. I watched him for a second before realizing there was probably another, then yelled at the crew to look to the right for the second one. Sure enough, 5 seconds later the wingman passed under and behind us, this time about 200 yards back (right on the track of the first). They were really beautiful, moving smoothly along with their wings swung back about halfway, but I was beginning to think that they were targeting us.

I again relayed a call to base that they were in the area. They may have been pretty to watch, but they certainly constituted a hazard to the several CAP planes out in the search area at approximately the same altitude. After we landed, debriefed, etc. we got the word that search operations were being suspended temporarily until the mission coordinator, Bill Overton, could contact Cannon AFB, almost certainly the source of the F-111s, to have their A/C flying the 'oil burner' route stay out of our way.

***

In the 70s and early 80s, I was made the scheduling officer, so it was my job to line up crews for the aircraft whenever we had a search. That involved dozens of calls to find a few people willing to devote one or more days to the search. For long searches, it was difficult to find enough volunteers.

***

The following is an example of how the ELT system was designed to work. It is almost textbook perfect. Late in the afternoon, on June 10, 1981, an airliner flying over central New Mexico reported an ELT signal around the Anton Chico VOR along V-12 late in the day—there had been no report at that time of an 'overdue' aircraft. On receipt of the information, Paul Harbin, and an observer, launched early the next day in the T-34 and proceeded towards the area. They were the only crew able to respond on short notice.

20 **Being able to select the best altitude for the terrain and weather conditions is an important aspect of the search profile.**

Rather than being directed to the Anton Chico local, the DF on the T-34 led the crew north—about 75 miles into the foothills of the Sangre de Christo Mountains east of Santa Fe. There, in the Pecos Canyon above El Macho, the crew spotted the downed aircraft. Two National Guard Huey helicopters airlifted the badly injured survivors to safety, less than 18 hours after their PA-28 had crashed.

The flight of the Piper had originated in Lubbock, Texas, and was proceeding to Santa Fe. It may be speculated that, as the weather was exceptionally good, the pilot, a flight instructor with over 6,000 hours, elected to make a low pass at a cabin belonging to a friend. The physics of density altitude (estimated at 10,400') caught up with him, as he was headed up-canyon, and hit the tall pines.

Blood Transport Missions

At various times, New Mexico Wing has had agreements with United Blood Services to provide 'on call' service for delivering blood to various parts of the state. These missions, sometimes called 'blood runs,' require the CAP aircrew to be airborne within one hour of notification. This is a demanding role that requires rapid alert and response to achieve the time goal.

According to the Enchanted Wing News (Spring 1982 edition) there were six 'Blood Runs' made during 1981. The pilots paid $6.00 an hour to fly these missions.

The T-34 was a valuable asset, in part because it was the fastest aircraft operated by the NM Wing. This attribute was used in many operations where time was a critical factor. In October of 1981, a 25-year-old woman delivered a baby in Ft. Sumner, NM and experienced uncontrolled bleeding. Albuquerque Squadron II was notified and the United Blood Services delivered the required blood and platelets to Kirtland AFB where CAP pilot Phil Barrott was waiting. The precious cargo was delivered with 2 hours of the request and the woman, who was within an hour of dying, recovered.

In March 1982, Albuquerque Squadron II flew two life-saving missions by transporting blood to Durango, CO. In the first incident, a skier ruptured a kidney. In the second, a man fell from a water tower and was suffering severe internal bleeding. Ed Greenway and Paul Harbin were airborne in the T-34 just one hour after receiving the alert. They were met at the LaPlata airport by another CAP volunteer who transported the blood to the hospital

On one occasion, September 12, 2001, Squadron II was called on to deliver. John Lorenz recalls it well in this article that appeared in the Southwest Aviator.

> The assigned transponder code, 4354, was so hard to obtain that I recorded it in my logbook. We were assured by several authorities that we could be shot down if we deviated from that code or from our flight plan. Erratic lightning

flickered behind the immediate clouds, half-seen in the close, black night. Radio frequencies were quiet except for the low-key, one-sided conversations we could hear as Air Traffic Control directed military traffic.

We had been called to stand by on the afternoon of September 12, 2001. The mission was to transport pints of blood, collected from dozens of willing Albuquerque volunteers, to a collection center in Phoenix that evening. Repeated television images of crashing planes and crumbling towers from the morning before were seared into the national consciousness. I was one of the lucky ones called on to contribute my skills, however small and however briefly, to the national interest instead of suffering dumbfounded in frustration in front of the TV. We had been given a chance to be useful and we took it, but an unspoken question lingered in the back of my mind: "Given the magnitude of masonry and steel mixed in chaos with human bodies, will there be anyone alive to benefit from the blood we deliver?" The question was irrelevant.

We met at a CAP member's home at 8 PM. John and I comprised one crew; Lee and Ernie were the backup crew, but were also scheduled to fly a mission with the same profile on the following night. Lee had flown C-47 transports over the Hump to China during World War II; John and Ernie are highly experienced pilots in their own right. What was I doing there? We talked quietly in the living room while Dave, the Emergency Services director, and his staff straightened out the last of the intricate details involved in obtaining a nationally assigned transponder code prior to flight. Cooperation between the CAP National Headquarters, Air Traffic Control, and the Pentagon, under the plan developed for national emergencies ("SCATANA"), had obtained permission for CAP to fly a limited number of very specific missions. Dave's newborn slept in the next room.

My questions to a former military pilot earlier in the afternoon had been met with flat denial. He was sure that no non-military pilot would be permitted to fly for any reason whatsoever. Calls to Flight Service to file a flight plan and for a weather briefing had been somewhat more encouraging, but were inconclusive as to whether permission to fly would or even could actually be given. Moreover, whereas the flight to Phoenix carrying blood was deemed important, the empty return flight was not. If actually allowed to depart, we would launch not knowing whether or not we'd be returning by bus. The final disquieting factor was the weather: scattered rain and thunderstorms. A widespread layer of broken clouds covered the route of flight in the limited interval available to us, between minimum altitudes over the mountains and the higher altitudes that would require oxygen that we didn't have on board.

We loaded four cases of blood from United Blood Services into a CAP van and drove through the drizzle across town, streetlights shining on puddles, heading for the flight-line on Kirtland Air Force Base. Just getting past the guard gate and onto the base that evening was an effort. Our uniforms and the official van made entry possible, but not easy. A squad of polite yet very determined and very young soldiers conducted a thorough mirror-and-dog search of our bags and the van before we were allowed past the machine guns, floodlights, and hastily placed cement barriers. Our entire effort was then nearly thwarted by the recently changed combinations on locks to the flight-line gate. Hurried cell-phone calls to various knowledgeable people put us back on track after a minor delay.

John had managed to nap that afternoon, so we agreed that I would take the first leg in the single-engine Cessna 206, figuring he would be the fresher of the two of us for the return flight. We lifted off at about 10 PM local time. Being the only traffic using the vacant runways at the normally busy Class C airport, we were immediately cleared to join the victor 190 airway. That route goes westward across the nearly uninhabited, unlit, high, broken country of western New Mexico. Our flight would continue for three hours across the continental divide and over the dark and barren mountains of central Arizona. I was instrument current but I have minimal experience flying in actual clouds, since most New Mexican clouds contain either ice or lightning depending on the season, and are usually bad places to be, even with an instrument rating. Nevertheless, concentration derived from an intensity I usually reserve for FAA checkrides managed to keep me aware of our position and helped me keep the navigation needles centered.

Near silence on the radio and an absence of anything visible in the darkness were combined with disbelief in the reality of the 9/11 attacks to create a feeling of total detachment from the world. We were floating along in our own cocoon, even having to turn on the landing light to tell whether we were flying inside clouds or not. Ground lighting was nil—pinpricks from the few, widely-scattered ranch-house lights provided no reference to the horizon even when we could see them.

Lightning flickered on and off beyond the wingtips, marking storm cells obscured by the broken clouds. We avoided the cells easily enough with minor course deviations because they were prominently, if discontinuously, lit by concentrations of flashes in the darkness, yet I regularly replayed through my mind the storm-penetration techniques I had read. That exercise was less than calming because most of the remembered advice consisted of a terse "don't." However, radio calls to Flight Watch yielded the information that their radar showed the storms to be scattered and mostly to the sides of our route.

A pale, bluish glow tinged the outer arc of the prop from time to time, coinciding with extra static on the radios. Maybe we were, maybe we weren't doing something vital to help protect the nation, but we were doing something. It was a release to be active, a welcome change from watching the news with an ache in my heart while grinding my teeth.

Air Traffic Control and Flight Service both sounded professional and matter-of-fact on the radio. Operations were few but otherwise the procedures were normal. We could hear Air Traffic Control giving instructions to Air Force tankers flying holding patterns with long, 50-mile legs, waiting to refuel armed fighters, but the responses and the plane-to-plane communications were on military frequencies and hidden from us. The lone two-way interchange we could hear was between Air Traffic Control and a lifeguard flight on its way to the Navajo reservation. It seemed small, distant, and out of place.

An hour into the flight I began fighting the urge to drift off to sleep. It wasn't overpowering but the accumulated stress of flight planning in the overall atmosphere of the attacks was combining with my biorhythms and telling me I should have been in bed. The feeling faded after half an hour, but it had gotten my attention. I resolved to watch John's piloting carefully on the return leg, monitoring for signs of fatigue.

We were vectored toward Phoenix Sky Harbor, sliding down from the high, dark minimum enroute altitude of central Arizona into the warm and well-lit night of that desert city. Picking out the runway amid the city lights wasn't easy for a first-time night arrival, so we followed the navigation radios in. We landed with a strong crosswind, and were met as we turned off the runway by a Follow-Me truck that had been alerted by the tower. Friendly hands unloaded the blood, offered sandwiches, and refueled the Cessna. The feeling of unity of purpose was nearly a physical entity, and almost comforting enough to compensate for the vacuous inactivity of this large airport and the strangeness of numerous lifeless aircraft parked on the dark ramps. We stretched our legs and took our time getting back into the plane.

Air Traffic Control was, in fact, expecting our radio call, and we breathed a sigh of relief as we copied our clearance for the return flight. Phoenix departure assigned us a new transponder code, as apparently they had not been party to the instructions to the effect that we would be shot at if flying under any but the original code that night. We accepted the new squawk only after repeated assurances that we would continue to be recognized and would be able to fly safely under the new code when handed along to successive Air Traffic Control facilities. Our apprehension was not fanciful: what little we could hear on the Air Traffic Control frequencies had suggested that unseen fighters, manned by grim pilots and equipped with live ammunition, patrolled the sky this second night after the attacks.

We started the homeward leg with a takeoff eastward into the darkness, climbing hard to clear the unseen mountains. John had the controls while I watched for the Air Force tanker that departed close behind and soon overtook us. We never saw it. Halfway home, a strong diffuse yellow glow appeared on the horizon in front of us. It grew, glimpsed as we flew in and out of the clouds, into a friendly half moon that at last gave a hint of definition to the landscape below, when we could see it.

John suffered no obvious attacks of fatigue on the return trip, although his altitudes and headings began to drift during the last half hour. Nevertheless, I scrutinized his instruments for the entire flight, probably contributing more to my own stress and fatigue level than to our safety. We kept up a random conversation throughout the trip and I learned much about this quiet man who is also the chaplain for the squadron.

A hundred miles out of Albuquerque we tried to raise CAP Mission Base on the radio to let them know we were running about an hour behind schedule, but we were out of range. A friendly Flight Service specialist accommodated us with a phone call to Mission Base instead. They had been awake, waiting for our call.

We landed out of a visual approach into Albuquerque, but a rain squall closed in on the airport five minutes after we touched down and we became drenched and chilled while refueling the Cessna. A quick debrief and a call to my sleepy wife, and by sunrise I was in the truck, heater on full as I headed home. A sudden weariness and an irresistible urge to sleep demanded that I pull off the highway to catnap briefly on the shoulder before proceeding.

Lee and Ernie never got to fly their mission. The weather deteriorated and widespread embedded thunderstorm activity made similar flights impossible for the following two nights. The next shipments of blood were driven over the mountains to Phoenix instead. By the time the weather cleared sufficiently to allow more blood-transportation flights, it was becoming starkly apparent that the smoldering rubble piles that had been the World Trade Center and one side of the Pentagon would yield few survivors in need of transfusions.

In retrospect, the flight could almost be viewed as a metaphor. Changed yet familiar surroundings, ill-defined feelings of danger, a passionate desire to help, half-heard communications, flickers of light, unknown friendships, a mission successfully flown, and, hopefully, the dawn. Did we help anyone? Probably not any one individual, though the trip had intangible benefits for many. Did we feel better for having made the trip? Yes, marginally. Would we have still made the flight knowing for sure that the potential benefit was minimal? Without doubt. My irrelevant question had been answered in an oblique way that was appropriate to the setting.

Disaster Relief

The New Mexico Wing has been called upon many times over its 70-year history to provide disaster relief. Among these occasions was the disastrous Cerro Grande Fire that burned through Los Alamos in 2000. However, few disasters have had such a wide-ranging impact, both economic and political as Hurricane Katrina.

Hurricane Katrina—When this storm struck in 2005, the New Mexico Wing was called upon to provide qualified pilots and the most capable plane in the Wing's possession—the GA-8. LtCol Jerry Burton responded to the call and spent eleven days flying daily sorties in support of the disaster relief mission. This is his story:

"The Call" to go was received around noon, September 8, 2005. Within two hours a crew (Bill Drumm, Ernie Braunschweig and myself) was assembled, the aircraft was loaded for an open-ended commitment to provide undefined services made necessary by the devastation of New Orleans resulting from hurricane Katrina, and we were in our takeoff roll.

We landed in Fort Worth just after sunset. We over-nighted there and enjoyed what we were sure would be our last good night's sleep for awhile. We were right.

We departed Fort Worth on an IFR flight plan thinking that we would leave the area more expeditiously under positive control. We were really wrong! We were vectored around Dallas on the north side. It was a very long flight.

We arrived in Baton Rouge close to sundown and were immediately given a mission to take a passenger to Esler Field, Louisiana. We grabbed some crackers, loaded the passenger and his baggage and flew an hour out along the same route we had just flown in on, off-loaded the passenger, and flew an hour back to Baton Rouge.

By the time we arrived back at Baton Rouge, the meeting room used for messing (eating) was full of sleeping pilots. The 'billeting' officer had waited up for us and took us to our three cots in the store room. The store room was full of uniforms, equipment, and a few mice. To his credit, the billeting guy had chosen to sleep there too. After a couple of nights in the storage room, some space opened up in another small building. The billeting officer negotiated our use of the building and moved a bunch of us into a small empty room for the remainder of our stay in Baton Rouge.

The food was good during the time we were flying out of Baton Rouge. However, the duty day was always slow getting started. It seemed that nothing got airborne before about 9:30 or 10 in the morning. I think, but don't really know, that Air Force liaisons were having difficulty in obtaining permission from the Louisiana state officials to use Civil Air Patrol assets. Effective communication and coordination between Federal and State agencies was difficult to achieve. Damage assessment was still incomplete and it's tough to manage all the assets that were available without knowing the big picture.

Federal control of the restricted area of New Orleans was put in place expeditiously, but the whole operation was still a very dangerous one. Everyone who wanted to fly into the restricted area had to have a mission number and description. They were to first contact a ground agency operating out of the Louis Armstrong airport. That agency was used to prioritize and manage the flow of aircraft into and out of the restricted area. When the mission was validated by the ground agency, the flight was cleared to contact an airborne control agency operating out of an AWACS aircraft. There was no radar service provided. Aircraft were assigned block altitudes based on type.

The whole operation was similar to operating in a military restricted area except that there were as many as 4000 flights going into and out of the area each day, the aircraft were more varied in type and performance capability, and the level of piloting skills of the 'other' guy was largely unknown. To the credit of the mission pilots, there were no mid-airs. We only had one near miss. The biggest problem in the restricted area was the presence of civilian aircraft who were 'sightseeing'. They didn't know the rules and therefore we had to assume they weren't following any of the rules.

The press aircraft were using police radio scanners to help them show up at critical points, so they often arrived 'on scene' before we did. They were good about respecting the altitude separation and actually provided some very timely and meaningful information to authorities. Considering the complexity of the situation and the mix of assets, I thought the whole operation was run extremely well. The potential for chaos and disaster was extremely high, but it never materialized.

An interesting observation we had was that on the second day we were there, all of the ground controllers were speaking with a New York or New Jersey accent and were handling the traffic volume much more efficiently than the controllers from the previous day. Obviously, they had been brought in to handle the demands of the situation. To them, it was probably just another day at the office. They performed admirably.

The missions we were assigned were good ones – challenging and important. Our targets included damage surveys of the delta, villages and neighborhoods, weather-reporting equipment in the gulf, roads, bridges, waterways, and refineries. We, of course, were always looking for people in distress, fires, and... bodies.

Among the observations we made were that there was no real sign of wind damage – it all appeared to be water damage. And, there was water everywhere. Our charts showed about 80% of the delta was land or marsh and about 20% was waterways. What we saw was 80% water covered and maybe as much as 20% land mass. Another observation was a very serene one. As we were searching one of the waterways we saw several dolphins playing and racing up channel.

The passengers on one of our early flights included some people from the LSU Hurricane center. They confirmed our observations that the damage we were seeing was not caused by the winds from Hurricane Katrina, but rather from the high water surge (20 feet) that accompanied Katrina. The flooding in New Orleans was caused by the breaching of the levees. With the early and limited information we had at the time it appeared that New Orleans had successfully weathered the storm; hours after the Hurricane had passed, the levees proved to be too weak to hold. The levees were, in many cases, earthen. We saw water flowing through the mass of some of the saturated levees, not just over the top or through breeches.

Other sights we saw included coffins in trees, neighborhoods flooded from the ground up to the roof of each house, and sections of the Lake Pontchartrain Causeway separated like pieces of a toy bridge.

When we landed at the end of the fifth day, we were told to load our gear and depart immediately for Tyndall AFB in Florida. The sun was just above the horizon. Most of the flight was made in the dark.

We landed at Tyndall after hours, but we had received permission to do so. We were met by two very enthusiastic CAP personnel who became like 'mothers' to us. All we had to do was eat, sleep, and fly. Eating was good—USAF mess hall. Sleeping was a little tougher.

We had great rooms, real mattresses, and no mice. Half of our sleeping was in our rooms. The other half was in the lobby at the General Aviation ramp at Louis Armstrong Airport or in the shade of the aircraft while it was parked waiting for the ground damage assessment teams to complete their work.

The first mission profile we flew out of Tyndall (Sep 14) was as follows.

0430 The FL CAP guys (Mom) would pick us up outside the BOQ.

0445 Breakfast at the mess hall

0515 One of us would preflight the aircraft while the other worked with 'Mom' to get weather, routing, NOTAMS, and file the IFR flight plan. Everything was IFR because we were flying over water from Tyndall (PAM) to Naval Air Station New Orleans (NBG), in the dark of pre-dawn as well as night, and there were many, many Restricted Areas between Tyndall and New Orleans and IFR would better facilitate us transiting or avoiding them.

0545 Brief the passengers (assessment team), load the aircraft.

0600 Take-off. Bill Drumm in left seat; I was in the right seat.

0830 Arrive at NBG – passengers disembark

0900 Ferry aircraft to Louis Armstrong (MSY) for refueling

0930 Downtime between flights – sleep wherever we can find a spot; buy sandwich at FBO

0400 Load assessment team from PAM (they drove over from NBG to MSY)

0415 Depart for Biloxi, MS (I am in left seat; Bill is in right seat)

0515 Arrive at BLX; disembark assessment team; Biloxi shoreline looked like a giant steam roller had come through – the trees were not recognizable as trees – they looked like millions of toothpicks all laid down in the same direction (extreme wind damage); buy crackers and coke from vending machine (supper); sleep in PAX terminal chair

0745 Load assessment team

0800 Depart BLX for PAM (I am in left seat; Bill is in right)

0945 Both fuel low lights come on

1000 Make precautionary fuel stop at Destin (DTS) – The sky was clear but the Gulf was reflecting the moon and many stars very brightly. There was an instructor pilot in the pattern at Destin with a student. I told him our situation and that if the lights were right I needed to plan to get it right the first time because there may not be fuel for a go- around. He saw our anti-collision lights out over the Gulf and directed us onto final approach using a well-lit baseball diamond as a reference point for me. We topped the tanks. They took a lot of fuel!

1045 Depart Destin

1115 Land at PAM – Too tired to eat – Mom took us back to the BOQ. Ernie was not with us. He had flown another GA-8 with another assessment team into Mississippi.

The next day's mission had the same time schedule. However, I was alone on this one with seven team members. This flight went directly from PAM to MSY. The assessment team was inspecting damage to the Air National Guard radar site there at the airport. After refueling the aircraft, I sleep for short periods under the aircraft. This time the assessment team needed to be picked up at NBG. When we departed NBG the visibility was lowering due to haze. It was like being in a bowl of yellow, sparkly soup all the way back to Tyndall. I climbed up to 11,000 feet. Everyone on the aircraft was asleep except me. Darkness came quickly. As we approached Tyndall, I started a high-speed descent. The rate of descent was fast and so was the airspeed (maneuvering airspeed). The aircraft sang its song of speed and the passengers began to awaken as I announced our approach into Tyndall. The haze/fog was moderately thick; I was grateful for the instrument approach system.

The following day was a day of R&R, The next day, Sep 17, we (Bill, Ernie, and I) flew the aircraft in steady rain and marginal IFR to Clinton, AL. We were picked up at the airport and driven to Maxwell AFB where we received a tour of National Headquarters, CAP and spent the night. On Sep 18, we were driven to the airport in Montgomery to fly home.

In the airport, we talked with an army unit returning home from Katrina relief to spend 3 days with their family before departing for

Iraq. They expressed their frustration over being in place to help several days in advance of Katrina, but not being authorized by the State (Louisiana) to act until several days after the hurricane had made landfall. We thanked them for their service in the Army and they thanked us for ours in the Air Force (Bill, Ernie, and I all served), I asked God's blessing on them and we made our way to our gate. It was a good mission and we were proud to have participated.

Jerry Burton's Katrina Mission Log

Task	Date	Destination/Comments	Flight Time
Ingress	Sep 8-9	ABQ FTW FTW BTR	8.4 hrs
Transport PAX	Sep 9	BTR Esler Field BTR	1.9 hrs
Grant writer	Sep 10	BTR Air Abort – HSI Failure –	0.4 hrs
Orientation/SAR/Site rep	Sep 10	BTR Delta BTR	
LSU Hurricane Center PAX	Sep 11	BTR-BTR Near-Miss Army Caribou	2.3 hrs
St. Bernard Parish	Sep 12	FEMA personnel	3.2 hrs
Levee Breaks	Sep 12		2.0 hrs
Huoma Airport - Pick up PAX National Congress of American Indians	Sep 13	One PAX cryied as we flew over his village. Spotted a forest fire as we returned to Baton Rouge from Huoma after dropping off PAX	3.0 hrs
Moved to Tyndall AFB	Sep 13	Night	2.9 hrs
USAF CE's Long Day Day break to midnight	Sep 14	Fuel Emergency	
Naval Air Station NO		MSY (Louie Armstrong) Biloxi to Tyndall	6.1 hrs
USAF CE's	Sep 15	Another Long Day PAM to MSY to NBG to PAM	5.1 hrs
PAM to Clinton AL	Sep 17	Left aircraft there-returned home	1.8 hrs

Clovis Tornado Damage—Captain Joe Friel and the NM Wing Operations acted proactively by allowing CVN 060, CAP assets to participate in the damage assessment from the tornado in Clovis in March of 2007. David Hudson and Bill Russell flew a mission to assist Emergency Preparedness Director Ken De Los Santos with digital photos and a film that provided a tool to determine the strength of the storm. From this determination, decisions were made that dictated how much funding was made available from state and federal agencies.

Northridge Earthquake—When a magnitude 6.7 earthquake hit Los Angeles in January of 1994, Farmington and ABQ SQ II responded. The quake, which killed 57 and injured more than 9,000 people, is often remembered for the freeway overpasses that were destroyed.

21 CAP members Lloyd Sallee and Tom Soapes prepare to depart to assist with the relief efforts for the Northridge Earthquake in 1995. Dannie Roberts of Farmington was also among the contingent.

***

Many factors affect the judgment made by the search pilot. These range from concern for weather conditions, the terrain, as well as the sense of urgency to locate the victims— who may be in critical condition. Moreover, as the incidents related here convey, not all the decisions result in a safe operation. The key is to have seasoned, well trained crews, who can effectively evaluate the situation and make the best choices to minimize risk.

Falcon Virgo

Falcon Virgo is a nationwide collection of exercises that sharpen the skills of North American Radar Defense Command's (NORAD) response to domestic aerial threats. Southwest Region of the Civil Air Patrol participates in this exercise from the El Paso Area simulating aerial targets for the United States Air Force. It is a real-world opportunity for personnel to help in the defense of the homeland. Pilots, Observers, and Incident Base Staff are employed for this very large exercise. The New Mexico Wing, project officer in recent years has been Col. Frank Buethe.

These exercises comprise a series of training flights held in coordination with the Federal Aviation Administration, the National Capital Region Command Center, the Joint Air Defense Operations Center, the Continental US NORAD Region (CONR), Civil Air Patrol, the US Coast Guard and the CONR's various Air Defense Sectors.

Falcon Virgo is designed to test NORAD's intercept and identification operations, as well as procedural tests of the NCR Visual Warning System. Civil Air Patrol aircraft, Air Force F-16s and C-38s, and Coast Guard HH-65 Dolphin helicopters, typically participate in the exercise flights that occur throughout the day, including late night and early morning hours, on scheduled exercise dates.

As the Continental United States (CONUS) geographical component of the bi-national command NORAD, CONR provides airspace surveillance and control, and directs air sovereignty activities for the CONUS region. CONR and its assigned Air Force assets throughout the country ensure air safety and security against potential air threats.

Since Sept. 11, 2001, NORAD fighters have responded to more than 2,300 possible air threats in the United States, Canada and Alaska, and have flown more than 46,000 sorties with the support of

Airborne Warning and Control System and air-to-air-refueling aircraft.

The author had an opportunity to fly the Falcon Virgo Exercise in April 2009, whose multi-fold purpose was to validate and certify an Air Defense Artillery unit, and to exercise Homeland Defense Operations and the various command and control channels.

> The aircrew for each of eleven GPS equipped CAP aircraft consisted of two experienced pilots, representing five wings of the Southwest Region. I was impressed with the planning that assured a safe and well-coordinated operation between the various agencies. An overview briefing on the day of arrival in El Paso coupled with advanced availability of the Operations Plan and exercise routes provided a thorough understanding of the objectives and activities.
>
> Five routes (labeled A-E) penetrated the various restricted areas of the White Sands Missile Range and McGregor Range just north of the El Paso International Airport from which we flew. Our role as a 'target' was to enter a route at a designated Initial Point (IP) within one minute of a selected time and fly the route at a predetermined airspeed, with descents to selected altitudes, to arrive at the terminating point called the BULLSEYE at a specific clock time.
>
> The eight-day exercise rotated the crews to different launch times for succeeding days so that each crew would fly an early morning (0100) through a late night flight (2200) schedule. After completing a route, the crew was directed by the controlling agency (CUFF Control) to make an additional run over another route. A typical flight would consist of 3-4 routes flown over a period of 3.5 hours.
>
> What made the week so challenging was the high winds both on the surface and aloft that averaged about 30 knots for most of our flights. I was privileged to be paired with Craig Coulter, a former F-105 fighter pilot. We alternated the left seat—the right seat typically performed the navigation set-up and the communications, while the left seat flew the plane. We had been tasked to fly the routes with a ground speed of 90 knots, but with the tailwind and turbulence on some routes, this was not possible.

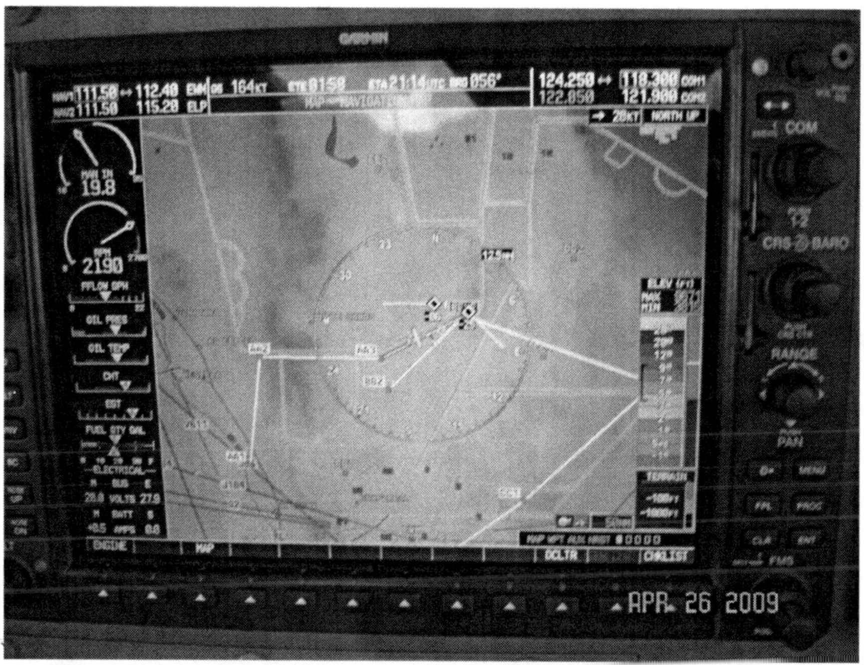

22 The C182 G1000 MFD shows the inbound track on the left and the other two targets (diamonds with dark centers) crossing over BULLSEYE in the center of the screen. The MFD shows a tailwind of 28 kts and a ground speed of 164 kts.

Four aircraft, of which only one was a CAP plane, typically worked each run from four routes simultaneously; crossing over the BULLSEYE at slightly different times and altitudes. Some of the other aircraft included a Learjet and an old DC-9 as well as a light sport aircraft. CUFF Control would periodically point out the other aircraft which we could see on the G1000 Traffic Information System displayed on the MFD. We were intercepted twice by a Coast Guard helicopter that briefly flew formation with us. It was an interesting experience.

***

23 A Coast Guard Helicopter intercepts a Falcon Virgo CAP target aircraft.

***

Walter Dutton, of the Las Cruces Composite Squadron wrote the following description of a similar exercise for an edition of the Cactus Corner Newsletter.

> Early one Thursday morning in December, Mission Pilot LtCol Paul Cline and Observer Capt. Walter Dutton prepared for a different type of CAP mission for the Las Cruces Squadron. At the request of the Arizona Wing, CAP, and the 162nd Fighter Wing of the Arizona Air National Guard, based at Davis Monthan AFB in Tucson , we were going to fly the CAP C182 just north of the Mexican border, on a homeland security training mission with the fighters.
>
> The Cessna was pre-flighted, weather checked, last minute details of the mission were confirmed with the162FW. A flight plan was filed, a flight release was obtained, and we were ready to depart for the boot-heel of New Mexico and the MOA in southeastern Arizona.
>
> At the scheduled time, we entered the MOA and started flying down one of the broad valleys. About 10 minutes after we entered the MOA, we heard 'Fight's

On', the code words to start the exercise. Shortly after that, an F16 flew past our left wing to 'check us out'. Another pass by the F16, and then we heard a call on the radio to "... *the white Cessna flying along the Mexican border. You have been intercepted by the United States Air Force.*" Since our instructions were to ignore any radio calls or visual signals from the fighters, we continued flying along.

After another visual inspection pass and additional radio calls, the forth pass by the F16 included rocking of his wings, to indicate that we should follow him – which we ignored. At one point, we heard the wingman say that he was at 17,000 feet, way above us at about 7,000. Then we heard the F16 pilot say that he was going to do a photo run, and his final pass was on our right side and just below us. Then we got a call to 'Knock it off', the code that the exercise was over.

We headed back to Las Cruces knowing that we had played some small part in helping the pilots of the 162FW train to protect our borders. We enjoyed it, and we and we would like to do it again.

Customs Missions

An interesting partnership began in 1987 when the US Customs Bureau called on CAP to help stop the influx of illegal drugs into the US from Mexico. Because of the restrictions placed on the military in enforcing laws in the United States, CAP is limited primarily to reconnaissance flights. The objective was to fly the southern perimeter of the state and look for suspicious activity such as vehicles or groups of people moving north across the border in areas that would not normally be traveled. A discrete air-ground frequency was used to communicate with the ground based border patrol agents who would then perform the physical intercept.

Ralph Meyerhein was one of the many pilots and crewmembers who volunteered for these missions. He recalls that NM Wing flew 2-3 missions a week during the period between 1997 and 2004. He noted that the position of the border was plainly visible with markers positioned each mile.

One of several mission profiles would have the crew fly from the Arizona state line across the southern boundary of New Mexico to the Texas state line. Flown at altitudes of 1000 feet AGL and low cruising speeds of about 100 knots, these flights could last up to four hours. Most of the NM Wing aircraft were involved in daylight missions that were flown at different times during the day. There were times when an early or late mission would require the crew to remain over night, typically in Las Cruces if they originated out of Los Alamos or Albuquerque.

Survey of Military Training Routes

No doubt, pilots are aware of the faint lines that often traverse the sectional charts used for in-flight VFR navigation. With designations such as IR-107, VR-212, or SR214, these are Military Training Routes. Tony Sobol, who has flown these routes many times as an FB-111 pilot, now flies them as a CAP pilot to verify each route. He provides the following narrative:

> Begun in 1987 for the NM Air National Guard to check for the possibility of unreported new construction, power lines, towers etc., these routes must be surveyed yearly at speeds of less than 250 kts for any uncharted obstacle over 100'. While any aircraft traveling at less than 250 kts can accomplish these surveys, the military has found Civil Air Patrol to be well suited for this mission. CAP provides disciplined pilots and crewmembers that are familiar with aerial search procedures. Many CAP members are former military aviators who have flown these routes while on active duty and are familiar with their usage. Finally, CAP is very cost effective. The typical IR/VR route can be surveyed for about $500-$600 and SR routes for $300.
>
> To accomplish a survey the time is coordinated with the route controlling agency to ensure it is not in use. The survey is flown at 1000' AGL at normal cruise speed. When an uncharted obstacle is found its position is recorded in latitude and longitude. Its MSL altitude is either estimated from the charts or recorded from the GPS system. Its actual AGL altitude is estimated. The new CAP glass cockpit aircraft are ideally suited for gathering this data. The type of obstacle; microwave, cell, or radio tower or other, is also noted. Finally, the obstacle is photographed. To survey the average IR/VR route takes 5-6 hours and the SR route takes 3 hours. At the completion of the survey, the data is turned over to the route controlling agency who then coordinates with the FAA to have these obstacles entered on the FAA sectional charts.

> Here in New Mexico we survey the following routes: IR 107, IR 109, IR 111, IR 112, IR 113, VR 100, VR 108, VR 114, VR 125, SR 212, SR 213, and SR 214. All the IR/VR routes with one exception, IR 112, terminate at Melrose Range and are used by the full spectrum of military aircraft. IR 112 terminates at a Radar Bomb Site (RBS) in Holbrook, AZ. The three SR routes are around the Albuquerque area and are primarily used by the 58 SOW.

SAREX Competition

Chuck Fairchild provided the following narrative about a SAREX he took part in June 1982 in a C172 (N5098R) with Walt Hatch and Robert Gibson.

"We had been selected to crew one of two NM CAP A/C going to the 1st annual regional search and rescue contest in Georgetown, TX. This was an Air Force sponsored test of 2 teams (2 planes) from each of the region states, AZ, NM, CO, OK, TX and LA. The contest was originally scheduled for 1 May but had been postponed because of rain. The last week of April we had gone to ABQ to get uniforms from wing and make other arrangements. I had gone to a couple of SAREXs to get a bit of refresher training before heading to TX. After the event was postponed, we didn't do anything for over a month except wait.

When the time came we were eager and ready to head for TX. One reason was that we would get about 15 hrs of flying for $5/h. But we were also eager because it should be a lot of fun. Anyway, the morning of the 18th finally arrived and we headed out with good weather and spirits. On the way, however, the weather started looking pretty poor ahead so Robert and Walt wanted to turn east toward Lubbock (I was a backseat non-driver). I suggested that they check with Flight Watch before turning east. The report indicated that we would be better off to continue SE to Roswell. At Roswell, the weather got a little worse, but not bad, and the trip was pretty pleasant, all in all.

According to prior agreement Walt flew 1st leg down (200 hr pilot), Bob flew the last leg down (500? hr pilot), and I was to fly the plane in the contest.

Everything went according to plan the first evening. After refueling, tying the plane in the CAP area, and going into town to get a room (and shower--boy was the weather warm and muggy), we returned to the airport via CAP bus for an 1800 briefing. The briefing was thorough and fairly professional in spite of the briefing officer (USAF colonel) being stung by a wasp mid-through.

Speaking of bugs... during the briefing, I found a spotted tick on my arm, so I took him off and threw him in the grass. The following afternoon after the contest, sure enough, while showering I found a spotted tick burrowed in my leg. This time, after removing him intact I flushed him down the John. There were many other nasty insect and spider varieties in that part of the country.

After the briefing, we drew lots for a takeoff time. We drew (or rather the other NM team drew for us) 1005 and 1350 times for the two sortie aspects of the contest. At the time, we wished we had drawn earlier flight because of expected turbulence and winds in the PM. We were right and wrong.

Next morning after a good but very slow breakfast, we got a ride out to the airport with a bird colonel who had joined us for the meal. We arrived at the airport about an hour before we were allowed to report for final flight briefing. So, we sat around reviewing our flight plan, checking over the plane, etc. The briefing didn't amount to much, just last minute weather (which wasn't too good), acceptance of our flight plan, and a time check.

A couple of planes on the earlier launches returned soon after take-off because of lousy weather in the search area. By the time our turn came, the weather was improving, and we prepared to launch. Again my crew was so nervous and antsy they made me so. We had a launch time of 1005+2 minutes and if we didn't make the time we would lose beaucoup points. I insisted that we not start the engine until 10 minutes before launch because I didn't want to sit at the end of the runway for 10 minutes before T. O. That made them really sweat, but they didn't complain. Wouldn't you know, the engine just turned over and over without a kick the first time I tried it. I was sweating then, and starting to think I had really goofed. While waiting 30 seconds for the starter to cool before trying again, tension in the plane was thick as mustard.

Fortunately, after about 10 seconds of cranking the second time, it started. As soon as it started, Walt said, "you might want to raise your flaps before taxiing". That snapped something in me and I blurted very foolishly, "come on guys, gimme a break. I'm a professional; I don't need to be reminded of everything." Immediately, I felt embarrassed so I lamely explained that we were all getting too taut and should relax and enjoy the day.

We did manage to take off exactly at the assigned time, and headed toward the ELT search area. When we arrived at the town where we were supposed to orbit until picking up the ELT, we heard nothing. I decided we had better cheat a little bit and go above our assigned altitude of 1500' AGL. At 2500 ft, just at the base of the overcast, we still didn't hear anything, but the directional needle was giving a weak indication to the NE. Without anything else to go on we headed in that direction.

After traveling about 10 miles, we started getting an intermittent, then a steady ELT signal. After a few minutes, since the signal was steady I decided to go back to 1500 ft. As we descended below 2000 feet, we lost the audio signal. For a minute I didn't worry about it because we had been losing it occasionally even at higher altitudes. But, after a minute and no signal I took it back to 3000 ft where the clouds were breaking up with bases at 3400. Still no signal and the needle response was weaker.

We started making a large square pattern, using wing dip and any other techniques we could think of to pick up the signal. We went back to the area and altitude where we had lost the signal, but nothing. I was concerned about the time we had been in the search area because another plane was supposed to enter the area 30 minutes after we did, and we were supposed to exit. So far, we hadn't seen him, but we had been in the area for 45 minutes.

24 Bad sun angles make a search more difficult.

All of a sudden, we heard the ELT again loud and clear. From then on we held it and started closing on it. When it was very loud and near, we all of a sudden started hearing another ELT. This double signal really confused the needle and us. After stumbling around for awhile we finally found the marker on the ground, 1 hr + 12 min after T. O. We talked to the ELT ground crew on FM radio and they asked us if we had heard both ELTs.

We skedaddled out of the area to clear it for the next plane. As we passed over the initial fix (town), we saw the next plane orbiting the fix. He saw us and made a beeline in the direction we had come.

The next sortie was a visual search at 1350. That gave us a while to rest and plan some. This time I relented and started the engine 15 minutes before launch. As you might expect we sat at the end of the runway about 6 minutes waiting for our T. O. time.

During climb-out, I could tell we had a pretty good tailwind on our first leg of the flight. Unfortunately, it was stronger than I thought and we reached our first fix about 2 min before time. I slowed it down more but we still reached the second fix about a minute early. The third fix we hit on the money, and the fourth, where we entered the search grid, we missed position by a half mile. Turbulence and wind corrections for the approximately 20 kt wind made flying an accurate pattern difficult.

Anyway, we spotted 2 of the 4 targets in the search area. We departed the search area about 3 minutes late and had to firewall it to fight the headwind and pass over the field 1 minute past our designated time. Well it was fun, but as we learned at the banquet that night, we hadn't taken any prizes even though we must have scored fairly high.

One thing that evidently counted against us was our appearance. The plane wasn't too clean, and we didn't have the radio-telephone license for it. But, the thing that probably killed us was the fact that I was wearing tennis shoes and a white tennis hat instead of regulation boots and hat. (I think also the fact that I was wearing Navy gold wings instead of CAP wings on my flight suit didn't set too well with the Air Force judges.) Nobody had told me that we had to wear regulation military flight duds, and since we didn't ever wear them on searches I hadn't even brought my boots for that warm country. Oh well, the foibles of man!

Actually, NM still took 2nd place in the competition, thanks mainly to the ABQ T-34 crew who won 1st place in the grid search and 2nd place in the ELT search. Nonetheless, we must have helped some, because Arizona, who took 1st in ELT and 2nd in grid search, won the best state award with us a close second. In fact, Bill Overton (our squadron CO and later NM wing commander) claimed that if I had been in proper uniform, NM would have won. Woe is me!"

Snapshot in Time

- 1981 nine aircraft in the Wing (six were certified for IFR)
  - 317 pilots, 189 cadets
  - 18 base radio stations
  - 125 mobile radio stations
- 1982 dry rate C150 N50929 $14/hr.
- 1987 average 106 hrs per A/C
- 1988 average 200 hrs per aircraft, one A/C recorded 700 hrs.
- 1989 3893 total hours, average 324 hr per A/C
- 1990 there were 16 funded SAR missions for 290 hrs.
  - two FINDS
  - two SAVES.
  - 200 customs missions
  - 37 DEA missions
  - 3,365 hours for the year.
  - 1166 hr proficiency & training
  - 2036 hr mission flying
- 1991 there were
  - 58 Air Force funded missions that generated
  - 308 sorties and 708 hours of flight time, resulting in
  - Nine saves!
- 2009 Farmington Initiated BLM flights to observe Native American archeological sites

5. Cadet Programs

When the Civil Air Patrol first formed, membership was limited to persons at least 18 years of age. However, it soon became apparent that many younger people were deeply interested in aviation and in helping their country. On October 1, 1942, the CAP program expanded to include teens between the ages of 15 to 17. These 'cadets,' as they were called, proved willing volunteers to help in ground duties to relieve the 'senior' members. It also provided training for such vital functions as first aid and communications. Soon, regular ground schools offered aviation training for aspiring pilots. Within six months, the cadet program had grown to 20,000 volunteers.

A September 1943 clipping noted that NM Wing goal was to have 100 cadets by March of 1944 and 600 by 1945. The Wing placed 4th in the recruiting competition for cadets as reported in a March 7, 1945 news item. CAP set an ambitious goal of 250,000 cadets nationwide by 1945 (Cadet membership in 2009 is about 25,000).

From the *CAPP 50-5, Introduction to Civil Air Patrol* we learn more about those early requirements to be a Cadet:

> Requirements for cadet membership were necessarily strict: each adult male member of CAP could sponsor one boy, and each adult female member could sponsor one girl. Cadets had to be between 15 and 17 years old, physically fit, maintain satisfactory grades, and be native-born American citizens of parents who had been citizens of the United States for at least 10 years. Although these restrictions seemed severe, they were deliberately imposed to hold down membership levels until a solid base could be established. They attended weekly meetings in classrooms or other places, studied in groups, on their own, or with their senior member counterparts. They spent nearly every weekend at the airport, applying what they had learned in the classroom.
>
> The cost to the Office of Civilian Defense to recruit 20,000 cadets was less than $200, which consisted mostly of administrative costs. Not a bad return on such an investment.

An excerpt from the *New Mexico Wing Senior Training Manual 1959 'Lesson Five — The Cadet Program'* provides a better understanding of the cadet membership in the early years:

> The CAP members were very busy in those early days of World War II doing many tasks for the nation in time of war. It is remarkable that they would consider a cadet program so important that they would have started it right when the CAP was at its busiest period. It shows that the farsighted people of the CAP considered the cadet program so important that it could not be postponed for war or any other emergency.
>
> And there were precedents of course. Numerous teenage auxiliaries have been attached to certain parent bodies. Most fraternal orders have such detached groups. The American legion and a number of service clubs sponsor youth groups as a part of their programs. Churches have always paid great attention to their youth programs, realizing that a church that does not raise its own future member dies out and is gone.
>
> In the spring of 1943 when the Army Air Force became responsible for the CAP as an auxiliary, cadet programs were given added stress. Courses were provided in military courtesy, military drill, navigation and meteorology. Those who were about to turned eighteen were treated to a special pre-induction course that was designed to prepare them for life in the Army.
>
> It was found that young men with a CAP background where more easily absorbed into the armed services. The CAP training gave them the jump on those without it. This advantage was reflected in quick promotions, adjustment to service life, and rapid progress in the ground school classes. A number of the CAP graduates went into flight training.
>
> During the war, CAP had a goal of 100,000 carefully selected cadets though this objective was never attained. At one time, the records showed something in the order of 60,000, but this estimate was probably somewhat optimistic. As there was no annual renewal, the record did not reflect the number that had dropped out. For instance in New Mexico Wing the record showed 500 cadets in early 1953. The actual number of active cadets at the time was something in the order of 250. In 1956, there were about 325 active cadets.

The cadet numbers for the wing probably peaked in the late 1950s. Attendance records from March 4, 1959 for Albuquerque Composite Squadron No. 1 (now Eagle Cadet Squadron), the largest squadron in the state at that time, showed 115 active cadets on March 4, 1959, with 78 cadets attending the meeting that night. By June 1961, the squadron's number of active cadets had decreased to 67. In September 2009, the largest cadet squadron in the state, Albuquerque Thunderbird, had 51 cadets.

25 Parades are always a great way to stimulate recruiting such as the Sqdn 1 Drill team at the 1960 State Fair. Left front: Ric Himebrook, followed by Stan Roeske

Although NM Wing had 388 cadets in 2009, some believe membership could be many times that number if an effective and on-going recruiting campaign were instituted. Others cite the wide array of other activities now available to those in their early teens as sidetracking any such program. The unfortunate part of the issue is that CAP offers so much to help stabilize the uncertain teen years and the lack of moral leadership that now exists. The opportunities and experiences for cadets is virtually unlimited. Andy Selph, a former Spaatz cadet and Squadron Commander observed, *"I also have always thought that another limiting factor to the growth of the Cadet program was (is) the size of the Senior membership, as without adequate Senior staffing, a large Cadet program would be difficult to manage.*"

In addition to the extensive formal Cadet Aerospace Education program, cadets often find themselves using their CAP expertise in their schoolwork. In 1969, Las Cruces Cadet Gary Schwede of the Las Vegas Composite Squadron won honors at the International Science Fair in Fort Worth, Texas, with his project "*Research on the Suitability of the Conical Configuration for Sub-sonic Astrodynamic Vehicles*". In 1989, three Alamogordo cadets were winners at the local Science Fair. Cadet Leslie Himebrook's *"Problems of Propagation of Radio Waves in Finding Lost Aircraft,"* Cadet Jason Bailey's *"Aerodynamics of Wings,"* and Cadet Don Fuqua's presentation on *"The Effect of Friction on Airfoil Parasitic Drag,"* showcase the aeronautical knowledge gained by some of our CAP cadets.

Pat Chochrell Balok, who became a cadet in 1959, recalls, *"I remember working the radio at the command center during REDCAPS (real search). Cadets did a lot of radio work and we had our own home crystal radio units that we used for net communications. We went all over the state for SARCAPS (practice search missions) and we would go out and do practice ground searches. We had our O-flights in a Piper and it seems we did a lot more flying than cadets do now."*

The cadet program plays an increasingly important role in today's culture. With more than half our young people being raised in a single parent home, their ability to understand the full spectrum of a complete family is in jeopardy. Often the single parent is working to support the children and there is little unity. Young people need to feel a part of a family and if they do not get that relationship at home they will find it elsewhere—all too often in gangs.

The CAP cadet agenda, like the scouting program, provides an organization that has a wide variety of activities that can keep our young people focused and involved in educational, challenging, and fun activities. Having a core group of motivated youth, in which the new cadet can find friendship, is a critical part of CAP.

Carol (Sawyer) Roeske, who also became a cadet in 1959, remembers, "*There were so many cadet activities, we could have been busy all week with just CAP. Beside weekly meetings with classes, we had drill practice and competition, marching in parades, SARCAPS (practice missions), REDCAPS (real missions), summer encampments, Special Activities, orientation rides, air shows, Armed Forces Day displays, and lots of community work. CAP always worked the Cerebral Palsy telethons, and for the Mother's March of Dimes we would set up a communications unit at 4th and Central. We put out collection cans, one with the name of each state, and encouraged people to donate money on behalf of their favorite state. Our squadron (Albuquerque Sqdn I) had a bus, with terrific seniors who would take us all over the state for our activities, and we had lots of fun during those bus rides, and even afterwards when we made a game out of washing the bus. The friendships we formed in CAP were a valuable part of our experience in the program.*"

Cadet Advisory Council

Some of the things cadets gain knowledge of in squadron activities are military courtesy, chain of command, and following orders. In the Cadet Advisory Council, cadets have the opportunity to learn the democratic process, including open debate and parliamentary procedures. Representatives from squadrons assemble at the wing level, elect officers, and appoint committees to accomplish wing cadet business and advise wing staff on the cadet program.

The 1969-1970 Yearbook lists the CAC Executive Committee:

C/LTC Warren Harkins, Hobbs, Chairman
C/Lt. Barbara Cole, Otero County, Vice Chairman
C/Maj. Beverly Vito, Central Group, Secretary
C/2 Lt. Thomas C. Scalf, T-Bird, Parliamentarian

Accomplishments cited were:

A new Constitution, 8 February 1969
The Yearbook Committee established, 8 February 1969
Honor Cadet 1968 Award presented to C/Sgt Mike Dillon, a representative from Central Group
Drill Competition Committee set up, 3 August 1969
NCO, Drill and Officers' Schools reported, 11 October 1969
Military Ball Committee set up, 8 February 1969

In some years, cadet advisory councils were formed at region and even national levels, and NM Wing has had a presence at both. In 1972, Beverly (Pepe) Vito was NM Wing representative to Southwest Region CAC and Chairman Pro-Tem of National CAC. Kaycee Gilbert served as Chair of the National CAC for the 2004-2005 term.

26 Cadet Advisory Council member Gayle Pinney of T-Bird created CAP recruiting bookmarks in the mid-1960s.

Spaatz Awards

While aerospace education and leadership training have been constants in the cadet program over the years, there have been many changes. For instance, the minimum age requirement for cadets was lowered during the 1950s to 14, during the mid-1960s to 13, and now is 12 (with some circumstances even lower). Even the uniforms changed, as pictures through the years clearly show.

One major change in late 1963 was an increase in the various achievements to which the cadet can aspire. Before then, the *Certificate of Proficiency* was the highest level of accomplishment, and was a requirement for participating in such Special Activities as the International Air Cadet Exchange (IACE) or the Jet Orientation Program.

CIVIL AIR PATROL

AUXILIARY OF THE U.S. AIR FORCE

Be it known that

Cadet Richard F. Himebrook, C84-2570

has satisfactorily completed the Training Course prescribed for Civil Air Patrol Cadets

In testimony whereof, there is conferred this

Certificate of Proficiency

Given at Washington, D.C. on this 8th day of October, 1958.

National Commander, Civil Air Patrol

Chief of Staff, United States Air Force

27 Before the Spaatz Award came into being in 1963, the Certificate of Proficiency was the highest achievement available to cadets

Rank was awarded as a cadet progressed through the program and filled various leadership roles in the quadroon. One former cadet noted that, *"In the old days cloth chevons were sewn on the sleeve to denote rank. While we learned how to sew, it was a major hassle to have to do it to all your uniforms every few months. The use of the metal badge for the collar is much more convenient."*

Cadet Major was the highest rank that could be assigned outside of the annual summer encampment, when temporary ranks of Cadet Lt Col and Cadet Colonel could be assigned. Most Cadet Commanders of large squadrons in NM before 1963 could rise to the grade of Cadet Captain, if they met the other time and achievement requirements.

In the 1963 program change, the numbered achievement levels were given names of aerospace pioneers, and the Certificate of Proficiency became the Billy Mitchell Award. Recognizing the need to provide higher levels of advancement, additional leadership achievements were added after a cadet completed the Mitchell Award, including the Amelia Earhart Award and the Carl A. Spaatz award (named for the first Chief of Staff of the Air Force and an aviation visionary). The grades of cadet LtCol and cadet Colonel became available to cadets who completed the higher leadership levels, with promotion to cadet Colonel automatic for cadets who earned the Spaatz Award.

Requirements for the Spaatz award are set high—in academics, leadership, and service. As a result, few cadets will make the effort or find the time to attain it—thus it is numbered to provide the cadet with a means of understanding the significance of the accomplishment. Only one of every 10,000 cadets receives the award.

A 1965 news item noted, *"Gwen D. Sawyer was the first New Mexico Cadet to receive the honor on December 17, 1965 when she received Spaatz Award Number 8. The award was presented by Maj.*

Gen. John N. White, USAF, Commander of the Air Force Special Weapons Center at Kirtland AFB, Albuquerque, and is the highest award that can be earned by a CAP Cadet. Miss Sawyer is the eighth Cadet in the nation and the first young lady to be so honored. With the award goes an automatic promotion to the rank of CAP Cadet Colonel. Miss Sawyer is a 1963 graduate of Highland High School in Albuquerque, and is studying at the University of New Mexico."

28 Gwen D. Sawyer, first New Mexico Cadet to receive the Spaatz Award presented by Maj. Gen. John N. White, USAF, Commander, Air Force Special Weapons Center at Kirtland AFB, 1965.

Les Himebrook is notable in that he was only 15 when he was awarded the Spaatz in 1987—an almost unbelievable achievement until you understand the family in which he was raised. His father, Ric Himebrook, was a cadet at age 13 in 1957 and rose to command the NM Wing. His mother, Roberta has held many positions at the squadron and Wing level.

NM Wing was not the only one that benefited from the efforts of these cadets; their positive influence for CAP extended to Europe. It turns out that two of these recipients, #164 Beverly (Pepe) Vito and #560 James Elliott ran into each other in 1983 at Ramstein AFB, Germany. Jim was stationed there in the Air Force, and so was Beverly's husband. After they bumped into each other on base one day, they started reminiscing about their cadet days, and decided to see if they could find enough other former CAPers there to start a squadron on base.

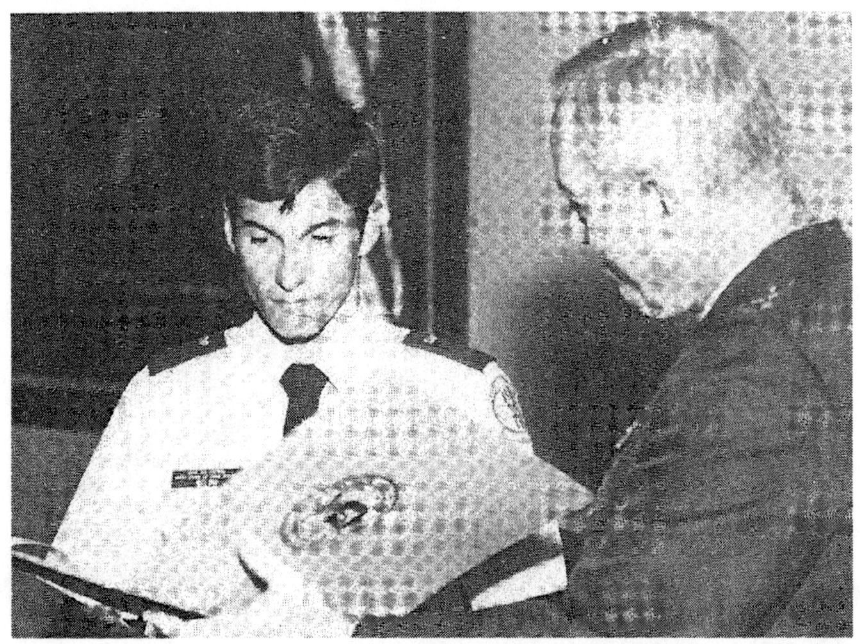

29 Cadet Andrew Selph of Thunderbird Composite Squadron receives the Spaatz award from Air Force Major General Richard W. Phillips.

While Elliott contacted HQ to set things in motion, Beverly used her PAO experience to put an article in the base newspaper asking any interested people to contact her. They recruited several other ex-members to join them and began meeting in a location Jim had obtained from the base CO. The squadron received a charter in

1984, right after Beverly's family had been transferred to Italy. Beverly reported hearing later that some other squadrons branched off from that one as members transferred to other bases in Europe.

New Mexico Wing Spaatz Award Recipients

Spaatz No.	Recipient	Date
8	Gwen D. Sawyer	17 Dec 1965
164	Beverly A. Vito	31 Dec 1971
243	Ben Klausner	02 Nov 1973
392	John Tor Bejnar	03 Jun 1976
560	James Elliott	01 Dec 1980
640	Andrew Selph	18 Apr 1983
670	Timothy Selph	02 Nov 1983
697	Michael Moore	26 Jun 1984
857	Leslie Himebrook	01 Sep 1987
921	Darrell LaRoche	29 Dec 1988
943	Matthias Girardi	12 Jun 1989
960	Scott McCarty	15 Sep 1989
993	Anthony Navarrette	18 Apr 1990
1274	Pamela Sever*	16 Jan 1995
1325	Luke T. Davis	16 May 1997
1356	Isaac A. Block	15 Jul 1997
1388	Jessica C. Block	13 Jan 1999
1434	Aleyna M. Farrell	01 Sep 2000
1449	Rebecca M. Lenberg	28 Dec 2001
1535	Kaycee D. Gilbert	19 Jul 2004
1570	Tyler J. Albright	24 Aug 2005
1670	Charles W. Matthews	29 Oct 2007
1726	Joseph O'Loughlin	19 Mar 2009

*Although official records credit this award to Florida Wing, that is only because NM Cadet Sever was attending college in Florida when she was ready to take her Spaatz exam, and was required to transfer to that wing to receive the exam. After graduation, she returned to NM and played an important role in School Enrichment Program (see below).

Summer Encampment

The 'Summer Encampment' is a pivotal milestone in a cadet's career. For many young people, this may be the first time they have had the experience of 'living away from home.' It is also an opportunity to expose the cadet to customs and courtesies, which might not be illustrated within their own squadrons. This is particularly true for start-up or rebuilding squadrons, where older and more experienced cadet leaders may not be available to provide these important legacy traditions. Thus, for many cadets it allows them, for the first time, to see how the rest of the CAP cadet world operates.

The summer encampment has its origins at the very start of the CAP Cadet program. A news item noted, *"A summer camp was held at the Roswell Army Air Field (RAAF) during August 15-25, 1945 with 45 cadets. The long 16-hour training days (from 6 am 10 pm) included cadets from Socorro, Las Cruces, Albuquerque and Santa Fe, plus 'Flights' from Deming and Silver City."*

"There were 106 cadets in attendance at the two week summer encampment at CAAF (Carlsbad Army Air Field) August 3, 1945. They were charged 75 cents per day for rations. Classes were held in military discipline and courtesy, physical training, Morse code, and aircraft recognition. Cadets were from Las Cruces, Hurley, and Silver City".

Living for a week in a 'barracks environment' also provides a measure of self-discipline for aspects as seemingly trivial as personal hygiene—how to handle a 'ditty bag' in a communal shower environment. It is interesting to visit the showers after the cadets have left and see the items left behind that 'mom' used to take care of.

The activities provided during an encampment can make a big impression on the cadet. Seeing the many aspects of an operational military unit, for example, gives a better appreciation for the training and maintenance that goes into preparing a plane and pilot for a mission.

Many encampment activities are participative and physical in nature, such as canoeing or rock climbing. These are performed under careful adult supervision and provide an opportunity for the cadets to grow in confidence of their own abilities.

30 This photo, identified as 'Los Alamos cadets attending Summer Encampment at Kirtland AFB—1947' (L to R) Johnson, T. E., Standlee, H. R., Garcia, W.J., Shane, C. C., Lathrop, last is unidentified.

The overall encampment has not changed much over the past 50 years. The more experienced cadets, who have attended one or more encampments, are assigned responsibilities of organizing and moving cadets from one activity to another, while qualified adults oversee critical aspects of safety and specialized instruction.

The NM Wing encampments of the 50's and early 60's were always attended by over 100 cadets. At the start of the new millennium that number dropped to about 60. In the 1950's and 60's, the encampments were often held jointly with Arizona Wing, at Air Force bases in Albuquerque, Roswell and Clovis, New Mexico; Chandler and Tucson, Arizona; and El Paso, Amarillo and Abilene, Texas.

NEW MEXICO WING, CIVIL AIR PATROL

AUXILIARY OF THE UNITED STATES AIR FORCE

THIS IS TO CERTIFY THAT GWEN D. SAWYER, 084-5178

ATTENDED THE 1959 CADET ENCAMPMENT AT KIRTLAND AIR FORCE BASE 6 - 14 JUNE 1959 AND SUCCESSFULLY COMPLETED THE TRAINING COURSE WITH THE FOLLOWING CONTENT:

USAF AND CAP ORIENTATION AND ORGANIZATION	2 HOURS
COURTESY, DISCIPLINE, LEADERSHIP AND COMMAND	8 HOURS
HEALTH, PHYSICAL TRAINING AND DRILL	4 HOURS
AIRFRAME AND ENGINE MAINTENANCE	4 HOURS
FLIGHT PLANNING, NAVIGATION AND WEATHER	2 HOURS
AIR TRAFFIC CONTROL AND AIR DEFENSE	5 HOURS
NIGHT AND INSTRUMENT FLIGHT	3 HOURS
RADIOLOGICAL DEFENSE	2 HOURS
SAFETY - GROUND, WATER AND AIR	4 HOURS
CHARACTER GUIDANCE AND CITIZENSHIP	2 HOURS
TOTAL	40 HOURS

DATED THIS 13TH DAY OF JUNE, 1959

J. GIBBS SPRING
COL CAP, WING COMMANDER

HOMER L. BIGELOW, JR
LT COL CAP, ENCAMPMENT COMMANDER

31 A 1959 Encampment Training Certificate. It details the type of formal instruction the cadet received.

When the encampments were distant from Albuquerque, cadets were usually transported by military airlift. By the 1980's, encampments were rotated between the various New Mexico military bases. In more recent years, most have been held at Kirtland or the Santa Fe National Guard facility. In the early 1990's joint encampments were held with the JROTC units.

Roberta Himebrook recalls one of her favorite encampment stories relates to her son Les. He discovered an old letter his Dad (a former cadet from the 1950s) had submitted to the Cadet Advisory Council (CAC) evaluating an encampment. So, he submitted that same letter to the CAC some 30 years later. Les read the report to the council—signed by 'Cadet Himebrook'. Then he gave the date of the report—from the early 1960's. The group thought it was a good description of some of the problems of their era...so apparently much [of the encampment] never really changes.

32 1959 Encampment Senior Staff, L to R: Major Amos Dolliver, USAF, Wing LO, Col. J. Gibbs Spring, Wing CO, L/Col Homer L. Bigelow, Jr., Encampment Commander, LtCol Julius Hollenbeck, Maj Juanda Sawyer, LtCol Robert Swain, Encampment Deputy CO, W/O Marsha Edwards

The 1981 encampment was held at Kirtland with 20 cadets from Six squadrons attending. The encampment commander was Capt. Ernest G. Inman with Paul Shirley as Deputy. 1st Lt. Susan Shirley was the Admin Officer. Cadet Michael Gordon of the Black Sheep Squadron received a 45-minute flight in a T-37. (Lt. Shirley passed away later in 1981 at the age of 33).

33 Female cadets review the standard survival pack as a part of one of the many classes during the 1966 encampment.

With respect to the decision to attend the Summer Encampment, Larry Zentner, in an article in the Spring 1997 edition of the Wing newsletter related the following:

> I was a cadet sergeant 15 years old, and had never been away from home alone before. We drove to Cannon AFB, NM and I spent seven days in pure agony. Well, it felt like agony at the time. When I returned home, to T-Bird Cadet Squadron, I was a transformed person. Seriously, I was different. My parents, teachers, choir director, minister, and close friends all commented that I was somehow changed in a special way. And no, I didn't look any different but I did act different. My room and closet was always cleaner. I made my bed all the time. At school, I volunteered more frequently to help. My schoolwork was not any neater, but it was always on time. At church, I spoke up with confidence and understood clearly how to be a team player. The real change was at CAP meetings. I understood why we did things the way we did. I was now contributing in a very real way to accomplish our CAP mission. Years later, as a commissioned officer there were many times when I called on my CAP experiences to accomplish the USAF mission. This experience all started with filling out a CAP Form 54 and attending a Type A Encampment.

34 Airlift returning from 1955 Encampment at Williams AFB, AZ. Silhouetted in door are LtCol Robert Swain and Maj Juanda Sawyer.

***

Charlene Reames, from Spirit Squadron attended the 2007 summer encampment and writes of her experience:

> After the [arrival] briefing we were taken to billeting … After unpacking some of our things we were taken to the chow hall. At the chow hall, we enjoyed MREs (yum yum) for dinner.
>
> The next day we woke up at 05:00 AM, rolled up our sleeping bags and went outside for PT. After PT we went to the chow hall for breakfast [and then] to the barracks to change into our BDUs.
>
> Our first day there we ran the obstacle course and went reppelling. On the second day, we learned self-defense from the state police and participated in simulated war games. The rest of the week when we weren't doing drill, we attended special activities or lectures.

On our fourth day at encampment, we went to Cochiti Lake. There we went scuba diving, rock wall climbing, canoeing, and learned how to turn our BDU s into life preservers. All in all, except for having to eat MREs for lunch every day, we had a great time. I finally met the PT requirements to be promoted to C/Airman. We all had a lot of fun and all who attended the encampment graduated.

35 1966 Encampment Senior Staff. Front row, L to R: Chaplain, LtCol David Beal (AZ Wing), LtCol Robert Barbaree, Maj Henry Moculeski, Encampment CO, Maj William Lane, Capt Paul Carroll

At the end of the encampment week, a graduation ceremony is held where the cadets 'pass in review' and where the outstanding cadets receive awards for their participation.

36 1959 Encampment Pass in Review. Carrying the flags are cadets Leo Zimmerman, left, and Raymond Alexander.

37 Thunderbird SQUADRON participates in numerous community service events. This Honor Guard team led the 2008 Veterans Day Parade with C/Lt Nathan Way as commander. Also seen (Front L to R) AMN Andrew Holets, LtCol Daniel Bracken, (hidden)

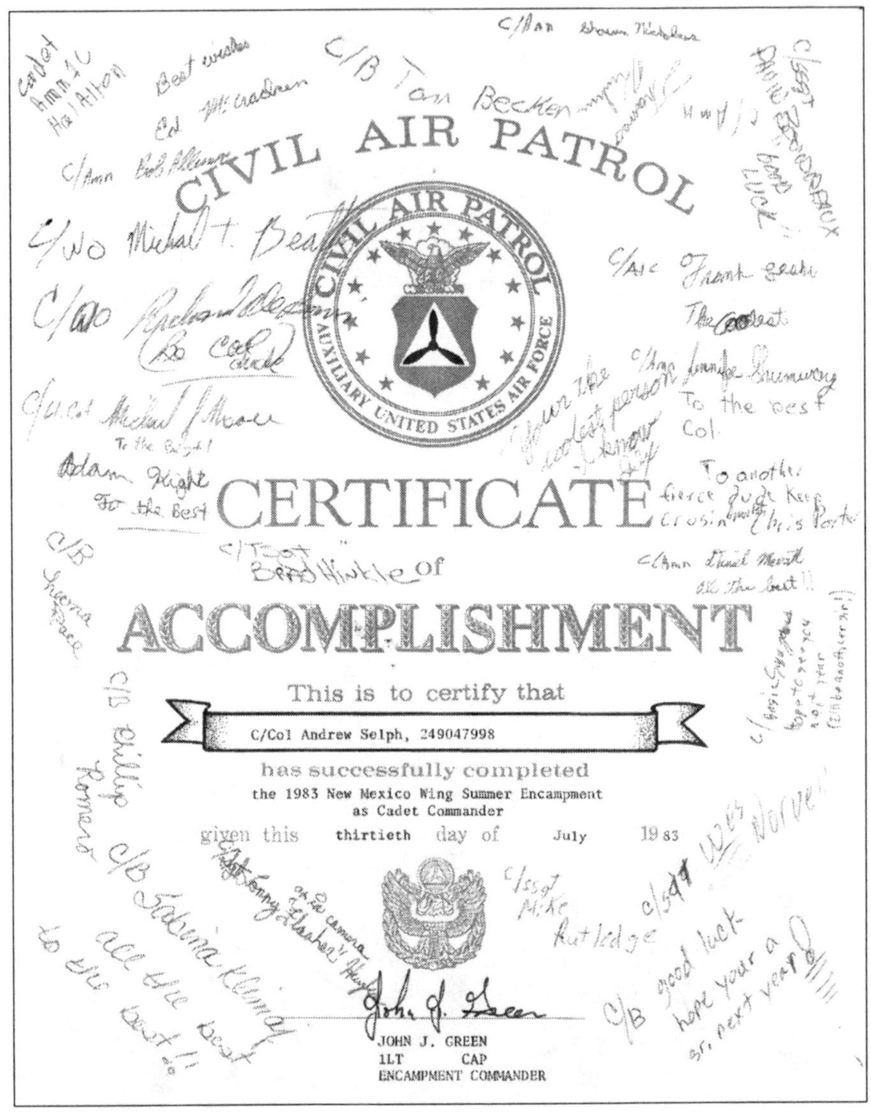

CIVIL AIR PATROL

CIVIL AIR PATROL
AUXILIARY UNITED STATES AIR FORCE

CERTIFICATE of ACCOMPLISHMENT

This is to certify that

C/Col Andrew Selph, 249047998

has successfully completed
the 1983 New Mexico Wing Summer Encampment
as Cadet Commander

given this thirtieth day of July 1983

JOHN J. GREEN
1LT CAP
ENCAMPMENT COMMANDER

38 An interesting way to add memories of an encampment is to have those with whom you shared the event, sign your certificate.

39 **The 1981 Encampment Program cover.**

And they said "it couldn't happen!"
Paul J Ballmer

Winter Encampment

While the Summer Encampment is often considered the high point for many cadets, NM Wing also offers a Winter Encampment positioned between the Christmas and New Year Holidays. LtCol Ballmer of Eagle Squadron originated the idea for the winter session in 2002, and NM Wing is one of the few across the country who holds both. Here is one cadet's view of a Winter Encampment.

The 2005 winter encampment was a success, regardless of its unusually small numbers. Cadets came from Farmington, Rio Rancho, Albuquerque, and one cadet came from the state of Maryland. The encampment included a total of nine basic cadets, nine cadets on staff, and five senior members. Lt Col Paul J. Ballmer was the Encampment Commander and the Cadet Commander of the encampment was C/1st Lt Dustin T. Wittman.

One of the many activities that cadets participated in during the length of the encampment was a tour of the flight line, where they saw aircraft such as the C-130. Cadets also got a tour of the Albuquerque International Control Tower, to see what it's like to direct air traffic. The encampment included PT at the base swimming pool, and a game of volleyball. In addition to these activities, cadets also found themselves drilling and participating in many classes.

During the encampment, cadets stayed at the Roadrunner Club, where they slept on air mattresses they were given. Cadets enjoyed all meals at the base dining hall during their stay at Kirtland.

The Honor Cadet of the Encampment was C/Amn Destiny L. Milleson of the Farmington Composite Squadron. C/ CMSgt Shawn P. McGowan of the Eagle Cadet Squadron was the Honor Staff Member. The Bravo Flight was selected as the Honor Flight of the Encampment.

Those attending the encampment included C/A1C Christopher Kaczorowski from the Caroll Composite Squadron, Maryland Wing; C/SrA Gerald Feltman from the Rio Rancho Falcon Composite Squadron; C/SMSgt Esteban Villa, C/

Enchanted Wings

TSgt Nathaniel Way, C/Amn Samantha Hyatt, C/Amn Sean Kilbane, C/Amn Brian Pascullo, and C/Amn Megan Robbins of the Albuquerque Cadet Squadron (James Monroe Middle School); C/TSgt Alexander.

From the Eagle Squadron Newsletter;

The 37 attendees at the 2006 New Mexico Winter Encampment endured the largest snowstorm in fifty years in the Santa Fe area. The encampment was held at the Oñate Complex of the New Mexico National Guard in Santa Fe. Cadets began their week by learning quickly how to make 'white collar beds'—the kind that you can bounce a quarter off of—in the dormitories where they stayed. They were also responsible for having their lockers all appropriately arranged with the proper spacing of their uniforms and their shoes lined up under the bed.

Cadets were given a tour of the FAA Tower at the Santa Fe airport and got back to the Guard base just before the big snowstorm began. Many of the activities planned were not completed due to about 24 inches of snow, which fell for the next two days."

Another edition of the Eagle Squadron Newsletter notes the, "The 2008 New Mexico Wing Winter Encampment, at Kirtland Air Force Base, graduated 47 cadets, 31 of whom were first-timers. Activities included classes on aeronautics and aerodynamics, a class on national cadet special activities and a session dealing with the physical and psychological effects of long-term drug use.

Cadets also explored two aircraft at the CAP hangar at Kirtland Air Force Base. A Gippsland GA-8 crew showed the cadets the airplane's cockpit and explained the ARCHER— Airborne Real-time Cueing Hyperspectral Enhanced Reconnaissance—system in detail. Cadets visited the 58th Air Base Wing and their aircraft, and asked questions of the pilots that flew each aircraft.

They also made simulated parachute jumps with the 58th Air Base Wing's virtual parachute, and tried the new radios and night visiongoggles used by the U.S. Air Force. At a trip to La Luz Starbase Academy, cadets flew flight simulators.

Cadet Orientation Flights

Of the many Cadet activities, the opportunity for a cadet to not simply fly in an airplane, but to operate the controls, is a significant motivation. That was certainly true for Stanley Roeske (a cadet in Albuquerque from 1957 to 1961) who says that cadet orientation rides were his favorite part of CAP. He recalled having flights from the old Seven Bar (Alameda) airport in an L-16, an L-5 and the PA-18 Super Cubs. Stan took flying lessons as soon as he could, and soloed at 7-Bar on a day that other cadets were receiving orientation flights.

One cadet who watched him solo, Carol Sawyer, became Stan's wife twenty-five years later. Flying has remained Stan's passionate avocation all his life, and he credits CAP with helping him get started as a pilot.

40 Three cadets receive their pre-flight briefing from Capt. Chuck Grubert prior to their O-Flight in the Helio Courier

One of Stan's more interesting experiences with orientation rides came in 1959 or 1960 but he was not the cadet involved. *"The engine of the L-5 quit during the flight (fouled plugs), and the pilot did a great job of gently setting the aircraft down on the west mesa, close to where Double Eagle II Airport is now."* They could not get a truck in to haul the plane out until the next day, so Stan and some other older cadets, who were working on developing a survival class, volunteered to guard the aircraft overnight—not so much from people, but from cows! It seems that cows loved the sweet taste of the dope used on the fabric aircraft, and the plane was in danger of being eaten. It got cold that night, but the cadets practiced their survival techniques by draining gas from the aircraft sump to light a fire of the dried cowpats they collected from the field.

In the 1950's cadets were allowed up to 10 orientation rides, (later reduced to 5) depending on availability of pilots and aircraft. The orientation ride syllabus described what was to be accomplished in each flight. After glider orientation rides were added (see below), the total number of authorized orientation rides for each cadet returned to 10. Unlike 50 years ago, only cadets below the age of 18 are now eligible for orientation rides, perhaps because there are many more opportunities for older cadets to qualify for flight scholarships to become pilots themselves.

Back in 1988, SM Thomas Seals, who had been a cadet in the early 1960s, recently rejoined the Farmington Squadron. He recalled that one of his O-Flights was in a C-47 and noted, *"That was quite a handful to fly and I'm really glad I got the opportunity."* If you are not sure what a C-47 looks like check page 120.

Cadet Special Activities

All cadets who meet basic criteria are eligible to attend summer and winter encampments, to receive orientation rides, and to participate in activities arranged at the squadron, group, or wing level. There are also special enrichment programs at the national level, called Special Activities. Cadets compete for available slots, based on cadet accomplishments. These activities range from cadet exchanges to flying encampments, to leadership schools, to special programs focused on possible career choices in aviation. One of the best changes to the cadet program over the years is the increase in number and variety of special activities, which have expanded from six in the early 1960s to 21 in 2009.

It is not possible to give a comprehensive list here of all the NM Wing cadets who have been selected for Special Activities during the past 60-odd years. The following are a few examples.

An article in the *Albuquerque Journal* in 1962:

> ***CAP Reveals Scholarship, Trip Winners***—Seven Civil Air Patrol cadets, all from Albuquerque, won CAP trips and scholarships Monday night at Kirtland Air Force Base. Four alternates were selected. The winners were chosen by a five-member board. The cadets were judged on proficiency and knowledge of CAP and Air Force affairs, manners and conversational ability.
>
> Four-week international exchange trip: Richard Himebrook, Sq. 1, Alternate Dean A. Smith, Socorro Composite Squadron.
>
> Boy's Jet Orientation scholarship (10 days at Perrin AFB, Tex):Charles M. Pyetzki, Sq. 1; alternate, Richard Brandiger, Alamogordo Composite Sq.
>
> Boy's space age scholarship (10 days at Chanute AFB, Ill.):Raymond L. Alexander, Sq. 1,
>
> Boy's Federal Aviation Agency Orientation (10 days at Tinker AFB,Oklahoma City): Jon T. Daffer, Sq. 1; alternate, Oliver L.Marianetti, Sq. 4.
>
> Two girls for two-week inter-regional trips: Regina Weber, Sq.4 and Patricia Chochrell, Sq. 1.
>
> Girl's jet orientation (10 days at Maxwell AFB, Ala.): Carol Anne Sawyer, Sq.1
>
> Trip to congressional anniversary dinner in Washington, D. C., Lynn Brusin, Sq.4.

41 1962 NM Wing Cadet Special Activities Selectees. (L to R) Pat Chochrell, Regina Weber, Lynn Brusin, Carol Sawyer, Ray Alexander, Jon Daffer, Ric Himebrook, Charlie Pyetzki. Note there are four styles of uniform.

Drill Teams and Honor Guards

The ability to perform in a drill team or honor guard is often not one of the first objectives of a cadet. However, after observing the precision and camaraderie of a team, many young people see an opportunity to accept this challenge.

Military drill was always an important part of the discipline and teamwork training for cadets. Cadets marched in many parades and competitions. Gwen Sawyer, another cadet who joined in 1959, recalls the Albuquerque Christmas parade on November 27, 1959: *"The Squadron 1 boys' and girls' drill teams marched in the parade, with a 3-person color guard. As a lowly cadet airman basic, I was thrilled to be selected for the color guard (not sure whether it was because of drill ability or height), between cadet squadron leaders Stan Roeske, and Ric Himebrook. The female cadets' class A uniforms then were our summer cords, with nylons and black flats. Unfortunately, there was a cold snap that day, and even though we tried to layer clothes under our uniforms, with our arms and legs bare, we froze! The next summer, the two drill teams competed against each other at wing level, and the girls won. See the picture where we are at a shoe shine party the day before competition."*

The 1969-1970 NM Wing Yearbook, organized by cadets, reports:

> 1969 was the first time since 1965 that New Mexico Wing held a State Drill Competition. In past years, only a few squadrons were represented, usually from the local area, but this year teams competed from Albuquerque – T-Bird and Squadron 1, Hobbs, and Santa Fe. The Wing Commander, Colonel W. Dale Parsons CAP and his staff reviewed the teams. After all the points were totaled, the cadets from Hobbs were named State Drill Champions and authorized to wear the drill cord.

42 An important part of the cadet program is the social interaction achieved while cadets participate in a 'shoeshine party'. This one was held the day before drill team competition 1960.

43 1960 Squadron 1 Girl's Drill Team, winners of the Wing competition. Left to right: Gwen Sawyer, Betty Ballard, Kay Milam, Carol Sawyer, (unidentified), Pat Chochrell, Julie Anderson, (unidentified), Mary Nell Hodges, team leader Rita Bartow.

The 1988 NM Wing drill team won 'Team Spirit Trophy' at Region Competition in Dallas. Les Himebrook recalls, *"The team was made up of cadets from Farmington & Alamogordo (about half and half.) They met in Albuquerque and even at a SAREX at the lakes near Tucumcari to practice. For two of the cadets the trip to Dallas was the first time out of New Mexico. A group from that team continued on and within a couple of years they won Region and went to National. I don't remember how they did, but by that time they only had one cadet left from Alamogordo and he spent the year in Farmington staying with another cadet and attending school there so he would be available for all the practices."*

With respect to the Honor Guard, this article comes from 'The Gallup Herald' in 2007.

GALLUP CADETS SERVE AS HONOR GUARD AT THE FUNERAL OF A BATAAN DEATH MARCH SURVIVOR

Upon learning of (Robert) Welch's death members of the Gallup's Civil Air Patrol were quick to volunteer their Honor Guard for the veteran's Final Salute.

Wyatt Hoy and Angela Sanchez, who live near Welch (a Bataan March survivor) approached (his daughter) Bobby Chandler with their offer.

"This was among the joys of living in a small community," said Chandler. "Dad would always see the kids practicing in their yards and comment how nice they looked."

Chandler said the Civil Air Patrol's Honor Guard made her father's graveside service all the more meaningful. "People have commented to me how they were moved by the Honor Guard," said Chandler.

Dressed in their blue uniforms, the smartly dressed cadets meticulously and reverently provided the Final Salute afforded veterans. After removing the American flag from the coffin, they folded it into the symbolic triangle that was then presented to Chandler. "This meant so much to me," said Chandler.

Honor Guard Commander Anthony Anaya-Gorman, whose grandfather was Navajo Code Talker Carl Gorman, was moved by his participation in the funeral.

"Memories of my grandfather shot through my mind also many times," he said. "This was more important than any competition or basketball game we have appeared at."

Cadet Captain Chris Pena said he was proud to honor a veteran that served the country with a 'willing heart.'

National Flight Academy

Flying Encampments were added in 1965, and expanded to two locations the next year at certified flight schools. Cadets were required to pass the FAA written exam before attending. During the 4-week (powered) or 2-week (glider) course, cadets received dual instruction, solo time, and check rides from FAA examiners.

Flying Encampment requirements have varied through the years as CAP worked to provide aviation opportunities to the largest number of cadets during times of changing financial support for the organization. For example, in 1970, cadets were required to have soloed before attending encampment. Cadets are now required to cover more of the cost of their flight training, as well. The total cost to a cadet in 1966 to go from zero time to a powered private pilot certificate was seventy-eight dollars—to pay for meals. In 2009, cadets attending powered encampment paid seven hundred and fifty dollars, which covered some of the flying costs, still a bargain compared to earning their pilot's license on their own.

44 Flight academy cadets in Oklahoma 1966

In 1969, there were thirteen Special Activities available, including some that are no longer offered, such as Nurse Orientation Course, Aerospace Career Counseling Seminar, and Spiritual Life Conference.

By 2009, Special Activities were organized into four different career categories, shown below. While the activities themselves have expanded, funding to conduct the activities and to transport cadets to the activities is another matter. In the early years, USAF airlift to the activities was available, as well as funding to conduct the activities. As both have been curtailed, participating in these opportunities now challenges the cadet to obtain funding for transportation as well as expenses at the course.

Air Force Careers
Spec Undergrad Pilot Training Familiarization Course (2 locations)
Air Force Pararescue Orientation Course (at Kirtland AFB)
Air Force Advanced Pararescue Orientation Course
Air Force Space Command Familiarization Course (3 locations)
Air Force Civil Engineering Academy

Aviation Careers
Aircraft Mfg & Maintenance Academy
MKS Aviation Business Academy
National Blue Beret (at Oshkosh during EAA Airventure)
National Flight Academy (9 locations)

Leadership Careers
Cadet Officer School
Civic Leadership Academy
Hawk Mountain Search & Rescue School
Honor Guard Academy
International Air Cadet Exchange
National Cadet Competition
National Emergency Services Academy

Technology Careers
Advanced Technologies Academy
Engineering Technologies Academy (2 locations)

This impressive array of aviation opportunities not only provides goals for individual cadets, but gives a hint of how the Cadet Program gives back to the country through helping develop aerospace leaders for the future.

Cadet Officer School

Many NM Wing cadets have attended Cadet Officer School. For several years, Dannie Roberts (Farmington Squadron) worked at the Cadet Officer School. Les Himebrook attended as a cadet and when he was at the Air Force Academy—his summer leave was being the cadet commander of COS ('91).

The following article By C/Capt Ben Andraka first appeared in the August 2005 edition of Cactus Courier. He writes of his experience at the Cadet Officer School held at Maxwell Air Force Base, Alabama.

> Cadet Officer School (COS) was a great opportunity. I met outstanding cadets from almost every wing in the country, as well as one from Japan. I saw so many "new" takes on problems and situations that come up in squadrons. I learned that there's not just one way to do things that is the "right" way. In the leadership manuals for CAP, leadership looks to be a simple line. Each lesson in the book builds on the previous achievement all following the same ideas on a given path. COS showed me that that barely scratches the surface. Leadership is much larger than I ever thought, with so many styles and paths and ideas that it would be impossible to know everything about leadership.
>
> Before I went, I was really thinking that leadership was going to be a dry topic, especially when it was being covered for ten days. When I went, my expectation was just to go, do what was expected of me to graduate. I got much more than that out of this. We had some of the best lecturers in the country come talk to us during this activity. There were Air Force Colonels; there were the highest authorities in the civilian world on writing, speaking and leading. There was a Korean War veteran who gave his story, there was even a man who planned desert storm who talked to us about strategic thinking.
>
> Outside of lectures, there were plenty of activities that required teamwork to accomplish them. Not the easiest thing for a flight made up of 13 officers. I saw through these activities that it's not always important to be right, to be the guy at the head of the room giving directions. No matter how high you go, you're still a follower. I've heard that plenty of times in the past, but it was never as clear as when I went to COS.

Cadet Charles W. Matthews adds his observations.

> Cadet Officer School was a life changing experience. I came into the program not knowing just what was in store for me. The atmosphere was a collegiate environment. All the cadets present were officers, and we were treated as such, given very few restrictions and rules. My flight was made up of some of the most amazing people I have ever come across in my CAP experience. In addition, my two instructors, Maj Wood and Lt. Col Maxwell were extremely helpful during the entire course of the school.
>
> My favorite part of COS was the people. I made some great friends from Oregon to New Hampshire. Our lectures were completely amazing. I can't give away all the details, but I can say that COS is one of the few places where you have so many great minds at your fingertips. The lecturers and staff were amazing. There was just too much information to recount. And of course, there was volleyball — man, I was terrible at volleyball. Our record was a dismal 3-19, but props to C/Capt Andraka and his volley ball championship flight.
>
> I would recommend COS to any officer who wants to gain a new prospective on leadership and gain an inventory of their leadership skills. While I was at Maxwell, I gained a new "strategic" view on leadership and was able to mold and frame a new leadership style and personal character from what I learned at Cadet Officer School.

Orientation Courses

CAP has offered a variety of 'orientation' courses down through the years. In the late 1950's the Jet Orientation course allowed selected cadets the opportunity to fly in a high performance two place jet aircraft. Ric Himebrook recalls attending the Space Age Orientation Course at Chanute AFB in 1960.

45 The high point of the Jet Orientation course is a flight in an Air Force jet—the ultimate O-Flight. Here Gwen Sawyer and her T-33 pilot, Capt. Dale Danning, USAF, Maxwell AFB.

Parajumper (now Pararescue) Orientation Course located at Kirtland AFB, requires cadets to have reached their 15th birthday by the start of this one-week introduction to the rigorous mission of the pararescue team. In the basic course, cadets learn land navigation, survival techniques, rock climbing, rappelling, and other skills used in rescue operations from pararescue specialists. This high-adventure activity also promotes physical fitness and builds character. Spirit Squadron cadet Kenneth Kietz attended the Parajumper (PJOC) course in 2007 and here are his thoughts:

> My time at Parajumper OC (PJOC) was incredible! Yes there was a little bit of PT, but the lessons learned have been, in my opinion, even more invaluable than those learned at Cadet Officer School (COS). COS gets into the details, but it's what you learn at PJOC that helps you accomplish those details.
>
> At PJOC you learn enough to become ground team qualified, going through search and rescue, navigation, first aid, knots, crossing treacherous ground, rappelling and more. But all of these are what help cadets learn the most important principle: How to work with your fellow cadets and with yourself.
>
> TEAMWORK is the grounding principle at PJ, you must learn to apply this concept or none of you will graduate. The definition of teamwork is: A group of individuals working together to accomplish a goal, while putting aside personal desires and comforts for that team. Individuals do not need to like or dislike the other individuals in the group; they just need to have the willingness to work with others as a team. This is something that I would like to bring into our squadron.
>
> Learning the extent of my endurance, how far a person can go before hitting their limit, is another of the most important and valuable lessons I have learned in my CAP career. One of the PJ's at the encampment put it very well, "Mind over body." You have the ability to push yourself physically so much further than you realize, and if you can do it with your physical abilities then you can do it with your emotions, mind, spirit and talent. A recent example of how I was able to practice this with quick and noticeable results was at COS. Our team was very tired and there seemed to be a disease of the spirit going around our team. None o us had any enthusiasm, energy, or motivation.
>
> This was detrimental to our ability to win at volleyball. I noticed this, after losing two games consecutively, with scores that weren't even close. Even

> though I felt very apathetic and lacked motivation, I forced myself to be cheerful, excited and enthusiastic. It took a little going, but the rest of the team caught the energy. By the end of that last game, we were jumping and shouting and enjoying ourselves to the fullest. We won that game, even though we knew we had lost the round. There was no way we should have won that game, but a change in attitude brought us around, making us the winners. Mind over body.

Andy and Dan Selph attended the PJOC course in 1979, and noted, *"It was a favorite for many New Mexico cadets at that time. Close to home, we kind of felt like the 'home team' up in the Pecos."*

46 Cadets are shown techniques using the magnetic compass during the 'Survival' portion of the second annual Pararescue Orientation Course.

Air Education Training Command Fam Course

C/Capt Curtis Christensen provided some insight into the working of the Air Education Training Command Familiarization Course (AETCFC) in 1999.

If being an Air Force pilot is your dream, then Air Education Training Command Familiarization Course (AETCFC) is a great national activity to attend. Of the two venues that CAP offers, I attended the AETCFC at Columbus AFB in Mississippi. The only constant in our days was that we began at 0545 with PT. I knew going into the course that it was going to be academically intense. But I was somewhat surprised at the level of competitiveness. Probably half of the students already had, at least, their pilot solo wings. The rest of us had some catching up to do. When we weren't in classes, we were studying or attending study sessions with the instructors.

Our instruction involved physiological training, flight principles, emergency procedures, and exposure to the various operating systems of the T-37. We had the unique opportunity to study a hurricane as Dennis passed overhead. However, many of our outdoor tours and activities were cancelled because of him. One of the highlights of the week was getting to fly for about a half an hour a full motion flight simulator with an actual Air Force Instructor Pilot. I got to do loops, barrel rolls, aileron rolls and spins.

International Air Cadet Exchange (IACE)

One of the exceptional Special Activities for cadets is the opportunity to travel to other countries as a part of CAP's International Air Cadet Exchange. The program was developed in 1947 when the Air Cadet League of Canada suggested their young people exchange visits with CAP cadets in the United States. Actual visits began in 1948, and expanded rapidly to include exchange visits with aviation-minded youth in over 40 friendly foreign countries. Selection to attend IACE has perennially been one of the choicest plums in the entire cadet program. After an orientation in Washington, D. C., participating cadets spend two weeks or more in a host country, representing the youth of their nation and learning about other cultures. A few of the NM Wing cadets selected for this high honor are:

1954 Clarence Nollsch, Cuba
1962 Ric Himebrook, Canada
1967 Gary Snyder, Great Britain
1968 Beverly Vito, Great Britain
1971 Warren Harkins, Australia
1982 Tish Dawkins, France
1985 Tim Selph, Norway
1987 Darrell LaRoche, Netherlands
1988 Mathias Girardi, West Germany
1989 Les Himebrook, Norway
1990 Gordon Weimer, France
1991 Emarae Garcia, Canada; Don Fuqua, Norway
1996 Isaac Block, Israel
1999 Adam Fachan, Japan, Alleyna Farrell and Jessica Block

Of the many Exchange programs that NM Wing Cadets have participated in, one of them was to the island nation of Cuba before the Castro revolution in 1959. Cadet Clarence Nollsch (also known a 'Bud') journeyed there in July 1954. Here are some excerpts from the local newspaper article of the time:

> This morning Clarence Nollsch boarded a plane for Washington D.C., first leg of his journey to Havana, Cuba... The Farmington boy, son of Mr. and Mrs.

Phillip Nollsch... is one of six cadets to participate in the program, and noting the honor, the Jaycees of Farmington presented him with a check for 50 dollars.

It's an honor that Clarence worked for entailing national eligibility requirements, than an eight-hour proficiency test and a forty-minute session with a board of inquiry in Albuquerque.

"It sure was worth it," Clarence said this morning at the airport. *"I feel that it is quite an honor and I'm certainly grateful to the Jaycees for their help. Was that a surprise.*

Clarence is a 1954 graduate of Farmington High School, was known for his appearances with his saxophone as a soloist in the band concert. He has been accepted at the University of Colorado where he plans to study electrical engineering.

47 Clarence Nollsch (3rd from RT) of Farmington with other cadets and chaperones in Cuba, 1954.

***

LtCol Sharon Lane provided the following story about one cadet's experiences on his IACE in 1999:

Farmington Composite Squadron Cadet LtCol Adam Fachan had set up three goals for himself in CAP. To date, he has achieved two of the three. One of the goals was to be the Cadet Commander, which he has been for the last

Clarence Nollsch Off For Cuba On CAP Cadet-Exchange Program

This morning Clarence Nollsch boarded the plane for Washington, D. C., first leg of his journey to Havana, Cuba, as a CAP cadet on the cadet-exchange program.

The Farmington boy, son of Mr. and Mrs. Phillip Nollsch of [illegible] North Butler, is one of six cadets all over the nation to participate in the program, and [illegible] the Jaycees of Farmington presented him with a check for 50 dollars.

In Washington, he's scheduled to meet the other cadets, 15 in all, from all over the nation, and the party will fly to Cuba for an exciting month's tour of cadet squadrons there.

It's an honor that Clarence worked for, including national eligibility requirements, then an eight-hour proficiency test and a [illegible] session with a board of inquiry in Albuquerque.

"It sure was worth it," Clarence said this morning at the airport. "I feel that it's quite an honor and I'm certainly grateful to the Jaycees for their help. Was that a surprise!"

The CAP cadet commandant in Farmington, Howard Chris-[illegible], feels that it's quite an honor [illegible] pride in the [illegible]

Clarence, a [illegible] graduate of Farmington High school, was well known for his appearances with his saxophone as soloist in the band concert. He has been accepted at the University of Colorado at Boulder, where he plans to study electrical engineering.

OFF TO CUBA: Clarence Nollsch, Farmington's honor CAP cadet, (right) gets a handclasp from Captain James McAllister of Albuquerque, at the airport this morning as he gets ready for the hop to Washington, D.C. where he will meet the 14 other CAP cadets of the cadet exchange program. The goal is Havana, Cuba, where cadets will have the opportunity of visiting other exchange students. Capt. McAllister is CAP liaison officer in the Duke City.

48 The Local Farmington newspaper prominently covered Cadet Nollsch's trip to Cuba.

49 This was the CAP plane that took the cadets to Cuba in 1954. Note the old `CAP insignia on the nose of the DC-3.

three years. One of the other goals he has had was to be a participant in the International Air Cadet Exchange and go to one of 24 countries. This past summer saw Adam traveling to the other side of the world and spending two weeks in Japan.

Adam left Farmington and flew to Seattle, Washington where he met his IACE group of six cadets and one senior member escort. Interestingly, two of the female cadets, Alleyna Farrell of Eagle Composite Squadron and Jessica Block of Los Lunas Composite Squadron, made the trip. The group, after IACE Orientation, which included a daylong intense study on how to use chopsticks, continued on to Tokyo. Japan's equivalent, the only sister organization in the IACE program, of Civil Air Patrol is called *Sky Friends* and is funded by the Japanese Civil Aviation Promotion Foundation, which can be compared to the American FAA. This Foundation funded the entire trip for the group of seven. In return, six Sky Friends Cadets and an escort came to the United States for two weeks, which was also funded by the JCAPF. Sky Friends cadets range in age from 6 to 18. They do not acquire rank but have positions based on their age and accomplishments.

The first two days of the trip were spent in Tokyo. Tokyo, the cleanest city that Adam said he has ever seen "smelled like soy sauce". He was amazed that he did not see homeless people and he felt "very safe" during his visit there. While there, the cadets were taken to the American Embassy where they met the American Ambassador and some of the Embassy staff. They went to Disneyland, Japanese style, shopped and were taken on a tour of the Tokyo Fire Department. Of course, when Americans think of a Fire Department we think of fire trucks and sirens. Not so in Tokyo. Because of the traffic gridlock in the world's third largest city, they have fire-fighting helicopters. Adam compared them in size to the "Huey" or the "Jolly Green Giant" and carry large of amounts of water and equipment to fire sites. The pilots and crew who fly them are considered "experts" in the fire-fighting field.

The second part of the trip began in Miazaki, a small island off southern Japan and is the agricultural center of Japan. It turned out that Adam liked Miazaki the best of all the places he went in Japan "because it is a pretty place and the people are very friendly". Many people there commute to Tokyo during the week and then return to the tiny island to be with their families on the weekends. The host family that Adam stayed with, Mr. And Mrs. Kamakawa and their children Kyohe, Arisa and Iima for three days and two nights. The family spoke little English but understood him to an extent. "We managed with sign language and pictures" Adam said. During the day Adam was delivered to his group activities. In the evenings, his host family took him to a Japanese festival and window-shopping at a local mall. While he was in Miazaki, a hurricane blew in, a first for Adam. While his family worried back in the US for his safety, he was taken to a shelter to ride out the storm. Once the weather settled down the IACE cadets continued their tour that included a trip to a local Japanese Air Force Base to see the Japanese Air Self Defense Force version of their *Top Guns*. The planes they fly are American made F-15's and the cadet group went to the maintenance facility to see them up close and personal.

The next city on the tour was Osaka where the cadets saw the Aviation College, Japanese temples, shrines and a fully restored castle. When asked how old the castle was, Adam replied "old...well actually about 1,000 years old." One of the most exciting adventures while in Osaka for him was a day spent sailing on an inland sea. Osaka is the industrial part of Japan.

In Kyoto, Japan, known for its historical sites, the group was taken to see the Imperial Palace. The entire outside of the building, covered with gold leaf, is approximately 1,200 years old. While in Kyoto, the group went to a Kimono fashion show. The people in Japan generally wear western style clothes but wear the traditional Kimono for evening functions. After visiting more shrines, temples and museums, they left Kyoto to return to Tokyo on the world famous "bullet train". The train, which travels at approximately 200 mph, made one stop and traveled 400 miles in two hours. When asked if he could actually see anything going that fast, Adam replied "yeah, if you looked real fast".

Upon their return to Tokyo, the business center of Japan, the group went to a disaster education center where Japanese children are taught what to do in an earthquake, hurricane or fire. The farewell dinner was at the hotel where the cadets were housed. When asked what he liked best about the trip Adam said "the food, especially Japanese barbeque." Two of the sites deliberately left out of the tour was Hiroshima and Nagasaki. Adam said "they wanted to show us only positive things in their country…not the sad parts of their history".

Adam, the son of Terry Fachan of Aztec, returned to Farmington to continue his second year of studies at San Juan College and his full time job as a lifeguard for Farmington Municipal Pools. His goal is to receive his Associate Degree and plans to become a SERE (survival, evasion, resistance, escape) instructor in the United States Air Force. When asked if his future plans included a return trip to Japan he said "definitely, most definitely".

As a postscript to the story, Lane relates that Adam DID go on to become a PJ (parajumper) and is in the military today.

***

In 1996, Isaac Block went to Israel. He writes:

> I did so much in those two weeks it is impossible to for me to condense it into a few paragraphs. Of the 19,000 CAP cadets in the United States [1996], I was one of one-hundred to be selected to participate. When I first joined CAP in 1990, I had three goals: to earn my pilots certificate, to get my Spaatz, and to participate in IACE. This third goal, a six year-old dream was fulfilled last summer.
>
> One of the reasons I chose to visit Israel was to see its people and to experience the culture. My parental heritage is Jewish, so I went anticipating the discovery of my roots. The land is steeped in history. As one European cadet put it "What do you Americans know of history? Two hundred years, what's that? Walking through Jerusalem on roads built by Romans thousands of years ago made me ponder the cadet's words.

While Americans may not have the long history of some countries, it is important for the rest of the world to remember that America has the longest enduring constitution.

***

NM Wing Hosts IACE Cadets—The 'Exchange' part of IACE means that CAP hosts aviation youth and their escorts from other countries each year. The visitors usually spend time in New York City and/or Washington, D.C. before flying on to host regions and wings. In the 1960s, NM Wing hosted cadets from Chile, Belgium and Peru. Cadets and their escorts were housed on base or in hotels, but wing cadets were invited to travel with the exchange cadets on visits to NM landmarks, such as Bandelier National Monument, in order to foster international communication, understanding and goodwill.

In later years, cadets and their escorts stayed with local families for a better in-depth exposure to American culture. Lt Col Jay T. Tourtel provides the following narrative:

Four families hosted six cadets and their escort during the 2007 International Air Cadet Exchange (IACE), which was held in New Mexico Wing. Two cadets from Canada, two cadets from Israel, two cadets from the United Kingdom and their escort from Canada spent ten days as guests of the wing. The cadets were treated to balloon flights at the Balloon Fiesta Park, followed by hiking up Sandia Peak, and watching the Albuquerque Isotopes play the New Orleans Zephyrs at Isotopes Park. On Sunday, after church services, glider flights were conducted that afternoon at Moriarty Municipal Airport, followed by a picnic lunch. The cadets toured the Grand Canyon in Arizona, and attended a pool party hosted by one of the families in the wing, That night, they attended a joint meeting of Eagle, Thunderbird, Falcon and Spirit Squadrons at Spirit Squadron's headquarters. This gave the IACE cadets a chance to interact with their American counterparts. The cadets were then flown to Alamogordo to visit White Sands Missile Range and Holloman Air Force Base, then a tour of Carlsbad Caverns.

50 1960 NM Wing Hosted Chilean Cadets.

Lloyd Sallee Glider Academy

The New Mexico CAP glider program was initiated and led in its formative years by former Wing Commander Colonel Lloyd Sallee. The main activity of the soaring program is a two-week long summer Cadet Soaring Academy. The goal is to take cadets from zero flight time to solo during that period. Cadets who had soloed previously, work toward the practical test for their private pilot (glider) certificate.

The first Academy in 1993, at Hobbs Industrial Airpark (HBB), was attended by 10 cadets. This airport was a WWII B-17 training base abandoned after the war and subsequently used as a soaring site. The cadets and an equal number of supporting senior members bunked in a clubhouse at the field. An SGU 2-22 trainer (N2770Z) was the first glider acquired by NM Wing for the 1994 Academy. This was augmented by SGS 2-33 trainers borrowed from the Albuquerque Soaring Club and the Hobbs Soaring Society and tow planes of the already established soaring facility in Hobbs. Sallee negotiated with the local college for housing and some meals. Early New Mexico supporters of the program included Allene Lindstrom (CFI-AG), Robert Gibson CFI-AG), Chuck Grubert, and George Applebay (A&P). All cadets who attended in 1993 and 1994 achieved solo.

This initial program was expanded by cooperative effort with the Soaring Society of America (SSA) in an attempt to broaden both the SSA and CAP Cadet Program to a wider spectrum of our youth. Working with other Sailplane enthusiasts, including the legendary LtCol Alcide Santilli, a nationwide program was begun in 1996 that provided for the addition of five glider flights to the existing five powered Orientation Flight (O-Flights). That the CAP Cadet program grew from 19,000 to 21,000 that year may be an indicator of the impact of the glider initiative.

The glider offers solo flight privileges for younger ages (14 as opposed to 16 for powered aircraft) and a lower cost and simpler operation than powered aircraft. The New Mexico program was quickly expanded to a week-long National Glider Academy that was hosted by several other CAP Wings. NM Wing expanded its inventory of aircraft over the years to include a variety of sailplanes such as a Blanik L-23. Several SGS 1-26 gliders were leased while Colorado Wing provided an ASK-21 (N221CP).

Tow-planes used at the academies are predominantly Piper PA-25 Pawnees borrowed from various commercial glider operators or CAP's own C182's with tow-hooks installed. In more recent years, the operation typically had 4-6 sailplanes and 3-4 tow-planes—often all active at the same time.

51 While one cadet prepares to 'run the wing' another in the cockpit of this Schweizer 2-22 is ready to launch

The 1995 Academy saw 460 flights totaling 109 hours of flight time. Because of the extreme heat, the activities began at 0600. The first student to solo was C/Sgt Debi Janer who was back on the ground after a flight of 7 minutes. The only Cadet who did not solo was C/A Robert Ortega, and that was only because, at the age of 13, he was too young.

On January 8, 1995, Cadet Shaun Stanton became the first New Mexico Cadet to earn his Private Pilots license in a glider. Capt Robert Gibson was his instructor. Following completion of his check ride, Cadet Stanton went aloft again and climbed to over 12,000 feet while remaining aloft for over one hour. The setting sun forced his return or he might still be up there.

52 Cadets attending the 2000 Glider Academy

Later Academies at Hobbs have provided for up to 25 Cadets, and an equal number of Glider Instructors (CFI-G's), tow-pilots, and support personnel quartered in dorms at the nearby campus of NM Junior College. The location was changed to Las Cruces for a few years but returned to Hobbs in 2008. Sallee's leadership role was subsequently assumed by Louis Braddi of Las Cruces (1996-2004), Brian Morrison of Albuquerque (2005-2008), and Roland Dewing of Rio Rancho (2009-present).

To describe the cadet's affinity to the Academy as inspiring would be an understatement. Cadet William Fitzpatrick was quoted in the

June 17, 2000 edition of the Hobbs newspaper as saying, *"In the air it's like the plane becomes a part of you.*" Santilli, whose first pilot's license in 1930 was signed by Orville Wright commented, *"When a 14-year-old goes up by himself in a glider, he comes back down thinking there isn't anything he can't do."* With a flight program that consists of 'boxing the wake', steep turns and spin recovery, the cadet builds confidence in their ability to master a new and exciting environment.

53 The late Lt Col Alcide Santilli, a lifelong glider pilot, instructor and Designated Glider Examiner, was instrumental in helping create the NM Wing Cadet Glider Academy. Orville Wright signed Santilli's original 1930 pilot's license!

Commanding the yearly Academy encompasses many tasks. Just ask Lt. Col. Chuck Grubert who held that responsibility in 1999 and 2000. Scheduling the gliders, instructors, tow planes, cadets and support personal is just the tip of the iceberg. Chuck had a few key supporters that including his cousin Janet Pearson, who managed to get many donations (T-shirts and hats) and special deals from local merchants such as half-priced meals from Furrs Cafeteria. Keeping the cost manageable is an important part of getting cadets enrolled.

Allene Lindstrom recalls her involvement with the program:

"Lloyd Sallee asked me to assist with the CAP Cadet Glider encampment in 1994 at Hobbs. My logbook says I towed. Tom Soapes was the first (known to me,) ground instructor. His classroom was the lunchroom. Not good, as there were constant interruptions with others needing to use the facilities. I don't remember bunking on the field. Lloyd located lodging at the dorm of the junior college where we were privileged to have lodging and in some years, breakfast. By the time I took over ground school, a classroom at the junior college became available.

The schedule was—up at 5:00 - 5:30 and breakfast then to the airport. The newbies flew the morning hours and went to class at 1:30. The second year attendees did ground assist in the morning and flew in the afternoon. Flying time lasted until late afternoon. Excitement ran high.

Lloyd would break about 4:00 PM, go back to the dorm and then Furrs for supper. As commanders changed so did the food arrangements and time schedules. During those encampments, everyone was allowed to fly until late in the afternoon. However, unrecognized fatigue was encountered and sometimes accidents resulted—nothing serious though.

The cadets were always well behaved. Cadet commanders had to deal with any behavior problems. Flag ceremony was held each morning before first flight. The home schooled cadets always impressed me with their study habits and ingenuity. Wal-Mart was the favorite shopping stop!

The Cadet Glider Encampment with the name change to Lloyd Sallee Glider Academy was a favorite experience. I retired from this in 2002. The loss of N6319H was my most unhappy event."

***

Eagle Squadron's Talon Newsletter of March/April 1995 provided some insight into what it was like for Cadets to fly gliders. C/TSgt John Grassham writes:

> *It began, as the most terrifying thought in the whole of New Mexico Wing's mind, the first cadets of the wing getting their glider pilot's certificates. People never thought it would happen, but it did. It started on Sunday morning February 4, 1995 and ended on Wednesday afternoon, February 8. Cadet Stanton was first. He and I got to the flight line at 0800 on Sunday to [help] preflight the tow plane we were taking to Moriarity. When we arrived, the aircraft N9455X had already been pre-flighted [by the pilot]; so we packed our stuff and took off...*
>
> When we had Moriarity airport in sight we circled the airport looking for 'The Wave.' During the winter, the [thermal] lifts aren't there, but 'The Wave' is. It's like a lift but it is concentrated in one or two down or up waves. They are created by the Sandia mountains when the [winds aloft] reflects off the mountains and pushes towards the east. However we could not locate the wave....
>
> *All this happened two days after a big snowstorm. The runway had been scraped clear and the taxiway looked OK but we where wondering whether we could park the aircraft on a solid sheet of ice...Col Santilli was already inside waiting for us so we went into the building awaiting a long preparation talk for Cadet Stanton to become a pilot. The time felt like it was standing still. And then Col Santilli pulled out a packed parachute and asked Cadet Stanton to check it. The tow pilot, Lt Col Soapes, and myself thought that was most interesting so we listened in.*
>
> *After the talk was over Lt Col Soapes and I went out ahead of Cadet Stanton to take the glider out of the hangar. Once we got the aircraft out, Stanton was there to preflight the glider so I helped and Tom Soapes hooked the tow-hook on the tow plane. When we were done pre-flighting, Col. Santilli pulled his car around and we hooked the glider to the car to pull it to the launch site.*

It took us about 15 minutes to push the glider to the launch site at the other end of the runway. Once we got down to the launch site we had to wait in line to use the runway. All morning we were watching a glider taking off almost as soon as the tow plane landed. The afternoon was no exception. When we got down there we were joined by Col Sallee, the other glider pilot. I was briefed on what I was supposed to do as a "Wing Runner" and went through a demonstration with the glider wing. Finally it was time to go. Five-Five-Xray towed the glider out to then runway and sped up. I ran the wing as far as I could to maintain the same speed as the glider, which wasn't very long. I wrote down the time off and the time down. When they landed we had to get the glider out of the way so other people could use the runway.

Cadet Stanton took off two more times with the same things; but the last time Stanton landed long so we wouldn't have to push the glider back. Glider flying is a fine sport. I encourage everyone to get involved and become pilots themselves.

54 A few final words from the instructor before this cadet solos for the first time.

A 2007 attendee, Samantha Reames, had this to say about her experience.

> Being able to fly a glider again was just amazing. This was my second year going to this Academy and because I had the opportunity to go again, I soloed. Some cadets have been lucky to have soloed at their first Academy, but for most it takes a second chance to achieve that goal. Actually, this Academy is two weeks put together. That's what makes it so neat, because the first week you learn the basics and the instructors fly for you just so that you get used to the feel of flying in an aircraft with no motor. Then the second week, it gets tougher. You have tests to make sure you understand what you've been learning, and you get to fly more and more on your own.
>
> We had two cadets from Rio Rancho, one from Albuquerque, four from Las Cruces, and three from Texas. There were eight cadets, total and eight senior members present. Plus, we had three gliders and two tow planes in operating condition. Our hosts decided that we would stay in Las Cruces, NM, instead of Hobbs, NM, because it was closer to where many of the cadets lived. A typical day was different from the next in terms of what we had to study, the tests we took, and what we learned from ground school, but the times were the same from day to day. This was how the day was arranged:
>
> - *Get up at 0500*
> - *Drive out to the hanger and eat breakfast*
> - *At 0800, take out the gliders, one by one*
> - *Preflight check each one*
> - *1000 hours, we had three cadets flying at the same time*
> - *1200 hours, break for lunch*
> - *1300 hours, continue flights*
> - *1800 hours stowed the gliders for the night*
> - *1900 hours, dinner and spent an hour with our flight.*
> - *2000 hours, we went back to the sleeping quarters ,were we spent two hours studying.*
> - *2200 hours, lights out.*
>
> In ground school, we learned about the different types of flying and landing patterns, different maneuvers we were allowed to do, and the emergency procedures we were to take if anything went wrong. We also learned how to get along as a team. Pushing gliders, each person had to walk a certain pace; otherwise none of us went anywhere.

> Working as a team to move gliders is especially handy when there's a glider coming in for a landing and another glider is in the middle of the runway. That's when everyone jumps into action to make sure there are no accidents. I can't give too much away of what we learned because 1) It would be much more fun if you went and experienced all of this yourself, and 2) This is just a sample of what all happened at this Academy.
>
> Flying gliders is fun, absolutely, but there are also safety precautions and ground work that you must learn. Other than that though, you just go and work as hard as you can, just to have fun! Even though this was my second year attending this particular glider Academy, if given the opportunity to go a third time, there would be no doubt in my mind. I would take it!

Newspaper headlines such as the one that follows are priceless for recruiting new cadets.

FRIDAY, AUGUST 4, 1995 — LOCAL/REGION — HOBBS DAILY NEWS-SUN 3

Cadets experience fright, thrill of flying solo for the first time

By HELENA RODRIGUEZ
Of the News-Sun Staff

"They don't need any private experience. They can join the Civil Air Patrol."
■ Lt. Col. Ruth Roberts

The only accident of any note in the NM Wing glider program involved the C182 tow plane N6319H on June 12, 2003. The CAP private pilot (who had recently been signed off to tow gliders—he had logged 24 tows) started his take-off roll with a glider in-tow. With a density altitude calculated to be 7,070 feet, he said that his initial climb pitch angle was approximately 20 degrees, and his airspeed was about 50 knots. Several witnesses said that the airplane departed at a high angle of attack, and then mush/stalled into a T-hangar.

The glider in-tow released when he saw the tow plane was in trouble and made an uneventful landing. There were no injuries although the C182 was destroyed.

55 Many ground school sessions are a part of the Glider Academy program.

Cadets at the Service Academies

Membership in CAP inspires some cadets to work toward appointment to one of the service academies—and provides them leadership opportunities to help them grow toward that goal.

The following is from the Cactus Courier 2007:

> Orientation is over, the boots have been purchased, and now the physical training begins in full force for two New Mexico CAP cadets. After years of hard work, Cadets Thomas Nichols and Curtis Christensen will realize their dream of attending the United States Air Force Academy (USAFA) on 28 June 2007, when they report to the Colorado Springs facility for in processing as Basic Cadets for the Class of 2011.
>
> C/Maj Nichols received a nomination for an appointment from Senator Pete Dominici and shortly thereafter, his Offer of Appointment from USAFA arrived in the mail. As a member of the Falcon Composite Squadron in Rio Rancho, Nichols has served as the Cadet Commander, Chairman of the Southwest Region Cadet Advisory Council, and Commander of the Falcon Composite Squadron Honor Guard. At two NM cadet competitions, Nichols won the "Fleet Foot Award." He attended two NM Wing winter encampments and in the

summer of 2005 was selected for the national cadet special activity Pararescue Orientation Course. Cadet Nichols is on the varsity cross country and track teams for his high school, Bosque High School.

C/LtCol Christensen, a member of the Los Alamos Composite Squadron, was nominated to USAFA by Senator Jeff Bingaman. Christensen also received offers of appointment to the United States Naval Academy and the United States Military Academy at West Point. But according to Christensen, "USAFA has always been my first choice. So I was thrilled when that appointment arrived in the mail." As a nationally rated fencer, Christensen, was also recruited to fence for the AFA Falcons. Christensen has served his squadron as the Cadet Commander, Deputy Cadet Commander, Executive Offi cer, and Public Affairs Offi cer. He attended three NM Wing encampments. Christensen was also selected to attend the Rocky Mountain Region Cadet Leadership School, Air Education Training Command Familiarization Course-MS, and International Air Cadet Exchange to Japan.

Although there is no NM Wing official record of cadets appointed to the academies through the years, some of the names include:

Charles Pyetzki (Albuquerque Sqdn. I) – Naval Academy (1960's)
Mathias Girardi (Farmington) — Air Force Academy—93
Randall Hyer (Los Alamos) — Naval Academy
Nola Neudecker (Los Alamos) — Naval Academy
Sharon Presley ( ) — Air Force Academy—94
Robert Woods (Thunderbird) -- Air Force Academy—93
Les Himebrook (Alamogordo) — Air Force Academy—94
Roy Caldwell (Los Alamos) — Air Force Academy
Thomas Nichols (Rio Rancho Falcon) — Air Force Academy —2011
Curtis Christensen (Los Alamos) — Air Force Academy —2011

School Enrichment Program — Group 800

The CAP Cadet School Program can be applied to middle schools as a 'for credit' elective course during school hours. This program is similar to a Junior ROTC course at the high school level in that military drill and customs, along with physical training are included. However, this program goes beyond that by teaching Leadership, Moral Guidance, Aerospace Education, Drug Demand Reduction Education, Emergency Services, and Life Skills. The course is taught by senior members who are either licensed teachers approved by the assigned school or under the supervision of certified teachers.

Included in the program are aerospace related field trips, orientation flights in CAP powered aircraft and gliders. A variety of other activities such as model rocketry, color guard, and drill team are available to the students.

The program is divided into sixteen (16) Achievements or teaching units. The goal is for the student to satisfactorily complete 2 to 3 Achievements each school year. As a cadet completes the testing for each Achievement, they move up one grade in cadet rank. They are also assigned leadership positions in their squadron throughout their training. Teamwork and collaboration are emphasized in their activities.

Twice a year, the weeklong CAP encampments which take place on military bases throughout the state, are available to the cadets as they progress through the program. Flight Academies are available which instruct cadets through to their first solo flight.

Parents and schools report that cadets who continue in the program demonstrate greater self-esteem, self-discipline, motivation, and improved grades. Further, the young people involved in these programs are far less likely to be involved in substance abuse, gang affiliation, truancy, and delinquency.

The CAP National Headquarters pays for:

- the first year's membership for any student on the free lunch program
- one USAF service dress blue uniform.
- all printed material and texts
- five O-flights in powered aircraft and five in gliders.

The origins of a Cadet School Program are believed to have begun in the Puerto Rico Wing, where it was introduced in many schools by the early 1960's. In New Mexico, it began around 1995 with two schools participating. Warren Johnson at Wilson Middle School and Van Sanders at Harrison Middle School, both in Albuquerque, operated these programs. Both individuals were previous U.S. Air Force veterans. At Wilson Middle School in particular Johnson had great success, and both schools had the program from 1995-2000. However, lack of support resulted in the demise of these noteworthy efforts. William H. Criswell commanded the Truman Middle School Program between 1995 until his passing in 1996.

In 2000, the New Mexico National Guard approached the NM Wing and suggested that a joint program be instituted at the schools where the Guard had a presence. This took place, and the Wing operated the Cadet Program in conjunction with the Guard at a number of middle schools quite successfully. The program was inherited by Lt. Col Claude Luisada in 2000 and has been steadily growing since that time.

During this time, it was decided to place all the Middle School Squadrons under a single organizational umbrella. This was accomplished and the unit became known as Group 800 with all the associated squadrons given 800-series charter numbers by National Headquarters.

It was also about this time that the New Mexico Senate Education Committee was approached for yearly funding. With the blessing of the State Legislature this became a reality and this funding is used mainly to pay teachers who participate in the Cadet Program either as an elective or as an after school program. In addition, the program was expanded to high schools.

As the funding has increased and the positive results of this program have been recognized the number of schools involved has slowly increased.

For the 2004-2005 school year, 221 students from five schools were enrolled. This placed New Mexico third in the country with respect to enrollment despite the fact that New Mexico ranks 36th in state population. Of this number, 46 attended encampments, and 15 received their initial O-flights. Availability of funding, planes and orientation pilots hampered efforts during these years.

In 2005-2006, eight schools participated with 470 students initially enrolling; a 113 percent increase over the previous year. Unfortunately, two schools were unable to implement their scheduled program due to a lack of teachers.

SEP 2008-2009 School Year Enrollment and Progress			
	Students enrolled	Became CAP Cadets	Achievements to Date
Rio Rancho High School	12	12	8
Espanola	69	69	69
Eagle Ridge	50	46	26
St. Therese	30	18	15
Village Academy	60	0	0
Horizon Charter School	13	13	6
Garfield	12	0	1
Totals	246	158	125

According to Luisada, the most difficult part of the SEP program is finding teachers who are motivated to participate in the program, and training and retaining the teachers who are under significant pressures in their normal classroom duties. Several outstanding teachers, such as Pam Sever of Monroe Middle School, herself a former Spaatz Cadet, implemented the program in their classes. Sever had great success over a period of just three years, but when she left the school, the program was dropped. Robert Will, at Eagle Ridge Middle School, has likewise demonstrated that with the proper preparation, the program can produce exceptional results.

AF JR ROTC 2009 Honors Camps

In late 2008, Major Elizabeth A. Fallon, Program Manager, Aerospace & Technology Honors Camps, sent a request to National Civil Air Patrol seeking Cadet Orientation Flights and Aviation Ground Training in support of their 2009 Honors Camp. The approved request was forwarded through channels to New Mexico Wing where the Commander, Col. Richard F. Himebrook accepted the task and assigned now Capt. Anthony M. Torres as Project Officer.

The AFJROTC Honors Camp effort was divided into four one-week camps during the summer of 2009; two in June and two in July. AFJROTC Honors Camp staff and cadets were hosted and housed by the University of New Mexico (UNM). UNM, the local UNM AFROTC unit, Kirtland Air Force Base, provided a variety of support to the Honors Camps.

The La Luz Academy classrooms, with Ronda Cole facilitating, were used for the NMWG Aviation Ground Training and simulator activities. Maj. Joseph R. Perea, MD, and Maj. Ted Spitzmiller were NMWG's primary instructors. LtCol David Simonson and Capt. Brian D. Morrison each instructed during an Honors Camp. Several NMWG CAP volunteers provided flight simulation assistance.

On flying days, AFJROTC cadets alternated between the tower tour, escorted by MNWG's Maj. Rich Rittmuller, and Cadet Orientation Flights provided by CAP Cadet Orientation Pilots. NMWG pilots and aircraft flew in from around New Mexico to support the Honors Camps effort.

Eleven aircraft and thirteen CAP orientation pilots conducted 218 flights totaling approximately 155 hours, allowing all AFJROTC cadets to experience the challenge of flight, many for the first time. Additionally, there were approximately fifty-five transport, ferry, and chase flights conducted to transport aircraft and pilots between NMWG squadrons and Albuquerque. The success of this effort, as noted by CAP National and AFJROTC, was truly an example of CAP NMWG support capability.

Col. Frank A. Buethe was Incident Commander for all four Honors Camps while 1st Lt. Walt Brown and Maj. James W. Steele stood in as Operations Officer, each for two Honors Camps. Larry Zentner held the Administrative/Finance Officer position for all four camps, as did Capt. William Fitzpatrick as Flight Line Supervisor. Bradley Jones was Safety Officer for two Honors Camps. 1Lt. Norman A. Reames was NMWG's PAO.

Snapshot in Time

1988 65 Cadets Attended the Summer Encampment.

Cadet Commanders Roster – November 1964

Alamogordo	C/Capt. Susan Oliver
Albq Comp I	C/Capt. Richard M. Anez
Albq Cadet IV	C/Maj. Oliver L. Marianetti
Albq Atrisco Cadet	C/MSgt. Charles Sandusky
Aztec Comp	(No name)
Carlsbad Comp	Cadet Rance Nymeyer
Clovis Comp	Cadet Randy Mason
Eunice Comp	(No name)
Four Corners Comp	C/2Lt. David Gaylor
Gallup Comp	(No name)
Grants-Milan Comp	Cadet Tom Bonomo
Hobbs Comp	C/TSgt. Pelham Jackson
Jal Comp	C/2Lt. Robert A. Walls
Las Cruces Comp	C/1Lt. Bruce Wood
Los Alamos	C/SSgt. Charlene Douglass
Roswell Comp	C/TSgt. Ignacio Ortiz
Santa Fe Comp	Cadet Craig Brown
Silver City Cadet	C/3C Danny Singleterry
Socorro Comp	C/1Lt. Wallace V. Nicholas
Tularosa Cadet	C/MSgt. Robert Gardner

6. Squadron History

As noted, many squadrons throughout the state grew during the war and then disappeared thereafter. The following table lists of all squadrons past and present with possible formation dates and current membership. Those with Designations (NM 0xx) are active as of 2009. This chapter contains a brief history of several squadrons.

New Mexico Wing Squadrons Since 1942				
Squadron	**Number**	**First Mention**	**Membership**	
			1988	**2009**
Albuquerque (generic)		1944		
ABQ Eagle	NM 012	May 1957	12	16/26 42
ABQ Thunderbird	NM 033		8	30/42 72
ABQ Heights Spirit	NM 083			14/14 28
ABQ Squadron II	NM 030		137	74/00 74
ABQ Squadron III				
ABQ West Mesa		1998		
Alamogordo	NM 073		78	26/14 40
Animas		1959		
Artesia		1946		
Belen		1944		
Blacksheep			16	
Carlsbad		1942		
Clayton		1943 (Flight)		
Clovis	NM 060			30/07 37
Cuba		Gone by 1959		
Deming		1944 (Flight)		
Edgewood High Desert	NM 085		27	05/'16 21
Farmington	NM 068		54	14/11 25
Gallup	NM 065	1944	14	07/05 12
Grants		1959		
High Plains			27	
Hobbs		1943		
Las Cruces	NM 024	1943 (Flight)	52	31/15 46
Las Cruces Dona Anna		1957		
Las Vegas		1944		
Lordsburg		1945 Active in 1959		
Los Alamos	NM 016	1950	94	25/02 27
Los Lunas				
Lovington		Active 1959		
Pecos Valley			19	
Portales		1946		

Raton		1945 Gone by 1959		
Rio Rancho Falcon	NM 077	1978		24/32 56
Roswell	NM 082	1943		15/03 18
Ruidoso				
Santa Fe	NM 018	1943	65	17/11 28
Sierra Blanca			13	
Silver City		1944 Active 1959		
Socorro	NM084	1944 Active 1959		15/13 28
Taos	NM 006			17/0 17
Tucumcari		Gone by 1959		
White Sands 387th		1970		
Gov Legislative Unit	NM 999			
NM Wing Staff	NM 001			22/00 22
Reserve Squadron	NM 000		35	69/5 74
School Enrichment 800				
Staff	NM 800			4
Rio Rancho Eagle Ridge	NM 805			03/49 52
Espanola Military Academy	NM 809			06/49 55
St. Theresa	NM 811			03/22 25
Horizon Academy	NM 812			04/12 16
Rio Rancho High School	NM 813			03/12 15
	NM 814			03/20 23
Gallup Middle School	NM 815			03/16 19
AIMS	NM 816			
Totals	29			489/389 878

Albuquerque Squadrons

Because of its size, Albuquerque spawned several squadrons almost from the beginning. As a result, it is often not possible to identify which squadron engaged in what activity as reported by the local papers. A news item that two CAP members, Oscar Sloan and Harvey Caldwell, were killed in the crash of their airplane on the west mesa made the headlines in July 23, 1945

These often short snippets of newspaper articles are intriguing as one Albuquerque paper reported that the "CAP Airport Opened" 6 miles north of city (and 1 mi east of Carlisle). It calls it the 'Cutter-Carr Field.' Yet another article dated Nov 27, 1945 calls it the Graham-Bell Airport, as it was financed by Lewis Graham and William Bell. The article describes a CAP sponsored air show where 5000 were expected to attend.

The Albuquerque units were initially labeled simply Sq I, II & III. SQ I was a composite squadron and is known today as Eagle. Sq II was a senior unit that still exists. ABQ III was also a Senior Squadron for Ground search operations.

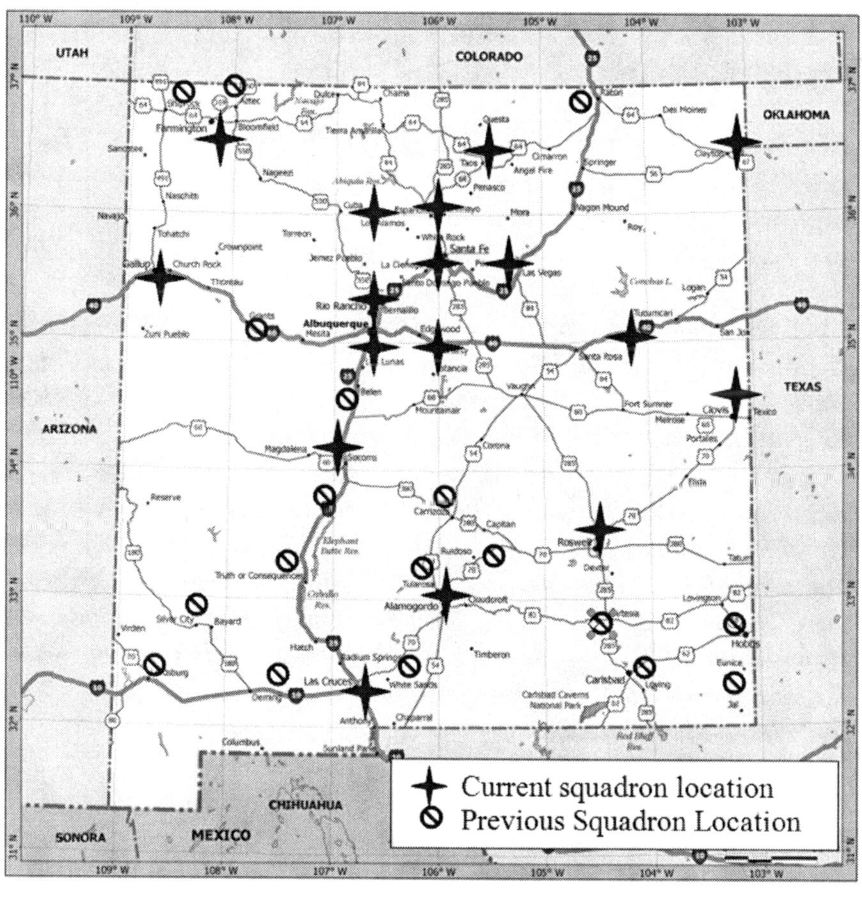

56 Location of New Mexico Squadrons past and present.

ABQ 'Eagle' Cadet Squadron

The squadron was chartered on May 22, 1957, and is one of the oldest continuously active units in CAP, according to LtCol Jay T. Tourtel, Eagle's public affairs officer. Since the squadron's charter number is 012, it was the twelfth unit in New Mexico and probably originated in the early 1940s.

Ric Himebrook sheds more light on the early years; *"When I was a cadet, I was in Albuquerque Composite Squadron I. It was originally organized during World War II and it was an old squadron when I was Cadet Commander and Jon Daffer was my Executive Officer.*

"We were mentors to help form a group at Borales Community Center that became a flight. Sometime later, the cadets from Borales were known as the Thunderbird Flight #4. Then the Squadron helped form the unit that became Eagle Flight #5. This is the way it was in the late 50's and early 60's. Over time, these became the Eagle and Thunderbird squadrons. As to the discussion as to which is oldest, Thunderbird or Eagle, the Albuquerque Composite Squadron I contained both and would be the oldest. Sq I seemed to have faded away when they both became squadrons in their own right. Thunderbird became a separate Squadron first; then, with Sq 1's charter number it is likely Eagle retained the old SQ I charter and changed the name."

Tourtel went on to say that in its 50-plus-year history, Eagle Cadet Squadron has consistently distinguished itself as one of the best squadrons in CAP as both a Squadron of Distinction—best in the region; and a Squadron of Merit—best in the wing. Ten of its cadets have gone on to receive Civil Air Patrol's General Carl A. Spaatz Award.

Squadron I also stands out as one of the few units in the country whose members participated in the earliest days of the space age. When Sputnik I was launched in 1957, the satellites were so small that they really could not be seen with the naked eye. Across the country, a series of about two dozen small telescopes were set to overlap portions of the night sky where the satellite was expected to appear. The setup was called the Mini-track system. Ric Himebrook, a former Squadron I member, recalls participating with other cadets who would intently watch for the faint point of light to cross their scope. They would then push a button that would record the position and the time.

57 Cadets Jon Daffer and Ric Himebrook 1960

By 1982, there were 13 active cadets with Major Dennis Kilrain as the CO and C/WO Robert Pfau as the Cadet Commander. Cadets Pfau and Roger Thomas completed solo flight training. Thomas also won the model airplane-building contest that year. Dennis and Kathy Kilrain received a plaque from the squadron in honor of their outstanding work. Thomas was the squadron's outstanding cadet.

Eagle Cadet Squadron's current regime began in October 2000, when LtCol Paul J. Ballmer assumed command of the squadron, after a nine-year absence from CAP. Ballmer succeeded Col Robert B. Haulenbeek, who was the interim commander at Eagle. As commander of Eagle Cadet Squadron, Ballmer was instrumental for the squadron receiving Squadron of Merit—best in the wing—for 2001, 2002, 2003, 2005 and 2006, and Squadron of Distinction—best in the region—for 2004.

Eagle Squadron was recognized as having the best aerospace education program in the Southwest Region. The squadron's commander was recognized as having the best cadet program in the region.

In October 2006, the squadron launched its quarterly newsletter, the Eagle *Flyer*, which won the 2007 Balsem Award (honorable mention) for outstanding newsletter and was recognized by CAP's National Headquarters as one of the outstanding newsletters in the nation.

Ballmer, in inaugurating the first edition of the Eagle Flyer, noted that *"we historically have been a powerful cadet unit in New Mexico Wing, looked to for advice from other squadrons on how to do things in the cadet program. We helped resurrect the Wing Cadet Competition in 2002. Many of our cadets have served as cadet commanders at the various summer and winter encampments during the past few years. Eagle Squadron led the way in initiating winter encampments beginning in 2001. In 2004, the Wing took over the responsibility for the winter encampments and they have continued ever since.*

We have sent our cadets to visit and assist with the institution of cadet programs in other New Mexico units, trying to get the Cadet Program started again. The Eagle Squadron has more cadets who have earned the Carl Spaatz Award (10) than any other unit in the New Mexico Wing. In short, we have an impressive record as a squadron in the New Mexico Wing." One Eagle cadet, Kaycee Gilbert, who went on to receive the Spaatz Award, chaired the National Cadet Advisory Council for the 2004-2005 term.

While most field trips are completed in one day, occasional outings extend for several days, as was the case with Eagle Squadron's Trip to Denver in 2006. Activities included a trip to the Wings Over the Rockies museum at the former Lowry Air Force Base, a tour of Buckley AFB, and a trip to the U.S. Air Force Academy.

.

NM Wing is privileged to have had many outstanding contributors and Eagle has had more than its share. Lt Col Jay T. Tourtel, Eagle's public affairs officer, was recognized with the U.S. Air Force Maj Howell Balsem Award in the newsletter category in 2007.

A CAP veteran with more than 25 years experience, Lt Col Tourtel originally joined as a cadet in 1971, earning the Spaatz Award. In 1978, he transitioned into CAP's senior member program, and served as his squadron's public affairs officer, leadership officer and squadron commander.

Eagle squadron has engaged in some interesting recruiting efforts over the years. In 2007, it held a contest to award $50 for recruiting at least three new members, $25 for recruiting two, and $10 for one.

An article by Kimberly L. Wright, published in Civil Air Patrol *Volunteer* magazine noted that Eagle Cadet Nicholas Quintero was selected to participate in two elite youth leadership programs in Washington DC in the same year—the Hearst Foundation United States Senate Youth Program and Civil Air Patrol's Civic Leadership Academy. The Hearst Foundation program, an all expense paid adventure, immersed youthful attendees in government activities for a week. Participants heard presentations from senators, cabinet and department chiefs and other high-ranking officials, and they met with a justice of the U.S. Supreme Court. Hearst delegates are required to possess noteworthy leadership abilities and a commitment to volunteerism and to rank in the top 1 percent academically in their state. In addition to the trip, the foundation grants each of the student delegates a $5,000 college scholarship.

Quintero said, *"The activities presented unprecedented opportunities to meet the leaders of our nation and the chance to witness firsthand the foundations of history in the making. My involvement in both programs furthered my respect and love for my God and country. Each activity was vastly different from the other in social and group dynamics. However, the differences complemented each other, allowing me to see each experience in a new perspective."*

ABQ 'Thunderbird' Squadron

Thunderbird is another very active squadron and was well represented in the 1969-1970 Cadet Yearbook:

> The highlight of events was the presentation of the Unit Citation to the squadron in 1967. This was the unit's reward for a lot of hard work by all the members...
>
> T-Bird has been under the command of five different men during this time. The one that most of the members will never forget is LTC Paul Carroll. He was an original member of the squadron when it was chartered in 1958. He worked his way up to the top through the years until his dream became a reality—a squadron of his own. Col Carroll was succeeded by LTC Fred Jarmin who was commander for only one week when he was moved up to be Group Commander. The command then passed to Lt. William Ronny. He was transferred by the Air Force to Thailand.
>
> By this time, needless to say, we were beginning to wonder who would be the commander the next time we came to a meeting. But, finally Capt. John Kamm was appointed and has been our instructor for a long time. He unfortunately had to resign because of a conflict of interest. This brings us to... the squadron's present command. 2Lt Darwin Erickson is a veteran of the Vietnam conflict and a holder of the Silver Star. At one time, he was a cadet in the squadron and came back as a senior member at the request of the squadron. He is very interested in search and rescue and wants T-Bird to have a qualified search team....
>
> Since 1967, T-Bird has strongly participated in special activities. In the summer of 1967, Gary Snyder went to Great Britain as a part of the International Air Cadet Exchange. The next year he went to Cadet Flying Encampment. James Crawford attended the one in 1969 in Oklahoma. ..
>
> On the fun side of things, T-Bird held a military ball, where a number of awards were presented including the Meritorious Service Award to Crawford. In October, T-Bird packet its bus and went to tour the Carlsbad Caverns. The last three years for T-Bird have been exciting, educational, and fun.

Donna Bracken, a former CO, said the Thunderbird Composite Squadron IV was re-chartered in November 1976. By 2009, dedicated members have grown this squadron to fifty-one cadets and twenty seniors (several are parents of cadets)—who have proven to be outstanding leaders in their community with the work they provide for Civil Air Patrol. They have been the recipient of Squadron of Distinctions for the last five years.

This squadron has grown and earnestly developed its Emergency Services tasking – participating actively in Wing SAREX's and has hosted intra-squadron emergency services training. In the area of Emergency Services: of its seventy members, 20 are Skills Evaluators; 36 have completed IS 100, 14- IS 200, 5-IS 400,11- IS 700 and 4- IS 800 courses. In GT qualifications, there are 14 GTM Level 3, 7 GTM Level 2, 14 GTM Level 1, and 3 Ground Team Leaders. Eight members are UDF Team qualified. Two members have their pre-solo wings and two additional have soloed. There is one mission observer, three mission scanners, and six mission radio operators and eight qualified for Flight Line Marshalling. These numbers significantly contribute to the readiness status of the NMW ES mission.

In addition, T-Bird proudly boasts in the accomplishments of Cadet Joseph Clark, the first cadet in the New Mexico Wing to receive the New Mexico State Search and Rescue Certification. This squadron has also participated with the US Customs and Border Patrol in joint exercises.

In the area of Cadet Programs, the squadron strives for excellence in cadets achieving their respective ranks. Currently, the squadron holds the record for the most Color Guard competition wins, representing the Wing at Regional competitions. Thunderbird has proudly participated in active duty and retirement ceremonies and funeral detail. Increasingly, the squadron participates in 4th of July ceremonies, the NM (CAPE) home school graduation ceremony and National Day of Prayer events. Thunderbird members exclusively recruited at the home school convention, the ABQ Home School Fair, the City of ABQ Volunteer Awareness Day, Talking Talons Day, and the NM State Fair. Receiving money through a grant,

Thunderbird provided rifles for new squadrons in the state, in hopes of spreading the enthusiasm of Civil Air Patrol in the communities. Thunderbird has become very active in fund raising projects with money targeted to assist cadets to attend National Cadet Special Activities. These numbers reflect the strong professional development advancements of the cadets in this squadron.

Aerospace Space studies have been lead throughout the years by outstanding educators in the New Mexico community. With the majority of seniors having earned their Yeager Award and the push for orientation flights, cadets soar in aerospace education. With the love for emergency services both seniors and cadets utilize their aerospace knowledge in planning SAREXs and evaluating search techniques.

Senior member professional development also strives for excellence. Over the years, Thunderbird has hosted and provided instructors for Training Leaders of Cadets, SLS, and CLC. The seniors have formed a study support group to complete the ECI 13. In an attempt to unite the cadet squadrons of the Wing, this squadron has sponsored dances, CPR/First Aid courses, Summer Encampment, and intra-squadron ES training at the EAA Fly-In. Thunderbird also hosted the AFRCC weekend and has represented CAP to the NM Pilot's Bash.

Recent Squadron commander have included (Marine Col) Frank A. Buethe, LtCol Robert Ross, Maj Russell Kappelman, Maj Donna Bracken, LtCol Donald Underwood, and Capt Charles Matthews.

58 T-Bird C/LtCol Bracken, Capt Irene Trujillo and Lt Nathan Way receive their Milestone Awards from Command Sergeant Major Kenneth Adair (Army National Guard, Onate Complex in Santa Fe). On their right is Lt Timothy Everhard (Deputy Commander for Cadets) and Capt Charles Matthews (Sq CO).

59 Summer Encampment has the strong support of the Army National Guard, Onate Complex in Santa Fe since 2006. Here a Guardsman instructs Cadet Vassar on the proper techniques of rappelling. The Guard personnel also instruct cadets in the obstacle course, self-defense training and drug demand reduction.

ABQ Senior Squadron II

As its name implies, Squadron Two (II) was the second Albuquerque squadron formed during WWII. Following the war, it became solely a Senior Squadron to reflect that fact that its membership was dominated by pilots whose primary interest was the Search and Rescue mission. Being headquartered on Kirtland AFB, it was natural for the squadron to gravitate to such a role.

Over the years, the squadron has often been the first to respond to a SAR mission and has typically had the highest number of mission pilots and assigned aircraft. Most recently with the disaster in Louisiana caused by hurricane Katrina, several SQ II members spend weeks flying in support of disaster relief.

The squadron peaked in 1990 when it had 120 members and 33 Mission Pilots. They were named Squadron of the Year. Many of the SAR missions described in a previous chapter were flown by SQ II pilots, observers and scanners.

Personal Reflections

Chuck Grubert, a former Egress Systems Specialist with the New Mexico Air National Guard recalls that when he came into CAP in 1973 Squadron II had three aircraft—the two T-34s and a PA-18 Super Cub. According to Grubert, one of the main differences with the way CAP was run was aircraft maintenance. In the 1970s & 1980s CAP members performed extensive maintenance on their aircraft (particularly the T-34's) under the supervision of FAA certified mechanics. Today, very little can be done.

He recalled a meeting where he, along with Harold Roberts, Ron Jacobson, and Larry Harrah, removed the tail of a T-34, and had the 500 hr tail-feather inspection done by an AI. The tail was then reinstalled and re-inspected with the aircraft back to the chocks by about 1 AM. *"Now that was a maintenance meeting,"* he said with some emphasis. *"Today we are considerably restricted because of FAA interpretation of 'owner maintenance'; CAP pilots are not considered 'owners.' Now we are going to a Part 135 type procedure and Wing is being required to participate in a centralized maintenance program."*

Grubert continued, *"As our squadron commander, Dwight went out of his way to create training, Mission training, A/C procedures, emergency procedures—not just theory but practical essentials. He made sure that each and every squadron meeting included some kind of practical training. Things like: "You can't search the trees; you have to search the ground". If you can't see the ground between the trees you are not going to find the aircraft. Spiral search is necessary to see the 'white spot'— that ground between the trees. This is a basic tenant of effective search flying that is overlooked by many people. The difference in flying a low-wing vs. high wing on missions is to be able to move that spot so the observer can see into that area. National was obsessed by the low speed, high wing A/C. But, in mountainous terrain where you are doing a contour search, the high wing can't do the type of search that is needed very effectively.*"

Regarding the criticism that SQ II was a flying club at that time he comments, *"We never thought of ourselves as a flying club. We had a certain pride of ownership that we felt we had earned by keeping and supporting the planes we loved so they could fly CAP missions. Some people in CAP still don't view the aircraft in that light. We wouldn't let just anybody fly the T-34 aircraft. The T-34 was a hot airplane for most CAP pilots and it took a higher level of ability to get checked out in it. It also took the willingness to put your own money up to fly it to stay proficient. Three pilots were identified as marginally competent and could not handle the T-34."*

"Harold Roberts was the T-34 Check pilot at that time. He required that you fly to Commercial standards—it's a high performance complex aircraft. He felt that you should be able to do this if you were going to fly that kind of an airplane. This attitude annoyed some pilots in NM who thought he was restricting them, and thought we were in a flying club. He was not intentionally leaving people

out because they weren't an 'insider' or Sq2 member, but he based his decisions on ability AND attitude.

"Yes, over the years from the 1960s when we got the T-34s, we lost some aircraft, but we lost far more Cessnas than Beechcraft. You also need to consider that CAP pilots have to fly in some pretty poor conditions, marginal weather and at low altitudes in high density altitude conditions. This is NOT the same as the typical GA pilot flies when he is going cross-country. Comparing the accident rates of these two types of pilots is like comparing apples and oranges. They just aren't the same.

60 The T-34 was an outstanding search plane for use in mountainous terrain

Unfortunately we had some lapses of judgment also... that T-34 we lost up East of Taos in 1980 (N421NM) was being flown by an active duty Major who was an Air Force T-39 pilot and was not doing his job as he had been taught... The T-34 we lost over the river had been out proficiency flying when a lost child was reported. He diverted, on his own time and at his own cost, to fly up the Rio Grande and search for this child. He was by himself and that is not good because he had to look down to search and was not able to pay full attention to what was ahead. As far as we could tell, he never saw the high power cable in front of him. That cable cut through the windshield and cockpit removing the canopy at the top of the fuselage before snagging on the tail. The aircraft then flipped over on its back and fell into the river.

He recalls hearing about Roberts and Jacobson retrieving the T-34 from Los Alamos, *"It was in pieces on a flatbed trailer. They went up there on their own time and money, brought it back, and, with a lot of help, rebuilt it to become N421NM.*

One of the keys to being mission ready was having the airplane in a hangar. Los Alamos had a hangar, it wasn't much but they made it happen. Eventually they got a second hangar. Their mission ready aircraft at that time was a Cessna 172, N5098R and it was in a hangar ready to launch... When they said they would fly a mission, I knew that at first light that plane would be rolling down the runway. It all comes back to attitude. People were interested in the mission. They were willing to give up their time and their money to make it happen." N5098R was one of the very first Cessna 172s in NM Wing that received the 180HP upgrade.

"When I joined CAP, Los Alamos had the Cessna 150, 70E. I don't know how they ever managed to fly that thing at those density altitudes. Years later, I was one of the people who pushed for that squadron to get one of the first Cessna 182's.

Grubert's heart is with the T-34; *"When we lost the original N422NM near Alameda Airport, CAP National was not going to replace it with another T-34. Earle Parks who owned Parks Industries in Amarillo, Texas was responsible for providing Sq2 with a rebuilt plane. He specialized in rebuilding the T-34. He was able to get the airframe donated and Wing used the insurance money from 422 to upgrade the engine and rebuild the airframe. Larry Harrah was Wing commander. Several years later Earle Parks and his team again upgraded 422NM by installing a new IO-550 Continental engine that gave it 300 Hp. Unfortunately, we lost Earle Parks in December of 2008 to an illness. Over the years, Earle had been a major supporter of NM Wing and the CAP Supply Depot in Amarillo. In a large part, it was due to his efforts that Sq2 was able to keep and maintain their T-34s."*

Over the years, Grubert has served in many capacities in CAP. He first became a mission observer. Then he got his Private Pilot certificate in N737MC (later to become N737NM) with Robert Haulenbeek as his instructor. He also served as Sq2 Air Ops, Sq2 Maintenance Officer and later became the NM Wing Maintenance Officer. Grubert was checked out and current in every aircraft in NM Wing until the GA-8 arrived. He also participated as a glider tow pilot at several Lloyd A. Sallee Glider encampments and became the encampment commander for two years in Hobbs. His proudest accomplishment was that of being a mission check pilot and teaching new people how to fly safely and effectively on SAR missions.

61 Chuck Grubert (l) previews a search area on a gridded sectional with JanDee Haag (c) in 1982

Not much went on in Sq2 or the NM Wing, of which Grubert he was not aware—and he has strong opinions. He firmly believes that

Senior members should not wear rank nor even the Air Force style uniform—*"Your 'rank' should be the job you are performing."*

***

Larry Harrah comments about bringing a T-34 back to NM Wing: *"I was commander for the National Staff College that year and held a meeting of the small staff at Maxwell that January [1981]. We had been given the T-34B from MS Wing after repair from a gear up landing. I flew commercial to Jackson, MS and was given an introduction to the differences from the T-34A but didn't realize that it didn't have a steerable nose wheel connection until trying to taxi for takeoff, but no problems after I recognized what was what!*

62 Larry Harrah delivers the T-34B from the Mississippi Wing in January 1980, to SQ 2 Commander Dwight Jennison.

I Flew to Maxwell and landed in N5357G as it was known then. Stayed about two days getting things set up with the help of the CAP-USAF commander and my chosen Curriculum Director. The senior programs director at National was on leave so things went well.

Left Maxwell on a Saturday (4 Jan '81) as I remember and refueled in Shreveport LA where I spent the night. Left the next day and flew in scattered snow showers to Amarillo where I refueled again. Into ABQ was a challenge as the snow was then fierce and the aircraft was not IFR equipped. As I recall I got here about 1600 on January 5 and was met by Dwight Jennison, then SQ2 commander and Chuck Grubert.

We took Dwight's picture in the cockpit as the receiving commander and I pointed out the differences between that aircraft and the T-34As. I was a T-34 check pilot in those days so I constructed a guide for aircraft differences for other pilots. The aircraft was a replacement for our PA-18, which had become non-use in the continental US except for Alaska (a tail dragger)."

63 Dwight Jennison inspects the newly arrived T-34B in January 1981.

***

Tom Godman recalls; *"I first joined CAP in 1989. Terry Wheeler a long time CAP member was my mentor and I had worked with Terry while I was in the Air Force. I wanted to get back to flying and CAP was the perfect opportunity. At that time, we had two T-34's, a C206 (N9375Z), a C172 180 HP with a constant speed prop, and after we got a C182 (N9455X) with 300 hours, reportedly confiscated from a drug arrest. My first checkout in the C172 was with Hugh Broadhurst. I hadn't flown for 10 years so it took several flights to get ready for the check. Over the next months, I progressed through the C182 and the T-34 and C206. I enjoyed the T-34 the most. It was very responsive and had super visibility over the nose and in front of the wing for searches. It was superb in mountain searches.*

Our main mission until 2001 was supporting Customs. You could fly every week if you were available and each mission logged up to six hours, split between the two pilots. At that time we had Loran to keep ourselves oriented. We had more searches then for downed aircraft and hunters/hikers. The advent of GPS and cell phones reduced the lost hiker/hunter searches a lot. I remember a downed aircraft SAR with Reed Mulkey in the T-34. We had a strong ELT, but could not see the plane. It turned out to be a composite aircraft which broke up into many small pieces and was not easily recognizable from the air to be an aircraft. We once did a mountain search in the T-34, where the slope was so steep you could only search down slope with throttle back and the gear and flaps down to reduce speed. The Mountain flying clinic in Durango was one of the best training opportunities to learn mountain search techniques. CAP sponsored SAREXs, night clinics, etc also greatly help.

Another memorable mission was in support of the Los Alamos fire. We mainly provided radio relay to mission control, but seeing the power of that fire and watching the fire tankers work was an amazing sight. Our ability to provide radio relay between the ground searchers and mission base is also invaluable to other successful searches. The opportunity to expand your horizons is participating in one of the periodic deployments out of state, such as Falcon Virgo is something to take advantage of if you can. Cadet orientation is another enjoyable mission that supports the community in a positive way.

The sophistication of aircraft has also changed. The C182T with the G1000 is the most advanced. It took a lot of study and help from able instructors to come up to speed and it is always a wonder to fly. The GA8 is also very advanced with its ability to search the ground for specific color signatures. Its avionics package is also up-to-date with GPS and a moving map display. I also enjoy the aircraft maintenance aspects of CAP. Working with the FBO, maintenance people give you additional perspective into the aircraft's operation.

We have an outstanding cadre of CAP instructors, who give freely of their time to not only provide the pilots with annual checks, but also impart their knowledge and procedures and techniques. The opportunities to check out in several aircraft and expand your ratings (e.g. instrument rating) are more reasons to fly with CAP. The camaraderie in CAP is one of the best rewards. Many of us have flown together for years and have all benefited from each other's experience and skills."

***

Ernie Braunschweig joined CAP in 1991 and, if legend has it right, has not missed a meeting since. He enjoys working with and supporting the community. He appreciates, *"associating with an excellent part of the aviation fraternity; serious pilots from the CBI* [China-Burma-India theater of WWII] *era up to recent special ops people. It is a privilege to fly with them."* But, like many in CAP, he is turned off by the growth in administrative tasks on flight crews dictated by ever expanding bureaucratic demands.

Braunschweig has several finds and one save to his credit, which he shares with Bill Drumm. He recalls, *"Bill and I were sent out before daylight to locate an ELT thought to be from an Archer rented by three Spanish nationals in CA. It had 4 hours of fuel on board when they took-off and 4 hours later it ran out of fuel at midnight north of Magdalena in the total darkness of NM. We were in 36L following the DF needle, when it suddenly swung left, I banked and there below us in the predawn light was the white Piper on the side of the mountain. It had come to the ground in an up slope arroyo donating landing gear parts and belly to the terrain as it slide up the mountain toward a large vertical out-cropping near a saddle in the ridge. At the last, the right wing tip snagged a bush, pivoting the plane into a steep grassy patch that stopped it without any frontal impact. One of the three passengers had back injuries; the others were OK. The State police helicopter came in, perched on a 10 by 10 foot flat rock and extracted them. We stayed to guide the ELT ground crew and then went home."*

***

Richard Pryor's current service to CAP began in 1979 when he first joined as a member of the Los Alamos Squadron. A friend suggested CAP as a good volunteer organization, and as a pilot, Pryor appreciated the opportunity to associate with other flyers. As Pryor recalls past events, he is still moved by the search that cold February in the Northern mountains for the doctor and his family of four who went down in a snowstorm. *"The dedication and willingness to help by the CAP and everyone at mission base was impressive. We wanted so much to find them alive. Unfortunately, the plane was not found until six months later. All aboard the plane died instantly in the crash."*

***

Perhaps because SQ II engages in so much flying activity, many of its members lament the encroaching legalism of CAP paperwork. One member echoed this sentiment when he said *"legal babble— the constant imposition of more restrictions as lawyers try to quantify common sense—something that is really impossible to do."*

***

Santa Fe Composite Squadron

The first reports regarding a CAP squadron in Santa Fe appear in a newspaper article of September 15, 1943 that indicated 85 cadets finished a CAP course in aviation topics. It reports that there were five squadrons in Albuquerque with 50 members, and squadrons in Roswell, Carlsbad, Las Vegas and Santa Fe with "Flights" in Clayton and Las Cruces. There were obviously several squadrons in Santa Fe at the time as a subsequent article states that Father Richard Spellman was named the commander of the 'new' Santa Fe squadron created a year later on August 17, 1944 and St Michaels Squadron formed November 26, 1944.

Another report says that St. Michaels College Cadets took first place in CAP Drill Competition that year. The St Michaels and Loretto Academy cadets were reported to have transferred to the Santa Fe Cadet Squadron for the fall term of 1945. Capt James P. Wheeler assumed command after Fr. Spellman.

***

The New Mexican (Sunday October 5, 1997 issue) had an article that was four columns wide with three pictures. Some quotes from the article are:

> On one recent evening, cadets in camouflage uniforms were helping set up and inflate a hot air balloon before rain and wind canceled the activity
>
> The program [Civil Air Patrol] is about a year old in Santa Fe but really has taken off since July, when Jan Lamm a registered nurse at St. Vincent Hospital, became (Deputy) Commander for Cadets. Lamm has increased the number of cadets from four to 21 and hopes to have 40 young people signed up soon.
>
> "I'm a real aggressive recruiter," Lamm said. She got most of her new members at the Santa Fe Air Show. I just basically worked the crowd," Lamm said. "I picked age-appropriate children and tried to sell them on program." Lamm became interested in the Civil Air Patrol through her

> son's participation in an Albuquerque unit of the cadet program. "I just think something like this is so important in Santa Fe, with things like our high dropout rate," she said.

Over the years, the Santa Fe squadron has held a prominent place in the SAR activities in Northern New Mexico.

Santa Fe Squadron received the following awards for 2006:

- Squadron of the Year
- ES Squadron of the Year
- Outstanding ES Service Senior Member
- AE Senior Member of the Year
- Safety Officer of the Year
- Squadron Commander of the Year

Los Alamos Composite Squadron

Bringing CAP to Los Alamos presented several problems in the early days. From its inception as a nuclear weapons laboratory in the early 1940s until the late 1950s, Los Alamos was a 'closed' city. Entry was restricted to those who lived there and to 'official business only.' In 1947, an airport was created on the east side of one of the many finger-like plateaus that extend out from the base of the Jemez Mountains. With the drive to Albuquerque being a long 3-hour ordeal in those days, the government had several flights each day between the two cities in both single and twin-engine Beech aircraft.

One of the early CAP members was Bill Chambers, a physicist with the Laboratory. Chambers recently opened his logbooks of that era to provide some insight into past activities. Bill was in the US Army during WWII where he was a pilot of Liaison aircraft assigned to Patton's 3rd Army in Europe. Chambers recalls flying L-4 and L-5 in reconnaissance missions and for artillery spotting. After the war, he went to graduate school before landing the job at Los Alamos.

Chambers remembers that Los Alamos had an active CAP unit in the early 1950s, long before the Los Alamos Airport opened to private aircraft. As a result, CAP members had to travel to Santa Fe to do their flying out of Ragle's dirt strip, *"now buried in a housing development,"* he says.

Chambers recalls Bill Lane being the Squadron Commander and at some point in the 1950s, Chambers assumed command. To provide a closer airport, Chambers and some of the Los Alamos pilots *"got involved"* in building the Espanola Airport. "*In 1954 I recall surveying and building the fence and grading the runways with Bob Klaer."*

Chamber's logbook records his first flight from Espanola in December 1954 and that *"we were flying the L-16 out of there by March of 1955 and* by *August 1956, we had an L-21.*" What is interesting about the Piper L-21 is that his logbook records the N-

Numbers as Air Force serial numbers AF-675 and AF-15895G. This is a bit odd since typically, these planes were normally registered with civilian N-Numbers. In addition, the second aircraft with a suffix of "G" would not have been a part of a standard AF serial. Chambers could not shed any light on these little mysteries. He turned over the squadron to John Durr when he got too busy with his job at the Lab and quit flying and CAP between May 1957 and April 1965. He believes the LAM squadron was dormant during much of that period. He renewed his CAP membership in August 1983

With the opening of the town to more normalization in 1958, private citizens petitioned the government to permit personal aircraft to be based at the airport. This was granted but the limitations were unyielding. Because of its unique location with a restricted area to the south, the town and mountain to the west, and the slope of the runway downhill to the east, the airport became a one-way operation. Only take-offs to the east and landing to the west were permitted. Operations were also restricted to pilots who had to apply for a "permit" to use the airport.

64 Identified as Los Alamos cadets from 1950; (Front l to r) G.R. Cooper, R.A. Plale, B.J. Patterson, H.E. Raymond, H.B. Alderete (Back) J.C. Colman, G.T. Wright, D.B. Okeson, M.B. White, Wayne Vanderford

Because LANL employees were well paid and highly educated, many chose to obtain pilot's licenses to allow them to travel more conveniently to other locals. By 1960, there were more than 20 airplanes based at Los Alamos, and a Civil Air Patrol 'Flight' was reformed. Perhaps because of limited membership at that time, the unit did not achieve the status as a squadron.

With a field elevation of 7,173 feet and density altitudes typically in excess of 10,000 feet during the hot summer months, Los Alamos Airport (LAM) is a demanding flight environment. Coupled with the often unpredictable winds that can have the wind socks pointing in opposite directions at either end of the field, LAM often requires better than average flying skills.

The requirement for currency and proficiency makes using the taildragger more costly as a viable resource. This issue was a problem for the Los Alamos 'Flight' in November 1971. They had a Stinson L-5 that apparently was not getting much flying time primarily because few in the Flight were qualified. This situation came to a head that November when Tom Cordell, the LAM Flight Commander stated in a letter to the Wing Commander, "*... the L-5 presently assigned... is detrimental to the continued growth and enthusiastic participation of this unit...*" In particular, it was noted that the plane did not have a heating system and it was almost impossible for two persons to converse in the noisy cockpit (ahh, the days before the intercom). A work order noted that the Annual Inspection in August of 1971 for the L-5 was $71.00.

Cordell requested that the yellow L-5 (N75060) be sold and the proceeds used to upgrade the fleet. In particular, he requested a C150. He addressed the difference in performance (the L-5 had a 185 HP engine compared to the 100 HP C-150) and assured the Wing Commander that the C150 would have no problems. He noted that several C150s operated out of LAM for the previous ten years without problems.

The L-5 was flown to Albuquerque by Allene Lindstrom and disposed of, and C-150 N5870E took its place. It saw many flight hours in the decade that followed. Used for primary training, proficiency and high-bird missions, the plane was a workhorse.

Having flown the C150 N5870E for many hours out of LAM, the author can say (without prejudice) that Cordell was being a bit optimistic. *"On one summer evening in 1974, I flew down to the Espanola airport (elevation 5790) to do some landings with a student and we had a very difficult time getting enough altitude to get back into LAM. It was also easy to operate the aircraft inadvertently over its gross weight limitation (1500 pounds)."*

The CAP Flight grew and became a major resource of aircraft and expertise for the Wing by the time it became a Squadron again in May 1973.

***

Airborne emergencies are uncommon. On the morning of March 8, 1981, the author and SM Robert Gibson, were about to cross the Santa Fe VOR inbound on the final approach to an instrument landing in N5098R—a C172M. Gibson was in the latter stages of his training for the Instrument rating. Without warning, the engine began to vibrate violently. We were not sure what had happened but recognized that we needed to get the plane on the ground as soon as possible. Reducing the power to idle did not totally eliminate the vibration. We were in visual conditions and had but four miles to reach the end of runway 33; however, we were unsure if the engine would remain with the airplane for the two minutes that it would take to reach that smooth surface.

I declared an emergency to the SAF tower and quickly debated setting the plane down on either I-25 or Santa Fe Downs racetrack—we had less than 1000 feet in altitude. The runway looked so close yet we knew we would have to call upon the engine for a bit more power to make it over the arroyo that separated us from the runway.

I committed to the runway, and was fortunate that the O-360 gave us that little bit of effort needed to make the threshold. We were met by 'the equipment' as we rolled out and shut down. As the propeller came to a stop, we could see that about 8 inches had broken off.

We learned that the STC for the 180 hp conversion used a prop that had a yellow caution zone on the tachometer. Operating continuously in that zone would cause vibrations that could, and did, fatigue the prop to the point of failure. A check of the tach revealed that it had an error of 200 rpm. Every time we had put the prop at an RPM setting we thought was in the safe zone—we were operating right in the middle of the yellow arc.

***

Cessna 150, N5870E met its demise on April 8, 1983 during a first flight lesson for SM Norm Elliott with CAP Instructor Pilot Robert Klaer in the right seat. Shortly after take-off, about a foot of the propeller broke off. It is hard to believe that two CAP planes, from the same squadron, would experience similar failures within 13 months of each other.

65 Cessna 150 N5870E lies broken following a forced landing.

Klaer was able to keep the violently vibrating Cessna under control and made an off-airport landing in relatively flat terrain. However, a small arroyo caused the plane to lose its left gear and the plane swerved, damaging it beyond repair. Neither Klaer nor Elliott was injured. Elliott went on to get his Private License and became a Flight Instructor (he was also winner of the 2001 AOPA Bonanza).

66 The point of fracture of the propeller on 70E is plainly visible

During the 1980s, Los Alamos rivaled SQ II as the largest in the state with more than 30 pilots and was was involved in many SAR efforts. In October 1984, a search for a missing Cessna 195 in the Sangre de Christo Mountains east of Santa Fe was conducted by Capt Walter Hatch and SM Charles Fairchild. The missing pilot, according to reports, had apparently become disoriented in bad weather. The plane's ELT did not activate and the pilot had prematurely closed his VFR flight plan so the search was delayed. The wreckage was located near the top of Thompson Peak. The three persons aboard the plane, who were from Illinois, did not survive.

***

Los Alamos was unique for other reason and one was its relationship to radiation monitoring. Allene Lindstrom recalls that SM John Brolley designed an exercise called 'Operation Hot Cloud'. He positioned a radioactive source in the C150 (obviously well within safe limits of exposure) and had its crew orbit in a designated area. A second aircraft and crew had a Geiger-counter and was tasked to locate the 'hot cloud' and determine its direction of movement and size. Allene remembers, *"This was one of the more ingenious and practical exercises devised. As Standard and Eval, we devised other exercises, but since most pilots had to pay their own cost of the planes, interest lagged."*

***

Los Alamos is an example of another squadron that prospered, in part, from community spirit. There were many who contributed to include Barbara Hoak, Vicki Johnson, Kathy Bostick… and the list goes on. Of course that might have been facilitated by the fact that most of the members worked for the Los Alamos National Laboratory and were somewhat sequestered in the northern mountains. Squadron Commander Larry Tellier was responsible for the first Squadron Leadership School to be held in Los Alamos in 1982.

Often parents become involved because of the desire to support their children's interests. In the case of SM Elmer Richberger, that involvement resulted in his helping to re-build the Cadet membership from two to 32 over a period of several years. He received an award from the local chapter of Parents Without Partners for his dedication.

There were occasional outreach programs such as the one in May of 1982 where the squadron, spearheaded by Allene Lindstrom, sponsored an Aerospace Education day at the LAM Airport. In addition to Tom McLaughlin's hot air balloon, there was Mike Clevenger's ultra-light, Wayne Bougianni's hang glider, a home built VariViggen by Clark Swannack, and Lindstrom's classic LK-19 glider. There were model airplanes, a flight simulator, and a wind tunnel built for the local science fair by a high school student who later became a CAP member (TJ Spitzmiller). Many in the town got a much closer understanding of aviation and CAP that day. However, an outreach program planned for the following year was cancelled when the city attorney required insurance coverage that the squadron could not meet.

67 A 1990 Open House at the Los Alamos Airport was presented by the squadron in conjunction with a community-wide festival. The theme was "Those Magnificent Flying Machines."

Having a monthly newsletter was also very beneficial to the squadron by keeping everyone informed and encouraging a closeness of spirit. It also contained the up-to-date "Mission Scramble" list.

While the Los Alamos airport's unique operating characteristics have been eased somewhat (students are now allowed to operate solo), it remains an airport that requires extra vigilance.

68 Wing Commander Bill Overton (top Left) presents Commanders Commendations to Molly Birely, Bob Cowan, Dick Fullerton, Larry Tellier, Allene Lindstrom, Kathy Firestone, and Bob Klaer (`1985)

Roswell Composite Squadron

The Roswell squadron formed with Al Vandergriff as commander in 1943, and with Capt Denny Moore assuming command by October 1944. In March 1944, the New Mexico Wing suffered its first fatalities when a CAP aircraft from the Roswell Squadron crashed into Pernal Peak six miles from Canones in Rio Arriba County. The two CAP crewmembers, 2nd Lt. Harry Mulroy, and Cpl Bruce Flegal (both of Roswell) had been searching for an Army bomber that had gone down near Santa Fe. The remains of their plane, which had been missing since the preceding Sunday was sighted by a search aircraft, two-thirds up the peak.

Joe Sides became the third commander of the Roswell Squadron on April 15, 1945. Later that year, Sides was piloting a CAP plane that tragically killed three people who strayed onto the runway during his landing at Tracy Field. Many aircraft of that era had poor forward visibility especially during slips (which was a common method of losing altitude during the landing). Undoubtedly, Sides had no way of knowing that the three had decided to cut across the runway and they did not hear his idling engine as he approached.

With the end of hostilities, some squadrons, such as Roswell continued to expand, as it was reported in January 1946, that radio classes began that month and two PT-17 aircraft were assigned the following month.

Las Cruces Composite Squadron

The earliest recognition of the Las Cruces squadron was a March 20, 1945 news item that says CAP Group 3 searched for a lost P-51 that was on a flight from Kirtland to Arizona. At that point, the state was divided geographically into four groups. Capt. Bob Crawford was the Las Cruces commander, while Capt. Carl Tyre was commander of the 'Third Group' headquartered in Las Cruces. In July 1945, a PT-17 was assigned to the Las Cruces squadron. That same month seven cadets attended the summer encampment at Carlsbad.

69 It would be interesting to know who these CAP members are and what they are doing in this photo from the early 1960s.

Judy Licht, a member since 1981, interviewed Eugene McKim, a former Las Cruces Squadron Commander, in March 2009. He joined the squadron in the summer of 1950. He thought that was the first year of the squadron; however, previous newspaper items reveal there was a squadron there during the war. It may have been disbanded and restarted.

McKim recalls those years were rather transitory.

"The squadron meetings were held near the railroad tracks in the old WW II prisoner of war barracks for a few weeks until they were torn down. Then we moved to two post WWII barracks on NMSU campus for a few months, until they were also torn down. Then the squadron was offered two barracks on the south part of the campus that had been moved from the air base in Deming. These barracks had 40 foot hallways with lots of small rooms, one of them big enough for a meeting place."

"The squadron commander was ex-Air Force officer, George Wilder. Rex Barrier, became commander when Wilder left (due to his construction job) who was then followed by Jack Weiss. The squadron had 20 to 30 senior members plus a cadet program.

At the time, Wing was getting state money ($5000) and, among other items, they bought binoculars for the squadrons. They had received a lot of military surplus gear, most unserviceable, but some is still being used to this day (2009). Wing also bought two transceivers that were stolen when building was broken into.

The squadron also got some vehicles, army/air force vehicles that were surplus. The LO said to go to Fort Bliss and pick out some vehicles, and send paper work to him. Power wagons and panel wagons were selected. Almost all of them had engine troubles. The old downtown Las Cruces high school had an auto mechanics department. So just for the squadron buying the materials, they rebuilt the engines.

In 1955, the college said they were going to build married student housing and the squadron would have to move again. They decided to move their two buildings to the college airport, and a third barracks the college offered. A truck and cranes were used to move three buildings in two days, with the help of the Navy operating the cranes. Buildings were set on blocks in an H shape.

70 Las Cruces Squadron Commander George Wilder (middle), Operations Officer Rex Barrier in front of an L-4 early 1950's

The first aircraft in the squadron that McKim recalls *"was an L-4 (in the picture). Later they had an L-16 for quite a while. The L-16 had one thing different from the Piper Cub - a fuel injected carburetor. It had 75 HP instead of 65 HP like the L-4."*

It was at this time that Jack Weiss became Southwest Group Commander. McKim was Communications Officer, Ray Raymond, E.S. officer and Hershel Vogan was Squadron Commander.

One Sunday, McKim accompanied another squadron pilot who was to fly the L-4 to a small dirt strip in the Gila. As the L-4 did not have an electric starter, McKim hand propped it several times but it refused to start. He called the Ops Officer who said the throttle had to be set half-open—a rather risky procedure—but it worked. *"We took off, had a sectional and a road map, (no radios) went up to the ridge, made two passes, couldn't find the airport. Went back to Grant Co. airport for fuel, taxied up to the gas pump, turned off the engine. Behind us was a Frontier DC-3 landing. We put 13 gallons of gas in that 13 gallon tank."*

"We asked the attendant where the Gila airport is. He said 'It's on the ridge, several airplanes, and a cemetery to the west'. We both remembered seeing the cemetery, but not the airport. So we go back and finally see the airport, with five airplanes. They had seen us fly over, but somehow we didn't see the airport."

This reminded McKim of a time in the 80's when one of the LRU pilots, who had been checked out in the squadron plane, went out to fly proficiency and had to call someone because he couldn't find the switch to turn on the radio. They hide those things in the darndest places.

As occasionally happens, there was some disagreement within the squadron and McKim left CAP for about five years. McKim recalls, *"In 1963, Ralph Raymond, a former Las Cruces member, dropped into NM Wing HQ one day to discuss the problem with the new commander, Harold Thomas. Thomas told Raymond he didn't know what to do about the Las Cruces squadron, they didn't respond to letters or phone calls. Raymond told him that there were a couple former members who knew how to run a squadron. Thomas said for them to send in applications and he would sign them. Ralph and I flipped a coin. I lost and became Commander!"*

McKim recalls that when he walked in the buildings after being gone for those years, everything looked just the same; all the equipment, desks, file cabinets, just as they left it five years before. Bruce Wood, a former cadet re-started the cadet program.

McKim continues, *"Around that time, a new member asked the Wing Commander that a second squadron be formed in Las Cruces, saying that Las Cruces was big enough for two squadrons. The commander said OK, and the Dona Ana Squadron began meeting at another place on campus, the old YMCA building. Within a couple of years, the two squadrons agreed to combine."*

In 1971, McKim went to the National Staff College in Montgomery, Alabama, on the regional LO's Convair 240. *"We landed at the naval air station in New Orleans, with an elevation of minus eight feet.* When they stopped at the Naval base in Dallas, the wheels were sprayed with a pesticide, to prevent proliferation of some bug attacking agriculture. *Flew on into Maxwell AFB, where we stayed in barracks just a half a block from air-conditioned classrooms. It rained every afternoon at 4:00 for fifteen minutes! The temperature was in the 80s, and the humidity 94 per cent."*

The squadron acquired a Stinson, after the L-16, which had an electric starter, landing lights, flare tubes, room for a stretcher with the back seats down, and drooping ailerons—it was a Short Take Off and Landing (STOL) aircraft. *"It could clear a 50' obstacle in 250feet ,"* according to McKim.

Jack Weiss and McKim took it to the old Alamogordo airport, which was where the fairgrounds are now. They had permission to follow Highway 70 across White Sands Missile Range. *"When we got close there was a large rain cloud right over Alamogordo, so we had to turn around and come back. This was the first airplane we had with a radio. "*

One time McKim and Weiss took the plane to El Paso to get the radio fixed. *"We had to fly around El Paso International several times until we got the green light to land - which seems strange today, but this was in the 50's."*

McKim recalls another time, *"Weiss was checking out a new pilot at the college airport, and the wind was blowing from the east, which was unusual. So, they took off toward the northeast and they pancaked it in about where the hospital is now. They both walked away, but the airplane was totaled. What may have happened was that with the flaps down, you need to gain altitude and speed before putting the flaps up. That STOL airplane with the flaps down had a lot of drag."*

When asked about SAR missions, McKim did not remember too many as there was not much air traffic through the southern part of the state at that time.

Between 1957 and 1963, the squadron had a Piper aircraft—2 place, with a starter! *"Here's what happened to it. Someone who had lost their radio control model airplane between here and White Sands, persuaded CAP to look for it. Unfortunately the Piper crashed and burned in that mission—don't recall why, but the crew walked away from it."*

About 1970, McKim relinquished command to Jack Weiss, and became Administrative Officer. In 1972, he transferred his membership to El Paso. Shortly after, Joe Gold, who knew McKim at WSMR, became a CAP member and asked him to rejoin him at the Las Cruces squadron. The squadron met on campus in Milton Hall and the commander Bob Abbott. McKim remembers each Wing Liaison Officer having a C-18 for a while.

71 The College Airport Las Cruces with several CAP aircraft visible (probably early 1950s)

The following article about Jack Weiss, and the Las Cruces Squadron was written by Lt Gregory P. French for the Enchanted Wing News in 1985.

> At approximately 5:30 am on 16 July 1945, Jack Weiss and a few other members of the U.S. Army Air Force at Alamogordo Army Air Base awakened not to the sound of reveille, but instead, to the dawning of the atomic age. Jack, at that time thirty-one years ago, was assigned to the Army Air Field as an Electronics Maintenance Officer. He and several others were shaken awake by the Trinity site test explosion that Monday morning. He had already served in the Army Air Force for three years by this time and in the Civil Air Patrol for two.
>
> Jack joined CAP in March of 1943 while on temporary duty at the Shawnee, Oklahoma Army Air Field. He has spent forty-three of his seventy-one years as an active member of Civil Air Patrol. After the war, Jack moved to Las Cruces. In 1950 he and other local CAP officers joined together to reactivate the Las Cruces Composite Squadron which has been operating continuously ever since. He became a Class II Mission Pilot in March of 1951, and in October of 1952 he completed the Air Rescue Training Service training program as a member of the first class to complete the course at March AFB, California.
>
> In March of 1953 and July of 1955, Jack served as Southwest New Mexico Group Commander. This group included the Las Cruces, Deming, Silver City, Alamogordo, and Truth or Consequences Squadrons. Jack has served in various offices with the Las Cruces Composite Squadron over the last thirty-five years. These include Personnel Officer, Finance Officer, two times as Deputy Commander for Seniors, and three times as Squadron Commander. He is qualified in every mission emergency services position including Mission Coordinator; and he has participated in more than sixty REDCAP SAR missions since 1950.

Judy Licht recalls: *"I have been a member of Las Cruces Composite Squadron since 1981. Our squadron has some interesting traditions that I think help to foster solidarity, as well as good fellowship. Over the years there have been many CAP campouts attended by quite a few members. Camping equipment has ranged from sleeping bags, to cots, tents, trailers and fifth wheelers. Camping areas include sites in the Gila National Forest, in the Lincoln National Forest and near Socorro. Who could refuse a cup of steaming coffee brought to you by Bob Abbott at first light? And playing dominos was a favorite and sometimes serious pastime for Bob and Libby and the rest of us. Bob Abbott also organized CAP fishing weekends.*

Memorial campouts have been held for Bob and Libby, in the years following their passing. Deanna Cline will be remembered in this way also.

A mistake in the squadron patch in the 80's led to the beginning of a new tradition, which has continued over twenty years. Instead of Civil Air Patrol, the patch read Civil Air Ratrol. A member suggested that this could be the start of the Goof of the Year Award, and it was presented to the member who first noticed the mistake. Each year the recipient of the award presents the award to the next honoree. We all try to keep our "goofs" hidden from last year's recipient! We have maintained a plaque with the original patch, and the names of each recipient attached. (We need to record what each year's recipient was honored for, as we are beginning to forget.)

For about ten years or so, we formed a gag gift committee, and this committee created gag gifts for just about each member of the squadron to be presented at our annual Christmas Party, along with the Goof of the Year Award and other more serious awards. We had many hilarious Christmas parties. I think the gag gift committee members needed a rest, so we haven't continued with that tradition. However, we each bring a wrapped gift to the Christmas party, and have fun as we take turns by number, opening a gift, and perhaps having our gift taken away by someone else, who chooses another gift, and so forth.

Another tradition that has had a long life is meeting at a restaurant for fellowship and maybe a little CAP business on Fifth Thursdays. Our regular meetings are held the first and third Thursdays, so when a month has five Thursdays that becomes our Fifth Thursday dinner.

Laughing together, enjoying each other's company, caring for each other are important to a squadron's ability to function well during the hard work of search and rescue and other missions."

An issue of the '1969-1970 Yearbook' produced by the wing has the following account prepared by the Las Cruces cadets:

> The Las Cruces Composite Squadron had a busy year in 1969. It was a rewarding year of excitement and knowledge of a job well done.
>
> One of the more exciting tasks in any squadron is the orientation flight. Our unit had two sessions of flying during that year, one during the first school semester, and one during the summer.
>
> The LCCS volunteered its manpower to the city during the summer by restoring an old building donated to the city for use as a museum. The job earned our unit a complete Civil Defense Course on medical self-help. This was our longest and most rewarding function during the year. Learning the fundamentals of life saving techniques was really fun. We all participated in the demonstrations and received an abundance of information from our instructors... the entire squadron passed with flying colors. Sgt. George Davis, Lt. Winfred King, and Officer Pamela Watenpaw, of the NMSU Police Department have received out deepest thanks...
>
> After our course, we initiated a weeklong membership drive to recruit new cadets. It so happened that the Southern New Mexico State Fair was coming up soon, so we made ready a booth depicting the story of the Civil Air patrol and handed out many thousands of leaflets. This proved to be a great success and added greatly to the number of cadets in our squadron...
>
> We of LCCS have found in the past years the importance of community service in the Civil Air Patrol. This is the only way to be well known in the community: To let people know that CAP is always there to contribute to the well-being of the community, and most of all, to help all people in need.

Alan Fisher recalls: *"The history of the Las Cruces CAP squadron is filled with great people, having a great time, serving a great country in the best way they knew how under the auspices of the CAP. The success and service over the last ten years has been on the shoulders of those that have served before. The inspiration from those that have gone before and have already joined the gathering host have motivated those that still labor to keep their legacy alive. People like Bob and Libby Abbott, who ran the squadron for so many years, were named the outstanding couple of the decade in 1980. Names like Jack Weiss, Gary Martin and Deanna Cline were also very instrumental in keeping the squadron going over the years.*

72 Squadron Commander Eugene McKim presenting Cadet Commander Bruce Wood with his Certificate of Proficiency.

The last decade has seen a number of events that have been significant in the history of the squadron. The operation of all of the main missions in the southern part of the state have involved the NM-024 facilities when all it had was an old communications trailer beside an old mobile home with the airplane kept in a borrowed sunshade.

Operations like the Felix Spade missions into Mexico, the Felix Keystone missions on the Tombstone MOA, the Border Patrol mission with slow scan equipment directly down-linked to the ELP

Customs office in ELP are just some of the key missions flown out of LRU. More recent missions like the Falcon Virgo and TARs mission are also depending heavily on the Las Cruces mission base and aircrews.

The Senior Squadron members have been involved in the wing and community activities. Colonel Joe Gold former NM wing commander; Colonel Joy Nelson former NY wing commander and currently the NM wing Vice Commander and Lt Col Paul Cline the NMW Director of Communications, along with many other members serving on wing staff. The squadron also hosted the wing conference and many officer development courses. LtCol Lou Braddi ran the glider academy for many years and even ran the regional academy from the LRU facilities currently serves as the NM wing Government Relations Officer.

Locally, members have supported the Las Cruces Int'l Air Show for many years and more recently the X-Cup Prize activities. They are also involved in the community helping the Balloon Fest and Whole Enchilada Festival.

The Cadets of the squadron are very involved in developing young leaders. Leadership training, aerospace education and PT are the core curriculum that has helped mature cadets into effective leaders in the community and beyond.

TWEF Fund raisers, volunteer balloon parking, color guards and many more have made the cadets splendid ambassadors for the CAP in Las Cruces. In '07, a group of cadets placed in the top 10 of the country in the Pete Conrad Space Initiative Competition in the International X-Cup Space Symposium, winning $500.

To accommodate these activities, the Las Cruces Squadron needed better facilities from which to operate. Thanks to Senator Lee Rawson, who presented and helped appropriate state legislative funds, we now have an 80x80 ft hangar and are soon going to have a modular office building for ops and communications activities.

Squadron members like Paul Cline, Alan Fisher, Walter Dutton, Dave Bjorsness and many others helped get the hangar in shape and has been a wonderful improvement over the old trailers."

More recently, the following newspaper article details the excitement of the squadron in X-Cup Prize competition:

LAS CRUCES CAP CADET FINALISTS FOR X-CUP PRIZE PETE CONRAD AWARD — On the weekend of 26-28 Oct 2007, a team composed of Las Cruces Composite Squadron Civil Air Patrol Cadets, represented New Mexico as one of the ten finalists at the Pete Conrad Spirit of Innovation Award Competition held at Holloman AFB, NM. As the only contestants from CAP, the "Space Cadets" used their aerospace knowledge to impress the crowds at the Wirefly X-Cup Prize and Space Expo. The other contestants were high school teams from around the country who also competed for the most innovative product that would benefit people living in space.

The Space Cadets designed a gyroscopic Space Sports Stabilization Belt that would enable sports and other recreation to take place in microgravity. They demonstrated the concept with a backpack mounted wheel that counteracted the force of swinging a bat in a low friction environment. The device would be strapped on as a small box containing gyros and controlled by an Inertial Measurement Unit connected to a Central Processing Unit [IMU-CPU] to interact with body movements. The cost of the unit and marketing strategies were also developed.

The cadets also had an opportunity to get personal briefings from such notables as: Dr. Peter Diamandis, Anousheh Ansari, Nancy Conrad, Eric Lindbergh and astronaut Jeff Hoffman. The CAP Space Cadet team consisted of Caleb Rawson, Gabriel Fish, Jacob Verburg, Betty Ann Fish and advisor Lt Colonel Alan Fisher.

Previous Las Cruces Commanders

George Wilder:
Jack Weiss:
Eugene McKim:
Paul Ballmer : 1981-82
Deanna Cline: 1994 -1995
Judy Licht: 1997-1998
Walter Dutton: 2008 –

Rex Barrier:
Hershel Vogan:
Jack Weiss:
Bob Abbott:
Bill Prestridge: 1995 - 1997
Alan Fisher: 1998 - 2008

73 C/SA Betty Fish, C/Am Jacob Verburg, Lt Col Alan Fisher, C/SA Gabriel Fish enjoy the X-Cup Prize Gathering in Las Cruces (2007).

74 On Memorial Day, 2007, Las Cruces cadets honored Cpl Lloyd Hackenberg, who served as a member of Merrill's Marauders (Special Forces in World War II). Next to Hackenberg is Cadet Abdiel Candelaria. (rt side) Cadets Gabriel Fish, Betty Fish and Lemuel Fish.

Gallup Composite Squadron

The Gallup Squadron first formed on October 13, 1944 with J.D. Dowling as commander and met at Clarke Field. One of their first searches in November of that year was for two Army BT-13 planes missing over NM enroute from Liberal, Kansas to Carlsbad. Another early search, centered 50 miles north of ABQ, was for a C-47 on a flight from Wichita to Long Beach. A few days later the newspaper quoted Dowling (who operated a flight school) as saying Gallup is well located for Post-war travel.

Five Gallup Cadets completed the 1945 encampment at Carlsbad Army Air Field. Their regular meeting place had moved to the Gallup Armory. On February 2, 1945, E. Parke Sellard succeeded Dowling as commanding officer.

A ground search was conducted on February 10, 1945 for an 'old man' who had become lost. Perhaps something befell the squadron in the months that followed, as an article on May 2, 1946 says that Maj Charles Phillips wants to 'reactivate' the Gallup unit.

We do not hear again from the Gallup Squadron until January 4, 1980, when the Gallup Independent newspaper headline announced 'Gallup Civil Air Patrol has new airplane.' Lt. Col Lloyd Sallee and Col. Earl Livingston delivered the Helio Courier to Lt. Roger Sturgeon, then commander of the Gallup unit. The aircraft, which had seen service with the CIA in Vietnam, was newly painted. The Wing Information Officer Margret Kilgore commented the short takeoff and landing characteristic of the plane. The story notes that the Gallup squadron had about 55 members, and was reactivated the previous year.

A new unit was again organized in 1989 with 50 cadets under Cadet Commander Rick Acevedo and DCC Sandra Aragon and Sister Judy Franz of St. Michaels (AZ).

Gallup participated in one of the more unusual emergency relief missions when they assisted the Navajo Nation during Operation HASHTKLISH in 2005. The event is recorded by Capt Jim Stephens:

> At approximately 0945, on Sunday, Jan 16, 2005, the Gallup (NM) Raptor Composite Squadron received a request from the Navajo Nation Emergency Operations Center for manpower assistance in support of Operation "Hashtklish" (the Navajo word for "mud").
>
> The Navajo Nation had been in a state of emergency since Jan 7, 2005 when Navajo Nation President Joe Shirley Jr. signed an emergency declaration due to the melting snow and ice all over the Navajo reservation making most of the dirt roads impassable with thick, gooey mud. Most of the roads had mud ruts over a foot deep and were impassable even for military off-road vehicles like a 2.5-ton (deuce and a half) truck. Since the majority of the roads on the reservation are dirt roads, there were entire communities cut off from the outside world and residents were running low on the necessities of life such as, food, water, medications, firewood and coal, livestock feed, and other basic commodities.
>
> Roughly the size of the state of West Virginia, the Navajo Nation Reservation is the largest Indian reservation in the United States. The majority of the reservation lies within the state of Arizona but also extends into areas of New Mexico and Utah.
>
> Once the Gallup Raptor Composite Squadron received the request for assistance, the call went out and the Gallup Squadron was on scene with 7 cadets and 4 adult members within 90 minutes of the original request.
>
> The tasks the Gallup squadron members were assigned included making "food bags" where they filled burlap bags with canned food and dry goods for distribution to stranded residents. They also loaded a number of trucks with several tons of potatoes and numerous hundred one-gallon containers of drinking water.
>
> The Navajo Emergency Management personnel were very impressed with the vigor and determination that the Gallup squadron showed by completing their assigned tasks within 6 hours. As a direct result of their efforts, several hundred families had food that night.

In addition to the manpower support, the Emergency Services Director for the New Mexico CAP Wing, Major David Simonson and his crewmate, 1stLT Jason Zentner also responded and gave a demonstration at the Navajo Emergency Operations Center on what additional CAP services and support are available if needed. They shared some historical information and representative aerial photographs and video of what CAP can provide.

This was the first time that Gallup Squadron had been asked to assist in any kind of emergency operation. An Memo of Understanding between the CAP and the Navajo Nation government was negotiated.

The Gallup CAP members who responded were: Capt Dean Trombley, Capt Jim Hoy, Capt Darlene Stephens, Capt Jim Stephens, C/2ndLT Anthony Anaya-Gorman, C/CMSgt Michael Fernandez, C/MSgt Madison Selleck, C/TSgt Wyatt Hoy, C/TSgt Taylor Trombley, C/SrA Merritt Selleck, and C/A1C Joe Sanchez.

The Gallup Squadron held their second annual winter 'Mini-encampment in 2005 that was open to the entire NM Wing. The event was held at Kamp Kiwanis, a resort type facility located about 18 miles south of Gallup in the hills.

The first year had been focused on cadet advancement and AE, which was quite successful. The second year the emphasis was on basic ES training, although there was an AE segment to kick off their Model rocketry program.

Although the event did not count as a regular encampment, it was run using the ICS system so that members could see the ICS system in action in ways other than a SAREX or REDCAP.

The cadets were divided into two groups. Group 1 took Basic First Aid and Adult CPR/AED course. This all-day event was limited to 20 people and led to certification and a patch to wear on the BDUs.

ICS-100 enables members to take the online GES test. BCUT, is the basic communications course where members earn their CAP Radio operators card.

To build leadership and management skills, the Cadets managed the training schedule. Cadets kept their grade and unit integrity (i.e. Gallup Cadet Leaders supervised Gallup Cadets, etc.) We had room for 180 people for this event. A Registered Nurse was on site for members with health issues. Cadets performed fire-watch and KP duties.

The Gallup newspaper reported the following in June of 2005:

On June 11, 2005, the New Mexico Wing of the US Air Force Auxiliary-Civil Air Patrol (CAP) announced that the Gallup Raptor Composite Squadron (a.k.a. Gallup CAP) will be issued one of the New Mexico Wing aircraft with an anticipated arrival date of the 2nd weekend of September 2005! At this time we do not know which of the 15 single engine Cessna type aircraft we will receive; but we will be getting one.

This will dramatically increase our functionality to the local communities in the areas of search and rescue, homeland security, aerospace education and many other types of operations.

To support this new asset, we are actively looking for aircraft pilots (minimum of a private pilot's license) and aircrew (no pilots license required) to man the new aircraft for search and rescue and homeland security operations.

To support this, Gallup CAP will be hosting a CAP Aircrew School at the Gallup Airport on the weekend of August 6 and 7, 2005. This school is the first step in becoming CAP aircrew and mission pilot rated and being awarded the coveted CAP wings. This training is also required for ALL CAP mission pilots.

The training will be followed up with an actual CAP Search And Rescue Exercise (SAREx) on Sept 9-11, 2005, at the Gallup Airport where students will be able to put to use the knowledge and skills they learned in the Aircrew School and work on becoming mission qualified.

We are excited about this new development and we couldn't have done it if it not for the dedication and hard work of all 70+ of our members.

To Jim & Pat Norvell –
It's a delight to work with you!
Mark Smith

Northeast Heights 'Spirit' Composite Squadron

Chartered on July 11, 2005 this squadron meets in the far northeast heights district of Albuquerque to provide a more convenient location for cadets who live in that part of Albuquerque. Despite its young age, it has already enjoyed considerable success.

The squadron's first commander, Lt Col Beverly (Pepe) Vito, a former Spaatz cadet, served from July 2005 to January 2006. Lt Col Mark Smith then served as commander from January 2006 to March 2008 at which time Lt Col Vito again took command. Other charter members who are still active include Lt Col Russell Kappelman and 1Lts Aida and Norman Reames. Their daughter, C/Lt Samantha Reames, is the first Spirit Squadron cadet to earn the Mitchell Award, which she received from the National Commander, MGen Amy Courter at the 2008 New Mexico Wing Conference.

Spirit Squadron received its first Subordinate Unit Inspection on December 1, 2007. Despite their relative inexperience, Spirit Squadron received an EXCELLENT rating! Spirit Squadron was also asked to host the 2008 New Mexico Wing Conference. Working as a team, Spirit Squadron organized and executed a highly successful wing conference that set records for attendance. The quality of both Senior Member and Cadet programs garnered praise. The wing conference's featured guests included the National Commander, MGen Amy Courter, and the famous aviatrix Mary Feik for whom the Feik Award is named. During the wing conference, Spirit Squadron was named New Mexico Wing's Squadron of the Year for 2008.

Although relatively small, Spirit Squadron is healthy, growing, having fun, and is an active participant in Wing and National events. Spirit Squadron's growing number of members embraces CAP's missions and enjoys serving and making a difference for their community and country.

The squadron has grown and prospered with its members taking part in a wide variety of CAP activities. For cadets these have included the Summer Encampments, the Gallup Winter Mini-Encampment, visiting the FAA Air Traffic Control facility and Glider Encampment.

Spirit Squadron volunteer service has included support of the Balloon Fiesta, Fourth of July activities at the Balloon Fiesta Park, providing snacks at Upward Basketball games, and lunches at monthly New Mexico Wing staff meetings. They have also had "just for fun" events as attending the IMAX Theater, putt putt golf, and even a cadet shoe shine party.

Senior members have attended Squadron Leadership School, Corporate Leadership School, and the Southwest Region Staff College.

75 Cadets Jacob Verburg, Caleb Rawson, Gabriel Fish and Betty Fish receive a signed Feik Achievement Award from Mary Feik, for whom the award was named, at the 2008 New Mexico Wing Conference.

Rio Rancho 'Falcon' Composite Squadron

Formed in 1978 on the west side of the Rio Grande as Albuquerque Squadron III, Falcon was originally named *The Roadrunners*. It was a spin-off of the Thunderbird Squadron and meetings were held at the old Alameda Airport.

In 1981, James Norvell assumed command from Richard Baron and held a contest to rename the squadron; *Falcon* was chosen. The unit had about 40 cadets and a vigorous program, fielding both a drill team and an honor guard. They were named Cadet Squadron of the Year for 1984—the same year that Cadet Michael Moore earned the Spaatz award.

76 Falcon Squadron hosts the 'brass'. (Back row l t r) 1st Lt. Chamless, Major Pomeranz, Col. Rice, Col. Bienko, Cmdr Criswell, Col. Jakusz, SM Judy Lawson, Lt. Falbo, (Front row) 1st Lt. Descamps, Capt Selph, SM Shawna Selph, Major Beverly (Pepe) Vito

Cadet Moore became a senior member and then commanded the squadron until 1986 when Beverly (Pepe) Vito took over. When the Alameda Airport closed in 1986, the squadron moved to Rio Rancho.

Following Vito, were LtCol William H. Criswell (a former naval aviator), Maj. Andrew Selph from October 1995 to April 1998, and Capt. Michael Mason April 1998-2002. David Simonson took over for the period of 2002 to 2009 when Lt. Michael Livesy took the reins.

77 Captain Mike Mason (l) turned over Falcon Squadron to Major Andrew Selph (r) in 1995. Wing Commander Colonel Dennis Manzanares (c).

As with many squadrons, parental involvement can make a significant impact. Several families have stood out over the years that have included Robert and Barbara Venable, whose son was Cadet Commander. More recently, the McNicol and the Feltman families have supported the squadron in many ways. The Feltman's two sons and daughter were active participants in the squadron, two of whom became Cadet Commanders.

SM Robert McNicol, whose son Brad is a former Cadet Commander, provided some input for Falcon history over the recent years noting, "*...to my own surprise, the squadron and its cadets have accomplished far more than I ever imagined. These cadets have made a significant impact on the lives of those in the community, and in the lives of the cadets and their families.*

In the past 5 years, civic activities have included Blue Star Mom support, Colors presentations (Triple A Isotopes Baseball and UNM Basketball and Volleyball games), Funerals, Parades, Charity Fund Raisers, and Graduation Ceremonies.

Numerous Wing, Region, and National Activities including coordinating the Wing Dining Out Events and Wing Cadet Competitions. Falcon Cadets have Commanded Summer and Winter Encampments, represented the Wing in Regional and National Cadet Advisory Council's and three were loaned out to assist other squadrons in getting established.

Falcon Cadets participated in the Wing Color Guard competition for the past five consecutive years. They represented the Wing at Regional competitions in 2005 and 2008 and participated in the Honor Guard Wing competition in 2005 and 2006."

Falcon cadets have attended the International Air Cadet Exchange (Thomas Nichols-Turkey, Jacob Fuentes-Singapore, Brad McNicol-United Kingdom. Other activities have included National Blue Beret (Bradley McNicol); Cadet Officer School (Gerald Feltman, Amanda Mackley, Paul Hoisington, Samuel Chesebrough); Para Rescue Orientation (Thomas Nichols and Jacob Fuentes); Air Force Space Command Familiarization Course (Ryan Sparks), and Honor Guard Academy (Bradley McNicol, Gerald Feltman, and Amanda Mackley

The Mackley sisters, Amanda and Caroline, and Ryan Sparks attended the Summer Glider Encampment in 2008, where they soloed. Sparks also earned his Private Pilot Certificate

Falcon Cadets have been accepted to the Air Force Academy (Thomas Nichols) , and received a Lifesaving Award (Gerald Feltman), and Spaatz awards. In this brief five years members of Falcon have been chosen Wing Cadet of the Year (Bradley McNicol, and Kenneth Keintz), Wing NCO of the Year (Tabitha Romero), Wing Cadet Commander of the Year (Gerald Feltman), and Wing Airman of the Year (Jordan Hill).

SM NcNicol added, *"As you can see, our cadets are very involved and take GREAT Pride to be 'Locked On' with the Civil Air Patrol. Our involvement as sponsors* [parents] *is insignificant to the accomplishments of the Cadets."*

Former Falcon Squadron Commander, David Simonson, has played an important role in Wing operations as well. He is conversant in virtually every aspect of CAP. His knowledge of communications, computers and Emergency Medical Treatment, has greatly enhanced the NM Wing programs. Simonson holds a private pilot certificate with an instrument rating, and is a Mission Pilot.

Socorro Composite Squadron

This unit was first established during World War II with its presence being noted in a newspaper article of the period saying cadets from Socorro attended the Summer Encampment at the Roswell Army Airfield in August of 1944. The squadron was later assigned an Aeronca L-16A (N6476C). We currently do not know when the original squadron ceased to exist, but it did contribute to the Wing '1969-1970 Yearbook'. Cadet Basic Joseph Martinez wrote the following input to the Yearbook:

> The Socorro Squadron has been very active in one respect—recruiting. In June of 1968, there was one cadet in the squadron. In January of 1969, the number had increased to three. Now the number of cadets in the Socorro Squadron is pushing on twenty, (including—AT LAST, three girls!)
>
> But, don't let the introduction fool you. The Socorro cadets have been busy in other areas. Cadet basics began filling staff positions to try and reactivate the squadron. Cadets worked with outdated, inadequate, and unserviceable materials and slowly converted the Socorro Squadron into a fast growing active and optimistic organization.
>
> We were ready for our first activity in September of 1969 and entered a display at the local County Fair. It was a feeble attempt but we were, as the saying goes, "just trying out our wings." Thanksgiving came along and the cadets thought about moneymaking projects to build up the treasury which stood at just over "point zero." Three turkeys were purchased with the last of the dwindling cadet money. Raffle tickets were printed up in accordance with all laws affecting such a sale. Over a period of one week, cadets sold raffle tickets at fifty cents each or three for a dollar. The local public actively supported the activity and the squadron received over eighty dollars in 'donations,'
>
> Well, right after winter began, the squadron should have begun to slow up, but we were going too fast to stop. The Deputy Co of Cadets was qualified as an instructor in Red Cross training and he gave interested cadets a course in First Aid which qualified them for their First Aid Cards.

> I am sure that you will find no one who will talk about our last money-making project for 1969. Actually, it wasn't a complete flop, but selling mistletoe didn't go over too well this year!
>
> That about wraps it up for our squadron, except that we were finally able to acquire a vehicle for cadet transportation, which really helped a great deal.

The only other solid detail uncovered from an earlier era comes from Bob Martin, of Channel 13 News. Martin, who is New Mexico's premier helicopter news reporter, was the cadet commander from 1970-71. Here are Bob's recollections;

I was a cadet in the Socorro Composite Squadron in the late 1960's and 1970-71. We had an active group of both senior members and about a dozen cadets. Cadets were offered flight training in the squadron's old 1940's era L-16 tail dragger for about $6 an hour...including fuel!

It had no radios and no electrical system. To start it, one person stayed inside the aircraft and held the brakes while the other went out and grabbed the prop and gave it a fling by hand. Navigation was by compass and looking outside.

Thanks entirely to my CAP training and the encouragement and support of Socorro Composite Squadron's senior members, I earned my private pilot's license as a senior in high school in 1971. I am tremendously grateful to those pilots who took the time to teach a young person the in's and outs of flying in New Mexico.

Several senior members at Socorro had their own planes and served as mission pilots. They all gave orientation flights to cadets on a regular basis.

The cadets held regular meetings, field training sessions and drill practice. We also were allowed to accompany senior members on ground search activities.

Regular squadron meetings and drill practice were held at the National Guard Armory in Socorro. I completed advancement to my Billy Mitchell Award before becoming a senior member at college in Las Cruces and joining the local squadron and becoming a mission pilot there later in the 70's. Civil Air Patrol remains a great opportunity for young people to learn about and experience not only aviation, but also personal discipline and responsibility.

78 Socorro Composite Squadron cadets, circa 1970 (Back l to r) Richard Baxter, Robert Martin, Joseph Martinez, (Front) Gary Sparks, Kelly Bryant, Cadet Nicholas

The following write-up details the resurrection of the Socorro Squadron in 2007. It is an excerpt of a document written by its new Squadron Commander, David Finley. The effort expended and the path they traveled is an example of effective planning and organizing—and persistence and patience.

As we began to once again bring the Civil Air Patrol to Socorro, it seemed useful to document how a group of people with practically no experience in the Civil Air Patrol went about forming a new unit from scratch and trying to merge it into the larger organization. It has been a great pleasure working with the members of the new Socorro Composite Squadron. They are a fantastic group of people who have shown great dedication to the goals and missions of the Civil Air Patrol and to their community and nation. It also has been a pleasure to be associated with the CAP's New Mexico Wing, whose leaders and staff have provided invaluable assistance as we labored to build a new unit.

As early as 2004, some Socorro-area residents expressed an interest in establishing a CAP squadron. Loradona Youngman, of Polvadera, contacted the NM Wing Headquarters that year and was sent an information packet. In October of 2005, Youngman was contacted by LtCol Claude Luisada, Group 800 Commander. That month, Luisada came to Socorro, met with Youngman, and went over the requirements and process for establishing a new squadron. He suggested she send a press release to the local newspapers to find additional people who might be interested. However, at that time, it appeared there were too few recruits to establish a squadron.

Youngman was primarily interested in CAP's cadet program as an activity for some of her children, whom she was home-schooling. By May of 2006, she had discussed CAP with several other home-schooling parents and gotten them interested in enrolling their children. Luisada and Youngman explored the possibility of Sarracino Middle School hosting a cadet squadron, but soon learned that home-school students could not join a middle-school squadron. Her discussions with Luisada turned toward including adult members and forming a composite squadron.

In July of 2006, Luisada contacted Dave Finley, of Socorro, who had filled out an inquiry form on the CAP National web site and subsequently received an information packet.. Luisada brought Finley and Youngman to collaborate on setting up an informational meeting in the community. Youngman had contacted the local newspapers and one of them ran an item urging interested parties to call her. Finley, the Public Information Officer for the National Radio Astronomy Observatory (NRAO), and a newly private pilot, began contacting people he knew might be interested. Luisada and Mr. Fred Harsany, the U.S. Air Force liaison for the New Mexico Wing, met Finley and discussed the organizational and procedural details of the process.

In September 2006, the initial informational meeting was held where Luisada and LtCol Roland Dewing, Director of Aerospace Education for the New Mexico Wing, gave presentations that introduced the Civil Air Patrol and its programs. Twenty-four Socorro residents attended this meeting, 11 of them adults.

At a second meeting, membership application forms were distributed. Jon Thunborg, contacted local police agencies and determined that the New Mexico Tech Police Department would take fingerprints for CAP applicants at no charge, unlike some other agencies that wanted significant fees for that service.

There were eight cadet applications and six senior applications. Then began a long wait. Everyone expected that processing would take some time. They faced the challenge of maintaining contact among themselves and maintaining enthusiasm despite their lack of any official CAP status.

The group met twice with the second meeting being at the Socorro Municipal Airport where they visited the hangar of Mr. Bill Marcy, a retired engineer, pilot and aircraft owner. Marcy provided cockpit tours of his 1947 Navion for the young people, explained the parts of his airplane, and showed his original airman certificate from 1944. This was a real hands-on experience, giving the potential cadets an opportunity to touch, sit in, and move the controls of a real airplane. The young people asked numerous questions and their enthusiasm was clearly visible.

Following the hangar visit, the group assembled in the small airport's "terminal" building. This, too, offered a learning experience as the group perused the various posters, charts and other publications in the building. They also enjoyed the display of pilots' first-solo cut-off shirttails that rings all four walls and represents flying achievements over more than a half century. . After the airport visit, there were no more meetings in 2006, but contact was maintained by electronic mail address to keep everyone advised.

Finley was designated as squadron commander by the group. The bureaucracy moved slowly and not without problems. However, the appropriate forms and materials were mailed on 5 January 2007

Just one week later, Finley received an email from National Headquarters announcing that the squadron was chartered as of 11 January 2007. Within a few days, members began receiving their membership cards and packets in the mail. The Socorro Composite Squadron was, at last, official.

The soon-to-be squadron received permission from Socorro County to meet at the County Annex Building. The first big project for the new squadron was to organize and conduct a public ceremony to receive the charter document from the New Mexico Wing Commander. The objective of holding this ceremony would be not just to receive the charter, but also to announce the squadron's existence to the community and to boost the morale of the members who had waited so long for official status. The date was set for February 20, 2007, and the ceremony planned for the Socorro Municipal Airport.

A press release about the event was issued and both Socorro newspapers ran it as a news item. Since the airport is owned by the City of Socorro, city government officials were advised of the event and invited to attend. Squadron members invited friends.

The weather cooperated and Youngman and Dawn Weaver, mother of one of the cadets, brought snacks and set up a refreshment table inside the airport terminal. A crowd of about 60 people waited as NM Wing

Commander, Col. Frank A. Buethe, and the Wing's Director of Operations, Capt. Joe Friel arrived in a CAP Gippsland GA-8 aircraft.

79 The Socorro Squadron charter is presented to David Finley

With the plane as an attractive photo backdrop, Buethe welcomed the members to Civil Air Patrol and presented the charter, an impressive document handsomely framed. Other special guests were U.S. Air Force Capt. Charles M. Holland, commander of a satellite-tracking detachment at White Sands Missile Range, Socorro Municipal Judge Frances Cases, and Mr. Ron Morsbach, representing Congressman Steve Pearce, a former Air Force pilot. Morsbach read a letter from Pearce, in which the congressman said, *"The Civil Air Patrol contributes to our safety, security and the quality of our lives ... I applaud your dedication to our country and your community by joining the CAP."*

Both Socorro newspapers, *El Defensor Chieftain* and the *Mountain Mail*, later carried photographs of the event. A photograph and story appeared in the national CAP News Online. The event greatly increased the squadron's visibility in the community. With this success behind them, the members began the formidable task of organizing, training, and building a functioning CAP squadron.

The Socorro Composite Squadron began with 14 members -- eight cadets and six senior members. The cadets ranged in age from 12 to 16; the seniors from 36 to 70. Only one senior member had any experience with Civil Air Patrol, as a cadet long ago. Three senior members had military experience -- two in the U.S. Marine Corps and one in the U.S. Air Force Reserve. In all cases, however, that military experience had been more than three decades in the past. The senior members included one private pilot and two who held both commercial and amateur FCC radio operator licenses

.

Socorro Composite Squadron Charter Members

Charles R. Chavez Senior	Alexander Cases-Weaver Cadet
David G. Finley Senior	Charles A. Chavez Cadet
Glenn A. Mauger Senior	Damon B. Hewitt Cadet
Jon E. Thunborg Senior	Weylin Melton Cadet
Larry R. Vanlandingham Senior	Tray G. Mishoe Cadet
Loradona Youngman Senior	Hanson Oxford Cadet
Joel D. Bowers Cadet	Trey A. Thunborg Cadet

The senior members would have to learn on the job -- and quickly -- as they undertook the tasks of establishing the organizational infrastructure and the programs of a CAP squadron. They relied heavily on the national CAP web site and found several members of the NM Wing staff who answered a myriad of questions about running a squadron. They also looked for potential new recruits who could bring needed expertise. Training was the first priority. The senior members had to complete the initial training that would permit them to officially participate in activities with cadets, then learn enough about the cadet program itself to begin teaching and mentoring the cadets.

In May, several cadets got orientation flights in gliders at Las Cruces. Powered-aircraft orientation flights were conducted at Socorro Municipal Airport in August. Pilots from Albuquerque's Squadron II flew to Socorro and presented the ground school and aircraft pre-flight operations. Eight cadets got in the air on these two days, and all were greatly enthused about their experience. Finley had alerted the local news media about the flights and a photo of cadets emerging from an aircraft appeared on the front page of Socorro's *El Defensor Chieftaint*.

The 50th anniversary of the launching of Sputnik I, the first artificial Earth satellite, came on 4 October, a regular meeting day for the squadron. Instead of a routine meeting, however, a public open house was planned to mark the historic anniversary. Holland prepared a presentation on 50 years of space history held in the auditorium of New Mexico Tech's Workman Center. The public was invited via a press release in local newspapers and on the NM Tech Web site.

At the end of the year, the squadron members could look back on a series of events and presentations that had brought alive several aspects of the aerospace environment and, particularly for the cadets, increased their knowledge of aviation and space operations.

With the nearly-complete lack of CAP experience among the charter members, training was the obvious first priority for the new squadron. Socorro's distance from other CAP squadrons made it relatively impractical for an experienced officer from an established squadron to be assigned as commander or advisor.

Col. Buethe and Capt. Friel conducted formal training sessions required to complete the orientation and CPPT certification for five senior members. A Squadron Leadership School (SLS) was scheduled at Kirtland AFB in Albuquerque in March, which Finley attended.

The Cadet Program was the area with which the squadron's senior members probably were least familiar in the beginning. Aerospace as a motivator of cadets cannot be overstated. Most cadets appeared to have joined CAP based on an interest in aviation and space. Their enthusiasm level was notably higher during AE activities and sessions than in many other areas. When they got to fly in CAP aircraft for their orientation flights, their joy was evident. These flights served as long-lasting motivational tools.

For the first few months, the squadron operated under the disadvantage of lacking uniforms for the cadets. The cadet uniform program was at a standstill at the national level because of a problem with a supplier. In the meantime, the squadron obtained T-shirts that served as a stand-in uniform as well as part of a PT uniform. Holland designed a squadron patch that first was applied as an iron-on graphic to plain white T-shirts, then was incorporated in professionally screen printed T-shirts. The T-shirts did a great job of helping build esprit de corps while the cadets awaited their CAP uniforms.

The squadron was fortunate in being able to recruit an exceptionally well qualified member to head the moral leadership training. The Rev. Phil Preston, a recently-retired minister and also a retired Air Force weather officer, eagerly accepted the invitation to join CAP.

In August, the squadron marked a major milestone -- the first cadet promotion ceremony. Cadets Trey A. Thunborg and Damon B. Hewitt were promoted to Cadet Airman. To celebrate the occasion, parents, family and friends of all members were invited to the promotion ceremony, along with prominent community members. The cadets received their new insignia with appropriate military formality, and the event ended with a reception and refreshments. A reporter *from El Defensor Chieftain* attended, and a photo of the two cadets appeared in its 11 August edition.

The second round of promotions, in which 10 cadets attained Cadet Airman rank, became a major celebration that marked a growing maturity in the squadron's cadet program as well as an exclamation point to end the year. On 13 December, New Mexico Wing Commander Col. Richard Himebrook made an official visit to the squadron. Again, parents, family and friends were invited to the event, and refreshments were provided. Himebrook encouraged the cadets, pointing out that he had begun his own CAP career as a cadet, and urged them to take full advantage of the program. A photo of the newly-promoted cadets appeared on the front page of the *El Defensor Chieftain.*

Charles Chavez became the squadron Safety Officer and began presenting regular safety briefings. One briefing he arranged featured a guest speaker, a State Police captain who gave a riveting presentation on methamphetamine and its dangers.

Glenn Mauger brought years of experience in electronics and radio communication to the job of Communications Officer. He presented the basic communications user training to the entire squadron, and by March, 11 members had completed the training. The next month, they received their Radio Operator Authorization cards from Wing.

Mauger also worked with the Wing communications staff to obtain radios for the squadron. As a result, the squadron soon had VHF communications capability installed at the Socorro County Emergency Operations Center and several small UHF handie-talkies for field use.

With an eye toward possible future operations at Socorro Municipal Airport (KONM) or even use of that airport as a mission base, Finley maintained contact with the city's airport manager and other officials, all of whom expressed support for CAP and its mission. The airport manager, Mr. Jay Santillanes, gave blanket approval for the squadron to meet at the airport and use the facilities in its small terminal building at any time.

In all of these areas, CAP has long-established procedures and regulations. The challenge for the Socorro newcomers was to learn these procedures and regulations, and that meant much reading and discussion, along with study of numerous forms used for these tasks.

In its first year of existence, the Socorro Composite Squadron did not mount any air or ground operations or obtain any vehicles or aircraft. Its members did, however, begin the long road to gaining the training and qualifications needed to turn themselves and the squadron into a CAP operational asset.

Alamogordo Composite Squadron

Alamogordo is one of the earliest squadrons mentioned in the NM Wing news clippings book indicating that it existed as early as 1942. The Army air base greatly expanded the town, but with the end of the war the Alamogordo paper noted concern over the Holloman Airbase closing. This did not happen and the base went on to expand its role as a major test and training facility. However, current records indicate that the squadron was chartered in 1952, so it may have been that the original squadron was disbanded or that a reissue of the charter occurred on that date.

The Alamogordo Senior Squadron and the White Sands Cadet Squadron were merged about 1980 to become Alamogordo Composite Squadron. John McGrann was the founder and commander of WSCS most of that time. John Green was also active during the unit merge. The Selph brothers (Andrew, Tim and Dan) joined WSCS in Oct 1978. The NM073 charter number belonged to the WSCS (probably chartered in the early 1970s - as it falls in line with the units issued charters at that time: WSCS NM073; Black Sheep NM076; Falcon NM077).

The squadron was extraordinarily active during a fifteen year period from 1983 through 1998 when it was awarded the New Mexico Emergency Services Squadron seven times. Records show that in 1995 the two squadron aircraft assigned flew almost 700 hours during 31 SAR missions and 50 missions in support of U.S. Customs and the DEA.

Alamogordo provided all the resources for a REDCAP in 1985 that involved a T-33. It had departed eastbound from Holloman AFB but was lost near Roswell. Due to icing and low ceilings, the squadron could not get its aircraft out of the Tularosa Basin. So they drove over to the east side of the mountains and rented a plane in Roswell. The search was not only hampered by low ceilings, drizzle, but an Air Force C-130 overhead. When the C-130 crew found out that all CAP members participating in the search were either Active Duty

AF or Dependents of Active Duty AF problems from the C-130 ceased. Upon finding the crash, the CAP ground team was asked only to secure the area—the remains of a person involved in such a crash can be very disturbing. CAP personnel were eventually replaced by several AF Security Policemen from Cannon AFB.

Another REDCAP is described in the following item from the October 1, 1991 Alamogordo Daily News.

> One of the most rewarding things that can happen to members of the CAP is to be credited with saving a life. That happened to two members of the Alamogordo squadron two weeks ago. Maj Carl Hendrickson, who flew the squadron Cessna 182 Skylane and 1Lt Robert Schumerth, who served as Hendrickson's observer, have been credited with saving the life of an 86 year old woman on September 20. The two men found Eugene Vavoufett in the desert about 5 miles southwest of Deming. Hendrickson and Schumerth were first launched on a search effort for Italian pilots reported missing on a flight from Albuquerque to Amarillo, Texas.
>
> *"The weather that day was pretty well horrible," Hendrickson said. After we took off and tried to go north, we couldn't get there because of the weather, so we turned around and came back to Alamogordo."*

However, Hendrickson and Schumerth did not make it back right away.

> *"As we were coming back our mission coordinator called us and diverted us to Deming. They had a missing person there,"* Henderson said.
>
> The weather again affected their flight. *"We wound up going to El Paso and then over to Deming because of the weather,"* Once in the area, Hendrickson and Schumerth radioed the ground search team, which included border patrol agents using dogs. The ground team instructed the two men to fly south of where they were searching. In just moments Hendrickson and Schumerth found Vavoufett.
>
> *"We flew down to the south and as luck would have it, and about five minutes, the flew right over the top of her,"* Hendrickson said. "She waved to us," Schumer said, *"that was good because we knew she was alive."*

> Searchers were concerned because the woman was not properly dressed to spend the night in the desert with the temperature near 40°. They were concerned about her age too. "*Usually, somebody that old, you fear the worst after a night like that in the wilderness,*" Hendrickson said.
>
> *"She had wandered off the desert the night before and when she went out into the desert, she just set down near a creosote bush,"* he said. The ground team from ground level, could not see her because she was just sitting down amongst the brush."

The CAP officers directed the ground team and an army helicopter from Fort Bliss to where the woman was.

> *"The ground team got to her first and gave her first aid. Then, the helicopter came in and took her to the Deming hospital,"* Hendrickson said. Hendrickson is retired from the air force and Schumer is the former chief ranger at White Sands National Monument.

Another article in 1996 entitled "New Mexico Wing aircrew saves lost hunter in rugged Gila Mountains Wilderness area" relates the following story.

> New Mexico - Just before midnight on Nov. 7, an alert aircrew from the Alamogordo Composite Squadron found a lost and exhausted 46-year-old hunter from Fabens, Texas. The man, in his second night of being lost, was alone in subfreezing weather in the rugged Gila Mountains Wilderness north of Silver City in southwestern New Mexico.
>
> Mission pilot Maj. Rock Hendrickson and mission observer 1st Lt. Katherine Ladd launched from Alamogordo shortly after 9 p.m. Flying to the general search area, the aircrew contacted the ground search party already in the area from the Grant County Search and Rescue team. After searching for an hour, the aircrew - in total darkness - pinpointed the location of the hunter by the muzzle flashes of his rifle which he fired into the air as the aircraft flew over. *"Considering the mountainous terrain and the fact that it was totally dark outside, this aircrew performed superbly,"* said Alamogordo Composite Squadron Commander Maj. Robert Schumerth. *"Their observations were remarkably alert and sharp under the circumstances."* However, the CAP aircrew's job was far from over. They served as a radio link between the ground teams until the hunter was reached - about 2:30 a.m. the next day.

> Refueling twice in Silver City and continuing to orbit the area while providing communications, the Alamogordo aircrew was finally released shortly after daylight when the rescue ground teams made direct radio contact with the other search and rescue teams. The CAP aircraft and aircrew finally arrived back in Alamogordo weary, but happy to have been of assistance.
>
> Hendrickson and Ladd were each credited with a "find" and a "save." According to Mission Coordinator Maj. Reed Mulkey of Albuquerque, as the hunter very probably would have perished if he had not been rescued in another eight hours.
>
> Hendrickson, a U.S. Air Force veteran and an eight-year CAP member, has several previous "saves" to his credit. For Ladd, a three-year CAP member, this was a first in the "save" category. Both members also have several "finds" to their credit. "This rescue operation was another outstanding example of dedicated and highly professional volunteerism by both the ground and air search teams," stated Schumerth .

Alamogordo was one of the first squadrons to get a dedicated hanger. Construction started in1996 and was completed the following year with the help of many community groups and the Materials Maintenance group at Holloman AFB. The 4400 square foot (55 X 70) K-span hanger, which also serves as a mission base, was built at Alamogordo-White Sands Regional Airport with funding from New Mexico Wing, Otero County, City of Alamogordo, civic organizations, and the Squadron. There are Communications facilities inside the hanger and facilities for an Operations-Missions Base for actual mission and training exercises.

In 1997, the Squadron was awarded not only the New Mexico Emergency Services Squadron of the Year but the New Mexico Squadron of the Year, along with Squadron Commander of the Year. This Triple Award had never occurred before in the New Mexico Wing history.

The squadron was meeting at Holloman AFB in 2006, when Clay Blevins came on-board. He ultimately became the Squadron Commander in January of 2009. Blevins notes, *"The Air Force had already designated the facility we were meeting in for demolition, so we had to find a new facility. After some work, the NM National Guard Armory agreed to host us in their facility in Alamogordo. Interestingly, the cadets had met there in years past. The facility had a very good classroom, and drill and exercise facilities indoors. We were required to keep it clean inside and out. Cadet numbers increased and decreased, with a high of 15, down to a low of four. These four cadets came on-board about the same time, and continued with the program as we moved to the Armory. These four cadets made up the color guard, and actively participated in all the volunteer activities we had in the local area. As we grew, somewhat, we had about 6 cadets then that made up the major cadre and were used to train new cadets as they came on-board. Two of those cadets were subsequently promoted to cadet officers, and one participated in 2009 National Blue Beret Program."*

Blevins continues, *"In December 2008, the cadets in the color guard, won first place in the non-musical marching class. They beat out the Holloman AFB Silver Talons, and the local AFJROTC color guard for that achievement. We also had our first model rocket launches, which were a lot of fun. We have an individual who pays us to clean up the trash that blows out of his commercial landfill. He is very generous. This is our primary fund raiser, and allows us to purchase items needed by the cadets, and the rest of the squadron."*

Alamogordo Squadron NM 073 Commanders

1952	1966	John Oliver	1990	1992	Ron Offley
1966	1968	John Maguire	1992	1994	Rock Hendrickson
1968	1972	Charles Nichols	1994	1998	Robert Schumerth
1972	1981	Sam Bednorz	1998	2000	Ron Offley
1981	1982	K.D. Kohlhagen	2000	2002	Paul Lazarski
1982	1986	Al Korzan	2002	2009	Shirley Kay
1986	1988	John Green	2009		Clay Blevins
1988	1990	Ric Himebrook			

Eagle Ridge Middle School Cadet Squadron

This unit is a spin off from Falcon Squadron and became a MSI (Middle School Initiative) Squadron in February 2005 (MSI later became SEP - School Enrichment Program).

Falcon Squadron was meeting in a commercial storage facility in Rio Rancho, commanded by MAJ Mike Mason, until September 2000. It was then that Mrs. Debby Morrell, principal of Eagle Ridge Middle School, invited Falcon Squadron to start the school program under the direction of the NM Army National Guard and had SSG Wil Romero teaching the in-school Cadet program. CAP member Robert Will then took over the program in 2002. Pam Thompson and Morrell provided a grant called 'Chilies' which was used as an in-school program one year and an after-school program for another. The School Cadets were signed up as members of Falcon Squadron until the school was chartered as Squadron 805 in February 2005.

At the celebration of Rio Rancho's15th anniversary of their public school system in 2009, CAP member Robert Will received a 'Special Recognition Award' from Superintendent Dr. Sue Cleveland and the School Board. Will was cited for his efforts with the School Enrichment Program at Eagle Ridge Middle School. Will has built one of the most successful SEP programs in the state since he became involved and acknowledged, *"much of the success for the program goes to the Eagle Ridge Principal, Mrs. Morrell for her support."*

The program for 2009 school year has expanded to three classes (sixth through eighth grades), meeting five days a week, with more than 30 Cadets in each class.

Horizon Academy West Cadet Squadron

Squadron commander John Wehner noted that this squadron has become a leader in student achievement and community involvement since its charter in July of 2008. The "Raptors" (their squadron moniker) are a comparably small squadron of 13 cadets and 4 senior members, but this tight-knit unit has impacted their school and community in a big way. Organizational alliance with the Civil Air Patrol has noticeably strengthened the esteem, confidence, and purpose of these young cadets.

Within their first year, the commitment of Squadron 812 brought several noteworthy accomplishments. Their dedication to training resulted in garnering top awards at the inaugural Group 800 drill competition. The unit has hosted or participated in events including service as Color Guard at the 2009 opening session of New Mexico's 49th Legislature, the Albuquerque Thunderbirds NBA D-League season opener and Horizon Academy West honors assemblies.

In September 2008, the *Albuquerque Journal* published an article highlighting the program and its cadets.

> "Pilot Program—Horizon Academy Expands Activities With Civil Air Patrol";
>
> Samuel Griego and Rumour LaJeunese want to be jet pilots.
>
> That is why they like the opportunity to go up in a plane and the aerospace education offered by the new Civil Air Patrol squadron at Horizon Academy West, a K-6 grade charter school near Coors Boulevard and I-40.
>
> Bailey Chavez likes the physical training, especially the push-ups.
>
> Griego, LaJeunese and Chavez are three of 13 Horizon sixth-graders participating in the squadron, which started at the school this year. They proudly noted that it is called Squadron 812.
>
> Fourth-grade teacher John Wehner is the squadrons commander and first-grade teacher Jennifer Lacey is its cadet instructor.

> Wehner said Horizon is always looking for enrichment activities for its students and the Civil Air Patrol program has national standards and a pre-established structure. Sixth-graders are the youngest students admitted into the Civil Air Patrol program...

Squadron 812 is dedicated to continuing a legacy of community service, aerospace learning and leadership development. Wehner said that he *"appreciates the support of the NM Civil Air Patrol, providing us the opportunity to inspire our youth to be the aerospace leaders of tomorrow."*

80 Horizon Academy cadets take top honors in the 2008 competition (Front L to R) A1C Rumour LaJeunesse, A1C Samuel Griego, A1C Roberto Perez (Back L to R) SSgt Nathan Brown, Squadron 812 Commander, Capt. John Wehner

Farmington Composite Squadron

Dannie Roberts, who joined in 1951 as a cadet, and is still an active member, tells us the unit formed in 1949. *"My friend Bobby Franks and his sister were going around trying to get other kids interested in forming a CAP Cadet unit. We met at the Old National Guard Armory atop airport hill. Senior Member Carl (Swede) Newholm was one of the first members as was Dr. Charles F. Bull (an instructor), and Howard Chrisman who taught air science at Farmington High School. Oscar Thomas, operated the Farmington Airport, and did cadet orientation rides, in an old tail dragger Taylorcraft."*

81 Cadets headed for Kirtland AFB for the Summer Encampment in April 1951. (L to R) Dannie Roberts, Leon Crabb, Sara Carpenter, Gloria Pousson, Derry Herring, Lawrence Stock, Bobby Flanks, Leland Noel, Charles Foster, Howard Ohr, Gale Knudsen. Note that passengers aboard military aircraft had to wear parachutes in those days.

He recalls, *"Farmington, Santa Fe and Albuquerque Cadets formed a drill team in 1952 to compete in National Drill Competition held at Francis E. Warren AFB Cheyenne WY. The USAF transported us there in a C-124 Globemaster. Back in those days whenever we were transported by the Air Force, we had to wear parachutes. They showed us how to put them on and what to do if we had to bail-out—how to pull the D-ring. It was pretty exciting"*

Roberts was one of the Cadets who participated in a Type A Summer Encampment in April 1951 at KAFB NM. He stressed the importance of the "Type A" encampment, *"This is the one that really allows the cadet to become a part of CAP. Once you have completed it, it opens the door to most other CAP activities."*

"The drill team was trained by an AFROTC instructor named Hotchkiss. We took 2nd place at the Competition; we were beaten out by a girls drill team from New York".

In 1954, when Chrisman was the commandant of cadets, Clarence Nollsch was selected to go to Cuba on the Cadet-Exchange program (IACE). This was an exciting time for all of us."

82 Cadet Clarence Nollsch from Farmington Squadron participates in the laying of a wreath at a Cuban Memorial site in 1954.

Roberts continues, *"The cadets participated in NM Wing Drill Competition in 1988 and 1989, then won at the Southwest Region level, and went to Maxwell AFB AL for the National Drill Competition in 1990."*

The team that went to the National Competition consisted of Chris Bacon, Kris Brack, Mike Coley, Cody Cornett, Nathan Evans, Tony Garcia, Emarae Garcia, K.C. Gauthier, Blake Hartsell, Eric Provencia, Frank Smith, Gerry Smith, Brian Tyson, Jamie Webb, Gordon Weimer, and Kalli Woodward.

83 **The Farmington Drill team went to Regional competition in 1988 and 1989 and all the way to the National competition at Maxwell AFB in 1990.**

Farmington Squadron Commanders

Bob Haulenbeek	1978	Steve Thomas	1993
Don Cooper	1979	Scot Mahon	1994
Joe Romero	1982	Dannie Roberts	1995
Will Stapleton	1985	Sharon Lane	1998
Ruth Roberts	1988	Larry Armstrong	2005
Michael Wick	1992	Scott Zenonian	2009 (present)

84 Farmington's Gordon Weimer earned top honors to represent New Mexico in France for the 1990 IACE. He was also awarded a life saving medal in 1990.

85 Farmington has been privileged to have many distinguished Squadron Commanders. Will Stapleton passes command to Ruth Roberts in 1988.

86 Some members of the Farmington Drill Team (Front L to R) Jerry Smith, unidentified, Gordon Weimer, Les Himebrook. (Back) Eric Provincio, Frank Smith, Emarae Garcia, unidentified.

87 Farmington's Dannie Roberts and Bureau of Land Management (BLM) Randy Tracy planning a survey of sensitive archeological sites in northwest New Mexico.

High Desert Composite Squadron

This unit was formed in May 2006 in Edgewood New Mexico to serve the residents east of Sandia Mountains in the Estancia Valley. Located 35 miles east of Albuquerque the squadron serves many small towns and villages that are often forgotten outside of the metro area. Primarily a cadet unit, the members take advantage of their rural surroundings to focus on expanding their horizons with the many activities that involve physical and mental challenges of Civil Air Patrol.

Having the command 'thrust' upon him in June 2007, Capt Chris Branan, a chaplain from Moriarity took on the leadership of CAP for youth in this rural area to build a strong Unit. The *High Desert Rats,* the moniker by which they prefer to be called, volunteer with the community by participating in the Pinto Bean Festival, Harvest Festival, Star-Gazing with Talking Talons, and other small town events in the area.

This Unit had the 2007 Winter Encampment Honor Cadet which proves the pride and dedication of its members. Each year a few cadets attend the Summer Encampment and always look forward to going to the next one.

The members do an annual camp-out at Villanueva Nueva Park further east, where they work extensively on their ground search and communication skills. Being from rural neighborhoods, these members think nothing of walking many miles to reach their goals, always finding the lost hiker or helping improve the state park, while enjoying the scenic beauty of New Mexico.

The members participate in the annual National EAA Fly-In at the Moriarity Airport, serving as flight line and aircraft handlers for the many glider pilots who travel to New Mexico to enjoy soaring in the high winds above and open terrain of New Mexico.

While regular meetings mean advancing their cadet and senior achievements, the members also participate in O-rides, Model

Rocketry, and Emergency Services training. Each year they actively participatc in the Wreaths Across America program, honoring fallen soldiers by placing wreaths at the National Cemetery in Santa Fe the second week of December. The members take great pride in their participation yearly and continue to expand their involvement in this outstanding program.

Bi-annual awards ceremonies recognize achievements made by the members while giving family members the opportunity to honor and participate in the advancement of the members.

This small but dedicated Unit continues to grow and strives to bring the pride of Civil Air Patrol to the rural area while utilizing the many talents of its citizens.

The *High Desert Rats* may blend into the scenery when in BDUs – but they shine through in every activity with their commitment and ease in participation of every activity of Civil Air Patrol.

88 Captain Kaycee Gilbert explains the use of the controls of a Cessna 206 to nine-year-old Sage Henson at a CAP Event in Moriarity in November 2007.

Ghost Squadrons — Many squadrons have come and gone over the 70 year existence of CAP in New Mexico. The following news clippings give but a tantalizing glimpse into their history.

Hobbs Composite Squadron — *"1969 was a very good year for the Hobbs Squadron."* At least that is what the '1969-1970 Cadet Yearbook' stated. The unit acquired a new headquarters building and had 16 new cadets "—and five were girls—" the item enthusiastically reported.

> Dale Harkins was the Southeastern Group Honor Cadet and Southeast Region Council Delegate along with Bill Azbill, while Warren Harkins was the Encampment MEO. Brad Williams received the Mitchell award. Encampment grads included Larry Hill, Bill Johnson, Gary Ralston, and Rhonda Sutton.
>
> Our first activity was a SAR test—one which no one will forget. Our bus did its best but just wasn't equal to the task of getting us up there and back, because it kept breaking down. Lt. Grizzell kept whispering words of encouragement but it was of no use. The bus has been a faithful servant but may have to be retired. Other activities included work activities that didn't seem like work, and orientation flights for all cadets. We also learned that Phyllis and Levena were delightful victims (simulated) for the ambulance crew on a SAR bivouac. In addition to regular classes were First Aid and radio operator classes, drill practice, the Miss New Mexico Parade, and because we believe in a lot of fun to go with our work, a few swinging parties.
>
> Last, but not least, was the bivouac to the Guadalupe Mountains when 31 cadets and 8 seniors retrieved a weather balloon. After a rough 12-mile ride in the four-wheel drive vehicles, and a mile and a half hike, we reached the balloon. It would have made a swell party decoration if only it hadn't burst because it was estimated to be 250 feet in diameter when inflated.
>
> Sunday was an anticlimax when we marked the wreckage of a plane in which, surprisingly enough, three people came out alive.
>
> As you can see, we had a very exciting year.

It is refreshing to hear such enthusiasm. One wonders what happened that caused the squadron to disappear.

Grants-Milan Composite Squadron—Few squadrons have documented their early history better than Grants-Milan. The squadron was activated on March 9, 1959 with Capt. Mervyn D. McKenzie as the first Commanding Officer. Doctor McKenzie, known as the 'flying Vet,' had moved to the area from Washington state where he was also a squadron CO.

We have a detailed history of their first years because someone made the effort to save newspaper clippings, radio announcements and some paperwork in a large scrapbook (now at Wing HQ) labeled "Grants History Book." If these old articles are any indication of a community's support for CAP, then Grants has to be among the top contenders.

The town of Grants experienced dramatic growth from 1945 to about 1970 because of uranium mining. Its population peaked at about 15,000 during that period and is now listed as 8,800 happy souls. Within a few months, the squadron reported a membership of 37 seniors and 52 cadets (30 boys and 22 girls).

It appears obvious that one of the keys to their rapid growth and early success was a closeness of the community as fostered by the local newspaper. Of course, this was the height of the Cold War and in the Sputnik era, patriotism was an attribute that young and old shared. Clippings relate how activities ranged from first-aid courses to bake sales. Yearly air shows were sponsored by the unit such as the one in 1961 in collaboration with the American Legion.

Coupled with the enthusiasm of the community was the growth in general aviation for travel, and New Mexico was a funnel for air traffic to California. The role of Gallup in SAR operations of the period was pivotal.

In May 1959, the squadron received its first CAP aircraft, a Piper PA-18, although it needed extensive maintenance to be airworthy—including a new fabric covering. With monthly dues of 50 cents and a variety of moneymaking enterprises to include raffles and dances, the squadron proceeded to complete the project. By October of 1960, a large bus was used to transport cadets to their weekly meetings at the Grants-Milan Airport.

89 Participating in community activities is an important part of being a cadet such as the Independence Day parade in Grants in the early 1960s.

March 28, 1960 saw the squadron's first REDCAP when a Mooney Mk 20 from El Paso enroute to Grants was reported overdue. The pilot, Ken Johnson had made his last position report to T or C Flight Service. The plane was found 50 miles SE of grants in rugged terrain by the Squadron Adjutant, Robert Peeples and wife, flying an Aeronca Tri-Champ. Snow showers may have been a contributing factor as the plane hit the ground at a very high rate of speed and the wreckage was strewn over a large area. There were no survivors.

In 1962, E.D. McLaughlin became the new Commander when the 55 year old 'Doc" McKenzie died in the crash of his red Bellanca in a remote canyon in northern NM.

***

In June 1963, a Globe Swift 145 N3299K piloted by Willard Wendell Tweed and wife began a trip from Albuquerque to Prescott, AZ. The pilot apparently encountered engine trouble just west of grants and tried to put the plane down in a small clearing but misjudged and hit some trees. When his friends in Van Nuys, CA (the final destination) reported the plane overdue, an extensive search began.

Richard Himebrook, who is among the few who's original CAP membership goes back more than half a century, participated in the search. He recalls, *"The plane was slow in being located because of thunderstorms. The woman who survived used the aviation maps in the aircraft to catch water and survive! When the thunderstorms cleared it allowed CAP to fly that area..."*

Eleven CAP aircraft including the PA-18 from the Grants squadron participated in the search and finally located the site. The pilot had died but his wife was rescued after a 6-day ordeal. This event was described in the book, *Minutemen of the Air.*

Because many of the CAP aircraft had no radios back then, the search pilot had to return to Grants to report the find. Himebrook continues, *"The Radio Operator immediately called the wing headquarters 'KKI722 this is Zuni 19 with a find, over.' Then the aircraft led a CAP ground team at the airport to the wreckage. A helicopter from the Uranium mine near Grants was called and they picked up the survivor and transported her to the hospital. She was released the next day."*

Himebrook noted that the call sign "Zuni 19" was a bus converted into a mobile communications unit. The communication officer was George Hankins (now deceased), the radio operator was Himebrook (NM Wing Commander 2007-present).

***

On another occasion, a parachute jump demonstration scheduled at the Grants airport was cancelled because of high winds—but a missing 12-year-old boy became the subject of an impromptu search that day. The hotdogs and coffee that had been prepared for the parachute event were transported to support the search which ended with the find that same day.

Numerous other missing persons were located, such as three Grant high school students, found after a night on Mt. Taylor in March 1964, when their car has become mud-bound on a dirt road. Three marooned hunters were rescued in November 1964.

The son of Edmund Ball required an emergency operation but needed permission from the father who was working cattle north of Mt. Taylor—another successful mission.

On March 1, 1966, the Grants squadron received an Aeronca L-16, which was delivered by Pat Patterson. The Scrapbook ends there. At some point, over the next few years, the unit was disbanded—one wonders why?

The **Carlsbad** squadron may have been one of the first to form as it was reported to have 20 cadets in 1942. The first commanding officer was 1St Lt. Malcolm Madera, who was succeeded by Irvin Murphy.

The **Las Vegas** Squadron had a bit of excitement in June **1944** when the newspaper reported "Escaped Convicts Hunted by CAP." Apparently, the prison authorities asked CAP for an aerial search of the area. There was no follow-up on any results.

In **1944**, 50 'cadets' from **Belen** were reportedly taken for flights at the new airfield on the west mesa. These were probably a form of motivational flights for prospective members because a January 18, 1945 article stated there were 15 cadets in the Belen Squadron.

On November 9, **1944** a CAP detachment formed in **Artesia** with B.N. Muncy Jr. as commander. There were 39 cadets meeting Tuesday and Thursday nights at the high school. As there were not enough senior members they are a "Flight" of the Roswell squadron. Lt. Hugh Barron assumed command in March 1946.

In **Lordsburg**, a January 31, **1945** article noted that Lt. Marshall Kuykendall was the new commander. A July item says the meetings will be held at his home where cokes and cookies will be served

Raton Squadron had its first meeting January 23, **1945**. and on Monday and Thursdays thereafter at the high school at 7:30. They reported 35 cadets enrolled with Mel Shipman as the first commander. At the other end of the state, **Silver City** held a meeting to organize a squadron February 16, **1945**

Portales was reportedly "organizing" in a May 1, **1946** article as was the **Clovis** squadron with Major Homer B. Bray listed as CAP "State Executive Officer" and R.H. Vandiver as "chairman" of the Squadron. These, of course, are interesting titles. The article goes on to say that Vandiver bought a Boeing N2S-2. The Cadet enrollment fee was $1.50.

The **Black Sheep** Squadron was chartered on November 29, 1978 and was commanded by LtCol Carl Stone. Most of the units 32 cadets were from the 51st JROTC Squadron at Albuquerque's Del Norte High School

The **Sierra Blanca** (NM081) was chartered in early 1982 and was centered around Ruidoso. A Cadet Program later started on the Mescalero Apache Reservation as an attempt at social involvement, but it had only limited success.

The **West Mesa** Composite Squadron was charted in January 1998 with Dave MacLauchlan as the CO. There were nine seniors including Steve Circeo as Deputy Commander for Cadets.

Snapshot in Time

Unit Commanders 1 September 1967
GENTRAL GROUP Don E. Raymond, LtCol
NORTHERN GROUP Harleigh H. ALLEN, LtCol
SOUTHEASTERN GROUP John SCOGGINS, LtCol
SOUTHWESTERN GROUP John McGUIRE, LtCol
ALAMAGORDO COMPOSITE SQUADRON Benjamin S. BROWN, III
ALBUQUERQUE COMPOSITE SQUADRON I Leslie P. CARTER, 1Lt
ALBUQUERQUE SENIOR SQUADRON II Zachary P. ORTIZ, 1Lt
ALBUQUERQUE SENIOR SQUADRON III David W. FARNSWORTH, Major
ARTESIA SENIOR SQUADRON Richard 0. GENTRY, SM
CALSBAD COMPOSITE SQUADRON Gene BENZ, 2Lt
DEMING COMPOSITE SQUADRON Dewey J. SLAPE, SM
ESPANOLA COMPOSITE SQUADRON Frank COX, 2Lt,
EUNICE COMPOSITE SQUADRON L. Evelyn YOUNG, 1Lt
FOUR—CORNERS SENIOR FLIGHT James KEENE, SM
GRANTS—MILAN SENIOR SQUADRON Gayland L. BROWN, W/0
HOBBS COMPOSITE SQUADRON Harold M. SMITH, Captain
LOS GRUCES COMPOSITE SQUADRON Julius N, WEISS, Major
LAS VEGAS COMPOSITE SQUADRON James F. SULIER 1Lt
LOS ALAMOS COMPOSITE SQUADRON WILLIAM LANEMajor
ROSWELL COMPOSITE SQUADRON Tommy DOW Captain
RUIDOSO SENIOR FLIGHT Robert KIRSCH, 1Lt
SANTA FE COMPOSITE SQUADRON George C. KNIGHT, Major
SOCORRO COMPOSITE SQUADRON David DOUGLAS, Major
TRES PIEDRAS SENIOR SQUADRON Jack S. ELDER, SM
LOVINGTON COMPOSITE SQUADRON Pauley ROGERS, 1Lt
TULAROSA COMPOSITE SQUADRON Charles NICHOLS, Captain
TATUM COMPOSITE ITO SQUADRON Johnnie GREG, 2Lt
THUNDERBIRD CADET SQUADRON Paul C. CARROLL, Major

Squadron Commanders June 1982

Wing Cmdr	Overton	**Gallup**	Ed Helmick
Alamogordo	Allen Korzan	**Highplains**	Terry Stidham
SQ II	Dwight Jennison	**Las Cruces**	Paul Watson
Black Sheep	Lynn Looney	**LAM**	Larry Tellier
Clayton	Harold Mock	**Pecos**	Lee Mitchell
Eagle	Ted Pfau	**Portales**	Norman Hart
Espanola	Nelson Cournoyer	**Quay County**	Wheeler Hughes
Falcon	James Norvell	**SAF**	Ted Price
Farmington	Joe Romero	**Sierra Blanca**	Ed Stalzer
Ft Sumner	Robert Addison	**T-Bird**	William LaRoche

Squadron Status 1987-1988

Unit	**Members 1987 vs 1988**	**Level I Completions**	**SLS 1987 vs 1988**	**ECI**
Wing	58 —57	40 —70%	21 —20	13 —12
Eagle	13 —12	11 —92%	6 —6	2 —2
Los Alamos	89 —94	75 —80%	18 —19	3 —4
Santa Fe	65 —65	52 —80%	29 —25	2 —5
Las Cruces	49 —52	47 —90%	21 —25	16 —15
SQ2	100 — 137	81 —59%	11 —12	1 —2
T-Bird	15 — 8	7 —88%	5 —4	2 —4
High Plains	28 — 27	23 —85%	4 —5	2 —4
Gallup	16 — 14	10 — 1%	2 —0	0 —0
Farmington	35 — 54	47 —87%	20 —18	4 —6
Alamogordo	79 — 78	76 —97%	33 —31	20 —17
Black Sheep	14 — 15	12 —80%	2 —2	2 —2
Falcon	11 — 5	3 —60%	4 —2	1 —1
Pecos Valley	19 — 19	14 —74%	3 —3	0 —1
Sierra Blanca	8 — 13	11 —85%	3 —S	1 —3
387th	15 — 14	9 —64%	2 —2	0 —0
Wing Hold	27 — 35	15 — 43%	4 —4	1 —1
Totals	**647 — 699**	**533 — 75%**	**189 — 182**	**70 — 79**

7. NM Wing Commanders

New Mexico has been privileged to have some exceptional leadership. This chapter contains a list of former Wing Commanders, their tenure and a brief biography of several.

90 Former Wing Commanders (l to r) Damerow, Livingston, Sallee, Harrah, Haulenbeek, Jakusz, Overton February 1995

NEW MEXICO WING COMMANDERS*

Maj Harlee Townsden	1 December 1941	14 June 1943
Lt Col James L. Breese	14 June 1943	18 January 1946
Lt Col Lewis W. Brahn	18 January 1946	18 March 1947
Lt Col Horner D. Bray	18 March 1947	15 September 1947
Lt Col Earl W. Stark	15 September 1947	23 March 1948
Col Kilbourne L. House	23 March 1948	20 January 1950
Lt Col Howard E. Livingston	20 January 1950	25 July 1950
Lt Col Herbert V. Scanlan	25 July 1950	20 February 1951
Col Harold E. Sanford	20 February 1951	22 March 1951
Col W. Randolph Lovelace, VII	22 March 1951	3 April 1951
Col Harold E. Sanford	3 April 1951	13 June 1951
Col J. Gibbs Spring	13 June 1951	30 November 1960
Col Homer L. Bigelow, Jr.	30 November 1960	28 January 1963
Col Harold D. Thomas	28 January 1963	4 October 1965
Lt Col Harry H. Crosby, Jr	4 October 1965	3 December 1965
Col Richard T. Dillon	3 December 1965	10 February 1969
Col W. Dale Parson	10 February 1969	18 March 1972
Col Richard A. Damerow	18 March 1972	6 March 1975
Col Earl F. Livingston	6 October 1975	27 October 1979
Col Lloyd A. Sallee	27 October 1979	20 November 1982
Col William C. Overton, Jr.	20 November 1982	26 October 1985
Col Larry A. Harrah	26 October 1985	4 January 1988
Col Robert G. Haulenbeek, Jr	4 January 1988	13 April 1991
Col Donald Jakusz	13 April 1991	24 April 1993
Col Joseph Gold	24 April 1993	19 August 1995
Col Dennis Manzanares	19 August 1995	14 August 1999
Col James Norvell	14 August 1999	20 September 2003
Col Frank Buethe	20 September 2003	19 May 2007
Col Richard F. Himebrook	20 June 2007	

* A 1946 news clipping says that Col. Lewis Graham had become the new NM Wing Commander. He does not appear in the Official Wing listing of Commanders.

91 Wing Commanders at the Southwest region Conference in Albuquerque, 2000 (l to r) Jim Norvell, Dennis Manzanares, Joe Gold, Don Jakusz, Earl Livingston, Bob Haulenbeek, Larry Harrah

W. Randolph Lovelace pioneered research in space medicine and was a member of the Mayo Clinic from 1941 to 1946 and Chief of the Aero Medical Lab at Wright Field in Dayton Ohio. No stranger to risk, Lovelace had parachuted from 42,000 feet to understand personally the environment and to test survival equipment. At that time, it was the highest parachute jump ever made. He held the rank of Brigadier General in USAF reserves and was a former CAP Wing Commander for New Mexico.

The medical facilities that bear his name became famous when NASA chose Dr. Lovelace to conduct the physicals for the first group of astronauts in 1959.

Dr. Lovelace and his wife were lost in a tragic airplane crash in December 1965 that was the focus of an extensive CAP search effort.

Homer Bigelow Jr. was member of the Civil Air Patrol since 1946. His experience with the organization includes being a squadron commander, a group commander, and many times the C.O. of State encampments.

Colonel Bigelow is originally from Boston where he embarked on an engineering career at the Massachusetts Institute of Technology. he served with the Corps of Engineers of the U S Army in both World War I and World War II. His work as a civil engineer took him over much of the West. His residence in New Mexico since 1935 has been marked by much public service, into which he has poured no small amount of his personal fortune. More important than this, however, is the fact that he has *given* freely of his own personal service as an organizer, builder and leader. The Nationally famous New Mexico Mounted Patrol is one such monument to his leadership. He was its organizer and its commander for the first ten years of its life. A newspaper article announcing his promotion to Wing Commander reports that the Wing had about 500 members

Harry Crosby Jr. first joined the CAP in 1942 in Buffalo New York and became a member of the New Mexico Wing in 1950. He held about every important assignment including Deputy and Wing Commander. Crosby was employed by the Prudential Insurance Company and became a pilot in 1938. He held several pilot ratings and licenses and his flying experience included search and rescue, cadet orientation flights, aerobatics, and barnstorming. He was a member of the OX-5 club and was its president in New Mexico.

His long time friend Eldred Harrington had this to say about Crosby, *"I am a professional educator with decided opinions as to how a job should be done. I possess more than a small amount of cynicism along with considerable liking for people of all ages. I have worked with many people in the educational business and some of them had been real heavyweights in the field. I have gone to many conferences, conventions, and educational meetings with Colonel Crosby. If I were to go again into any regional or national conclaves I would select Harry Crosby as my associate. Of all the educators I have been with during 40 years, he rates among the top ten. Together I think we could attack almost any problem and, at least, emerge from it alive—perhaps even triumphant. We make a good pair; Crosby for knowledge and experience; Harrington to insist on simplicity since it has to be that way for him. At this writing* [1966] *Colonel Crosby has assignments dealing with whatever the rest at the CAP staff might have left undone."*

Richard T. Dillon was appointed Wing Commander in December 1965. He made his home in Albuquerque with his wife and four children. He was born and raised in Pocatello, Idaho and attended public schools there and became a CAP cadet. At the University of Oregon he earned both his M.S, and a Ph.D., in mathematical analysis.

He became a pilot in 1945 and held single and multi-engine ratings, and single engine sea and an instrument rating. In addition to flying, Col. Dillion's hobbies were photography, skiing, amateur radio, and postal chess. He served in the USAF as a gunnery instructor at Lowry AFB, in Colorado.

He was employed by Sandia Corporation since his arrival in New Mexico in 1958, which is when he rejoined the Civil Air Patrol. He began as a pilot in Albuquerque Senior Squadron 2. For a time he was Special Projects Officer on the Wing Staff, and also director of emergency services for the Wing. In October, 1963 he became the Squadron II commanding officer. During his tenure he reorganized the Wing into three Groups; the Southeastern Group, the Southwestern Group, and a Northern Group.

Earl Livingston was an exceptional individual as judged by almost any standard. A native of Albuquerque, he was an expert ice skater in his early years and graduated from Abbey School in Colorado. Following in the foot steps of his father, who was a pilot and NM Wing Commander in 1950, Livingston first joined the CAP in 1948 and was an aircraft mechanic in the Air Force from 1950-1952.

While serving in the Air Force, he contracted Polio and spent almost two years in thc hospital. Because the disease left him without the use of his legs (a paraplegic), he was discharged on disability. But that didn't slow him down. He returned to college and earned a Bachelor's degree from the University of Albuquerque and also attended the UNM Law School.

He married Viola, who would be his life-long companion, in 1958. She became a CAP member and received several awards before she retired from CAP after serving for 29 years. Livingston became a realtor as well as being chairman of the DAV in New Mexico. He was diligent to ensure that veterans received appropriate consideration for employment. As Livingston also loved sailing, he was also a member of the Coast Guard Auxiliary, and an accomplished photographer.

92 Col Earl Livingston and Brig Gen Richard N. Ellis USAF and a formation of cadets at Kirtland AFB 10 Jan 1979

Livingston was an avid Private Pilot and continued to fly even after he was disabled. He owned an Ercoupe, Navion, and a Piper Tri-Pacer. A plaque on the wall in his home records that he placed second in a spot landing contest at Conchas State Park in 1976. Two of his five children were CAP cadets; Mary Therese and Patrick James. He is perhaps best known for his interest in the cadet program and is only one of two Wing Commanders who took a team to National Drill Competition. His family hosted international cadets from the IACE program in 1975.

He received numerous honors including the Distinguished Service Award from the CAP. He was also a member of the New Mexico Blue Max Society and received the 1978 Aviator of the Year award from the New Mexico Aeronautical Association. Because of his exceptional spirit, Livingston was featured on Norman Vincent Peale's radio show in 1976, 'The American Character'.

> EARL LIVINGSTON DOESN'T LOOK LIKE A LIFESAVER, BUT DON'T LET THOSE CRUTCHES OR WHEELCHAIR FOOL YOU. MANY PLANE CRASH VICTIMS IN NEW MEXICO OWE THEIR LIVES TO EARL AND HIS COMRADES IN THE CIVIL AIR PATROL. EARL'S LEGS HAVE BEEN PARTIALLY PARALYZED SINCE HIS BOUT WITH POLIO AS A YOUNG MAN, BUT THE DISEASE DIDN'T STOP HIS FLYING.
>
> EARL WAS JUST A BOY WHEN HIS FATHER TAUGHT HIM TO FLY. HE ALSO TAUGHT HIM THAT HE HAS AN OBLIGATION TO FELLOW AVIATORS IN TROUBLE. EARL REMEMBERS HIS FATHER'S WORDS TODAY AS HE RUNS CAP MISSIONS LOOKING FOR MISSING FLYERS.
>
> AS A COLONEL IN THE ALL—VOLUNTEER ORGANIZATION, EARL COORDINATES SEARCHES IN THE CENTRAL PART OF NEW MEXICO. HE'S ON CALL TWENTY—FOUR HOURS A DAY. THE WORK IS LONG AND HARD AND SOMETIMES DISAPPOINTING, BUT IT HAS ITS REWARDS, TOO. EARL HAS NO IDEA HOW MANY CRASHES HE HAS SPOTTED OVER THE YEARS OR HOW MANY LIVES HE'S RESPONSIBLE FOR SAVING. BUT HE STILL FINDS THE JOB REWARDING. *"THE BEST PART OF OUR WORK IS FINDING PEOPLE ALIVE,"* EARL DECLARES *"BECAUSE THAT'S WHAT THE CAP IS ALL ABOUT. WE'RE IN THE BUSINESS OF SAVING LIVES."* THAT'S EARL LIVINGSTON OF ALBUQUERQUE, A LIFESAVER WHO'S FLYING HIGH IN THE AMERICAN CHARACTER,

Livingston's granddaughter Kristi Owen is carrying on the family tradition when she earned her Private Pilot certificate in 2009.

Lloyd A. Sallee is best remembered for his involvement in the Albuquerque Soaring Club, the National Soaring Foundation, the Soaring Society of America as well as his dedication to CAP.

Lloyd was born in Oklahoma, but the family left because of the dust bowl. Lloyd's father was a construction superintendent and the family moved often. He graduated from high school in Utah and enlisted in the US Navy in World War II. At the end of the war, Lloyd remained in the Navy Reserves and was recalled to active duty and served during the Korean War.

He finished college in New Mexico where he earned an engineering degree. During this time he rose in rank in the Albuquerque Naval Reserve and was its Commanding Officer until he retired after twenty years of service.

He headed the Architectural Specialties Division of J. C. Baldridge Lumber and held a GB98 general contractors license. Some of the major projects that were completed were Albuquerque High School, St. Vincent's Hospital in Santa Fe, Plutonium Facilities in Los Alamos and the Marriott Hotel. Lloyd was also a vice-president of Baldridge. He was active in the American Subcontractors Association, serving a term as president.

Lloyd's other love was flying. He owned a Cessna, an ultra light and was a part owner of a twin Beech. He was IFR rated. He joined the Civil Air Partrol in 1974 and flew numerous missions, many times getting up before dawn to be ready to fly a SAR.

He held various positions, including mission coordinator, safety officer, and deputy wing commander and achieved the rank of Colonel. From 1979 to 1982, he served as Wing Commander for the New Mexico Wing. After he retired from Baldridge in 1990, he felt not many young people were becoming involved in CAP. Since Lloyd was active with the Albuquerque Soaring club, he thought an encampment for cadets to teach them gliding would be a way to get their interest in aviation. The first cadet encampment was held in Hobbs, NM at the Soaring Society of America facilities. It was an instant success since the cadets actually soloed in the gliders.

Lloyd has four sons and one stepson. At the time of his death in 1996, there were 11 grandchildren. The sons are employed as college professor, minister, project manager, police office and high school teacher. One of the grandchildren, Rick, has taken flying lessons and will, hopefully, become a pilot.

William Overton worked for the Los Alamos National Lab and was an avid aviator. He flew his own C172 on many CAP mission and eventually donated it to the wing.

Larry Harrah was born in Carthage, Missouri 16 January 1931. He attended school in Golden City Missouri graduating in 1949. He obtained a BS in Chemistry and a PhD in Physical Chemistry from the University of Missouri where he also instructed in physics and physical chemistry laboratories. His specialty there and subsequently, was in the area of molecular spectroscopy. Following his academic career he entered the Air Force and was assigned to Wright-Patterson AFB, Ohio in the Wright Air Development Center. He remained there on various assignments until 1966 when he left to take a research position with Sandia National Laboratories in Albuquerque, NM. He retired from Sandia in 1987 but continued to work in his field on full and part time employment until 2005. He holds 12 patents and published more than 70 articles on spectroscopy and radiation dosimetry.

Larry joined CAP in Ohio and was active in the Ohio Wing as an assistant to the Wing Communications office. On moving to New Mexico he continued to participate in CAP activities as a member of Albuquerque's Senior Squadron II where he was appointed Squadron Commander following the promotion of his predecessor,

Col. Lloyd Sallee, to Wing Commander. He was chosen as a check pilot for the unit in 1969 acting as check pilot in the PA-18, T-34 and L-16. He held several positions on Wing staff including: Standards and Evaluation Officer, Emergency Services Officer, Personnel Officer, Operations Officer and later after his Wing Commander tour, as Maintenance Officer and Safety Officer. He was appointed Wing Commander in 1985 and served until January 1988.

Prior to his retirement from the Air Force reserve in 1983, he served as an Air Force Reserve assistant to the New Mexico Wing. While acting as a Reserve Assistant he was chosen to participate in our National Staff College as a seminar advisor, Curriculum Coordinator and in 1981-82 was the Director. As a retired Wing Commander, he returned to NSC as a seminar advisor in 1989, 1990 and 2001 for a total of 9 years participation in that college. He is a graduate of the New Mexico State's SAR School conducted by the US Forest Service in 1997 and is qualified as a State SAR Operations Officer. He attended the National SAR School in 1986 and served on nearly all positions on SAR and SAREx for New Mexico Wing from 1967 to the present. For many years he taught SAR management courses for members of New Mexico Wing. Col Harrah holds a commercial pilot's certificate with Instrument, SEL and MEL ratings and has logged > 3500 hours in light aircraft, much of that on SAR.

Robert Haulenbeek has been a member of Civil Air Patrol since 1966. For four years, he served as Squadron Commander of the Farmington Composite Squadron, a unit which he organized. At the Wing level, he has served as Director of Operations, Director of Communications, Wing Standards/Evaluations Officer, and, under Col. Harrah, as Wing Deputy Commander. He is a Command Pilot and flight instructor, with over 3000 hours of flying time. He has earned the Gill Robb Wilson Award.

Haulenbeek worked as an Air Traffic Control Specialist at the Albuquerque Flight Service Station. His wife Rebecca was also a CAP member, and served at one time as Wing Finance Officer. The

Haulenbeeks have two children, Kimberly, and Robby, who was a Cadet with Falcon Squadron in Albuquerque. Col, Haulenbeek says that his hobby is "working with young people". Both he and his wife were Girl Scout leaders! His special emphasis on expanding and improving the Cadet program.

Don Jakusz moved his family to New Mexico in the Fall of 1969 after completing a 22 year tour with the US Air Force as a navigator. Jakusz pursued a second career as he worked for Public Service Company Of New Mexico (PNM) and attended UNM to receive a BS Degree in Engineering 1981

He joined the Kirtland Base Aero Club where he earned a Commercial pilots license and an instrument rating. Jakusz recalls "*Among my new friends in aviation was a young engineer and flight instructor named Mark Haag, who suggested that Civil Air Patrol could always use help and might be of interest. Not having been there or tried that, the challenge needed to be met, and I needed a mentor.*" Albuquerque Senior Squadron II seemed to be a fit both for needs and interests.

The association worked quite well, and when Col. Bob Haulenbeek assumed command of the Wing, Jakusz accepted the position of Vice Commander. He traveled extensively to other parts of the State to address different needs and special problems. He recalls being, *"armed only with a fire extinguisher and a blanket, my primary task was putting out fires."* While serving either as Vice Commander and Commander (87-93), Jakusz' involvement included the establishment of Lloyd Sallee's Soaring Encampment, the US Customs "Border Watch" program, and the US Drug Enforcement Agency support for the DEA mission. At the completion of Col. Haulenbeek's tour as Wing Commander Jakusz was appointed as his successor.

Shortly after Jakusz transferred Command of the NM Wing to Col. Joe Gold in 1993, family medical issues prompted a move to the Dallas Texas area. Jakusz continued his CAP affiliation serving as

Region Vice Commander until 2006. He entered the ranks of the CAP retired shortly thereafter.

Joseph Gold is a native of Appalachia, a small town in the southwestern portion of Virginia. He attended school in North Carolina, Virginia, and New Mexico. He came to New Mexico for the climate as he was bothered by asthma in Virginia. He attended New Mexico State University, obtaining an Engineering Degree. He then was employed at White Sands Missile Range.

While at the Missile Range, he joined the Las Cruces Composite Squadron in 1952. His duties included classroom instruction of Cadet members, which he enjoyed and did for about two years. His duties at the White Sands Missile Range for the first five years consisted of collecting flight data on the early missiles being tested, such as the V-2 missile. He also performed testing and evaluation of missile systems such as Redeye, Chaparral, and Stinger.

In 1979, he rejoined the Civil Air Patrol and was assigned as a pilot with the Las Cruces composite Squadron. At the time he held a pilot certificate with single-engine and multi-engine ratings, with instrument airplane and flight instructor certificates. He became a CAP Check Pilot and a Mission Check Pilot and served as Chief Check Pilot and Standardization and Evaluation Officer for the Wing. He was also a Cadet Orientation Pilot, a duty he greatly enjoyed.

Col. Gold was active in the Senior Member Training Program which he completed in 1987; his Gill Robb Wilson certificate is # 819. He is a graduate of both the Region and National Staff College and he served on the instructional staff of both as a seminar advisor. He also served as Deputy Director and Director of Southwest Region Staff Colleges.

He was appointed Vice Commander New Mexico Wing in 1990 and served in this position until April of 1995 when he became Wing Commander.

Under his leadership, the Wing purchased a glider and initiated a soaring program for Cadets as well as participated in a test program of CAP squadrons established at Middle Schools throughout the state. He instituted an Advisory Board of past Wing Commanders to instill an invaluable continuity of leadership and experience within the Wing. He restructured the Wing financial system to provide for a fully automated accounting program, which allowed access to vital data needed to support financial management decisions. For these accomplishments he was awarded the CAP Distinguished Service Medal.

He is a member of the White Sands Missile Range Hall of Fame and has served on the Board of Councilors for the Citizen Bank of Las Cruces. He and his wife, Fern live in Las Cruces and have three grown children. He is actively engaged in genealogical research and has written several books on the subject.

Dennis Manzanares has served in many capacities for the Civil Air Patrol since joining in 1981. In addition to his tenure as Wing Commander from 1995 to 1999, he has also served as Vice Commander, Squadron Commander, Wing and Region Legal Officer arid Director of Senior Training and Director of Recruiting & Retention.

Col. Manzanares received a law degree from Georgetown University Law Center, Washington, DC, in May 1976, and has served as an attorney for many years in northern New Mexico. He and his wife, Carmel, make their home in Taos, where they are involved in other community organizations.

As a licensed, instrument-rated pilot with over 1000 hours of Pilot-in-Command time, Col. Manzanares has served as an FAA's Accident Prevention Counselor, as Legal Officer for both the United States Pilot Association and N.M. Pilots Association and as a member of the AOPA Legal Service Plan.. He has also been a featured writer for NM Flying Magazine. Col. Manzanares is a Mission Pilot and a Chief Mission Check Pilot.

James P. Norvell Has served in several capacities for the Civil Air Patrol since re-joining in 1979. In addition to his tenure as Wing Commander from 1999 to 2003, he has served as the Wing Vice Commander, Wing Director of Logistics and as Squadron Commander for Falcon Composite Squadron.

Col Norvell began his CAP career as a cadet in 1956 in the Santa Fe Composite Squadron. He has many regrets that he did not continue his membership while at New Mexico State University and during his time serving in the United States Army Security Agency. Jim and his wife Pat joined CAP in 1979 while he was working in Gallup for the New Mexico State Highway and Transportation Department. He continued to serve in the Gallup Composite Squadron as a communication officer and emergency services officer until he was transferred to Albuquerque. At that time he transferred his membership to Albuquerque Composite Squadron IV and became the commander in 1981.

Col Norvell worked for the New Mexico State Highway and Transportation for nearly 31 years. During this time he served as survey party chief, assistant project manager and project manager.

Col Norvell and LtCol Pat Norvell were very active with the IACE program. They have hosted cadets from many nations from 1989 to1999. Many different languages were spoken in the Norvell household during these times with the exchange cadets

As of this writing Col Norvell is serving as the wing personnel officer and as the wing historian. He received his Gill Robb Wilson in 2000 and is a graduate of the National Staff College. He is a member of the Veterans of Foreign Wars and the National Space Society.

Frank A. Buethe has had a distinguished career having served in the Marine Corps Reserve, retiring as a Colonel. He was on active duty as a naval aviator with a combat tour in Vietnam and received decorations that include five Air Medals and the Meritorious Service Medal.

His CAP activities have included managing the CAP SWR air assets for the annual US Army ADA Culminating Training Exercise (Falcon Virgo) from 2005 to the Present. He served as New Mexico Wing Commander, for the period of 2003-2007. He was Albuquerque Senior Squadron II Commander for 2008, Thunderbird Composite Squadron IV Commander for 2 years and Director of Emergency Services for 2000-2003.

Col. Buethe served as Encampment Commander for five consecutive years, for which he received the CAP Meritorious Service Award. His was the Drug Demand Reduction Administrator and assisted in development of the Middle School Initiative in four schools in cooperation with NMNG. He was also a Safety/Accident Investigation Board member.

Col. Buethe's civic responsibilities include instruction for the Military Order of the World Wars Youth Leadership Conference, and Treasurer for the Order of Daedalians, Atomic Flight 17. He is a past member of Federal Reserve Bank of Chicago Advisory Council on Small Business, and state judge for the Blue Chip Enterprise Initiative awards. He earned a BA in Government from Dartmouth College, and an MBA in Marketing & Finance from Wharton School of Finance & Commerce. His work experience includes serving as Vice President, Existing Business Development (1996-97) for the Greater Albuquerque Chamber of Commerce. Prior to moving to Albuquerque in 1996, he held numerous executive positions in Green Bay, Wisconsin.

Richard 'Ric' Himebrook is the current Commander for New Mexico Wing, as of the date of this publication. He is a Gill Robb Wilson recipient, and a graduate of the National Staff College, and the Industrial College of the Armed Forces. He has served in various operational and staff assignments, performing duties as a squadron commander in 1988-1990 and Vice Wing Commander 1999-2007.

He received a Bachelor of Science, Electrical Engineering, University of New Mexico in 1965 and a Master of Science, Meteorology, Texas A&M University in 1974. Col. Himebrook began working on his Private Pilots License 1968, while stationed in Laredo, Texas. The flying club aircraft cost $7.00 per hour wet with the instructor. However, he had to interrupt his training when he became engaged. He eventually completed the requirements for his Private Pilot certificate and went on to become instrument rated in 1993.

The Himebrook family has been fully engaged in CAP activities for many years. Col. Himebrook's CAP association dates back to 1957 when he first joined as a cadet. He was also instrumental in the forming of the Thunderbird Squadron in the late 1950s. Son Leslie was named as 'Outstanding Cadet of the Year' in 1987 and the Colonel, his wife Captain Roberta Himebrook, and Leslie, were honored in 1988 as the 'Family of the Year'. In 1993, Ric and Roberta received the 'Decade of Dedication" award.

8. Wing Membership

The number of members in the New Mexico Wing has varied greatly over the years. Motivation for membership is often related to a few individuals who are able to tap into the community spirit. Often, for the cadets, this may take the form of a young person who provides a role-model for their peers.

There have been some whose voluntary service has spanned more than half a century as indicated in the following list with their initial date of joining.

Ben Brown 1941*	Joe Gold 1952	Jon Daffer 1957
Julius Weiss 1942-2006*	Bill Chambers 1952	Richard Himebrook 1957
Joy Nelson 1949*	Robert Will 1954	Ted Spitzmiller 1958
Earl Livingston 1948-2004	James Norvell 1956*	Pat Chochrell Balok 1959
Juanda S. De Witt 1949	Claude Luisada 1956*	Gwen D. Sawyer 1959
Dannie Roberts 1949	Roland Dewing 1956	Larry Harrah 1959

* Continuous service

Perhaps the record of CAP service in New Mexico is held by Julius Weiss who passed away in 2006 after more than 60 years of membership. Ben Brown is listed as still being active in the New Mexico Wing although his current address is in Illinois.

Family membership has also been an important part of the CAP tradition. In NM Wing, the Himebrooks are probably the only family where three members of the same family held the same position [at different times] of NM Wing Deputy for Cadets. Roberta held the position under Haulenbeek, Jacquez and Gold. Ric had the position under Manzanares. Their son Les held the position under Norvell while he was stationed at Kirtland (by then he was active duty AF).

The Role of Women in CAP

The status of women has changed greatly in our society since CAP was formed, and some of the early restrictions on women in CAP would be surprising to young people today, especially when the CAP National Commander, as of this writing, is Maj. Gen. Amy S. Courter. In CAP's first days, however, women were not allowed to fly the coastal patrol missions performed by CAP in World War II, a reflection of the roles for military women during the war. However, the cadet program included young women as well as young men from the very beginning.

Female cadet participation in National Special Activities was limited until the mid-to-late 1960s; activities were for one gender or the other, but not both. IACE was developed in 1947 as an international exchange of male cadets, and no females were allowed until 1968. On the other hand, female cadets held leadership positions in their squadrons and attended summer encampments from the start. While the drill teams were segregated by sex, there were female as well as male teams in New Mexico Wing. Women always played an important role in NM Wing, and a few of these women are profiled in this section.

At one time, there was a Wing staff position called "Coordinator for Women." The 1959 NM Wing Senior Training Manual lists the following duties for that position:

> The coordinator for women at all echelons, is responsible to the commander for monitoring of all matters affecting the selection, training, utilization, career progression, character development, discipline, military clothing, recreation, housing at encampments, public relations, and general welfare of female members and girl cadets in CAP.

The person who held that position for many years was Juanda Sawyer whose husband was also the Wing Liaison NCO, and whose daughter received the first Spaatz to be awarded to a female cadet in the nation.

93 Juanda Sawyer (2nd from right) with her two daughters (Carol and Gwen) who would become cadets. The Beech D-18 was used by the Wing LO for transport.

Juanda Sawyer DeWitt began her affiliation with CAP in 1949, first in the Kansas Wing and then with the Michigan Wing before coming to New Mexico in 1952. She held many positions in CAP, including Director of Administrative Services for New Mexico Wing. She was a TAC officer for many state encampments and had two daughters who also became members. She received her pilot's license in 1958.

94 Juanda and John Sawyer and daughters Carol and Gwen.

Joy Nelson, the current NM Wing Vice-Commander, became a cadet in 1949. She said her "*family traveled a lot and could be sure she was in good hands in a new environment because CAP had a good group of kids.*" Later, as a mother herself, she was happy to see her own son join. Joy was so successful in the organization that she was the first female Wing Commander of the huge New York Wing.

After losing her husband, Joy wanted to return to the dry heat she had enjoyed as a child in the desert southwest, and moved to New Mexico in 2004, where she was called on to help the Las Cruces

Squadron. She loved helping and mentoring the cadets, and says, "*The best award I've had was a surprise from the Las Cruces cadets. I helped them prepare a 10-year award for a senior member who was retiring, and after they presented it they unexpectedly called me up to receive a plaque that said 'In Recognition Of Her Outstanding Leadership Of The Las Cruces Civil Air Patrol Cadet Program.' That award means more to me than all the other awards, including the Distinguished Service Award*".

It is no surprise when Joy answers a question about why she has stayed in CAP so long, by saying, "*to give back what CAP gave me, to make a difference. Thirty-five years ago, I got discouraged because my squadron was so focused on Emergency Services, they were neglecting the cadet program. I was ready to quit until one of the cadets told me 'Lt. Nelson, if you quit, you can't make a difference.' That's why I've stayed all these years-to make a difference.*"

95 Maxine Murfin (grandmother of T-Bird Cadets Asa & Eric Ruth) posing in her CAP uniform in 1956.

NM Wing has the distinction of being the only wing whose first two Spaatz cadets were female, Gwen Sawyer (#8) and Beverly Vito (#164).

96 C/Col. Gwen Sawyer first female Spaatz Cadet nationwide.

Gwen reflects on her CAP experience: "*Because my parents were in CAP, I saw cadets having fun when I was still too young to join. I wanted to be a part of that, and couldn't wait until I was old enough. The day after my 14th birthday (the minimum age at that time), I turned in my application and attended my first squadron meeting at Albuquerque Composite Squadron I (now Eagle Cadet Squadron).*

For the next 10 years, CAP was an important part of my life. I was fortunate to have so many wonderful experiences in CAP. Some of the friendships have lasted over time, and the opportunities I was given made all the difference in my career. The experiences in studying hard and working toward goals, teamwork and leadership, have stayed with me for 50 years. We had great drill teams, encampments, Special Activities, Cadet Advisory Council meetings, community service outings, bus trips, and parties.

My Spaatz Award in 1965 was presented by the Commander of the Air Force Special Weapons Center, Maj. Gen. White. He was very kind, and I think he was touched that I took off my shoes for the pictures so that I wouldn't be taller than him. He invited me to be his special guest at the KAFB dining-in the following week, and arranged for his tallest lieutenant to be my escort. During the toasting (to the President and the Air Force Chief of Staff), the presiding officer also proposed a toast to me, which was pretty heady stuff until he added, 'after all, she may be the mother *of the chief of staff some day.' It didn't turn out that way.*

Although female cadets weren't eligible to attend the first national Flying Encampment in 1965, the next year we were. Since that was the last year I could stay a cadet, I was thrilled to be selected. It's worth noting that female cadets were accepted into Flying Encampment a full 10 years before women were accepted into the Air Force Academy. That summer Col. Richard Dillon, the Wing CO, flew his Apache out to the Summer Encampment at Dyess AFB in Abilene to attend the Pass-in Review, then flew me on to Lawton to start Flying Encampment the same day.

CAP was responsible for my career in more ways than one. My pilot's license helped me qualify high enough on the list to get hired as an FAA air traffic controller, and made a difference in understanding navigation and cockpit and radio procedures. More than that, my time in CAP gave me the confidence to handle the culture and succeed in the training. There were only a few women in Albuquerque Air Route Traffic Control Center when I got there (maybe 3 out of 300), but I knew how to handle myself in a male environment. Besides, a couple of former cadets were there and welcomed me—Jon Daffer and Richard Chavez.

Later, when I transferred to the FAA Academy in Oklahoma City as an instructor, I attended the Management Training School in Lawton, which was in the same building that had been the boys' barracks at the Flying Encampment. It was familiar because I conducted inspections there as the encampment Cadet Deputy CO.

When I was a cadet, I wasn't eligible to attend the special activity FAA Orientation Course at the FAA Academy (as my squadron mate Jon Daffer did), because it wasn't open to female cadets. By the time I arrived there as an air traffic controller (helped by my overall cadet experience), I saw female as well as male cadets come through in their CAP uniforms, and cheered for the progress. I completed my career there many years later as acting manager of the school.

97 Senator Barry Goldwater presents the Falcon Award Certificate to Gwen Sawyer in 1966. On left is Wing CO Richard Dillon.

Beverly Vito first joined CAP in 1964 as a cadet and explains, "*The adventure kept me in. My family moved a lot and I was always the* *newcomer in school, having a hard time fitting in. In CAP, I got to do things the other kids in school didn't, such as getting a ride in a jet and doing a barrel role by myself* (as Group Honor Cadet of the Year). *I remember a mission in 1967 when Earl Livingston was the mission PAO. He asked me to come out and be his assistant. Then he had to go fly a mission and he turned the PAO role over to me. When I got back to school the next day, some teachers told me they heard me on the radio, and looked at me with new respect."*

98 C/Col. Beverly Vito

The first year IACE was opened to female cadets, 1968, Beverly was selected as the Southwest Region participant, and went to Great

Britain. In 1969 she won a solo flight scholarship, and she completed her private pilot certification at the 1970 Flight Encampment. She earned her Spaatz Award (#164) in 1971, only the second cadet in NM Wing to reach that high level. Beverly was active in Cadet Advisory Council, and represented Southwest Region on the National CAC in 1972.

When asked what difference the cadet program made in her life, Beverly replied, "*It gave me self confidence to meet the challenges and different responsibilities. I felt 'If I can do this, what else can I do?' I was confident going into adult jobs, because I knew I could do them. You can achieve anything you want, but you must analyze, organize and plan. I also had the satisfaction of doing something for my country and community.*"

Beverly traveled the world as an Air Force wife after her cadet years, and helped start the squadron at Ramstein AFB in Germany when her family was stationed there. When she returned to Albuquerque, she re-entered CAP and began another distinguished record of service and achievement. She re-entered CAP as the Wing Senior Programs Officer in1986 before moving to Falcon Squadron in 1989 as the Deputy for Cadets. As the Squadron Commander, she increased cadet enrollment and was the Wing Senior Member of the year in 1991.

In 1992 and 1993, Beverly was the commander of the NM Wing Summer Encampments. She attended Staff College in 1989 and liked the training so well she still goes every year "*as a treat for myself*", although she now is the Commandant of Students. In 2005, Beverly helped start the Heights Spirit Squadron, and is the Squadron Commander—for the second time. She was honored in 2008 for her Decade of Dedication to NM Wing. Like many of the women recognized on these pages, Beverly enjoyed CAP as a family activity, first with her sister when they were both cadets, and with her cadet daughters after she was a senior member.

Beverly says that as a senior member, "*I not only have the satisfaction of doing something for country and community, but giving back by working with cadets, helping to prepare young people for a future that's not just video games, drugs, etc.*"

99 2LT Peggy Noltensmeyer (at controls of a T-34) and WO Austin Glover

The 1966 Convention issue of Southwest Times (a monthly publication of SWR), states *Mrs. Peggy L. Noltensmeyer of Cedar Crest, NM, recently became the first woman pilot in CAP in New Mexico to fly solo in the T-34 aircraft. She was checked out by*

Warrant Officer Austin Glover, CAP, Commanding Officer of the Albuquerque Senior Squadron 2. Mrs. Noltensmeyer is a 2nd Lieut. in CAP and the wife of D.E. Noltensmeyer. She has been flying since 1952 and holds a private pilot's license. She has been a member of CAP for two years, is a native of Albuquerque and graduated from Albuquerque High School. In 1943, she joined the WASP (Womens Auxiliary Service Pilots). As a member of WASP she completed her ground school, and had just begun her flight training when the WASP program was disbanded. Mrs. Noltensmeyer is the mother of four boys, one of whom is at the Air Force Academy in Colorado Springs.

A story in the CAP News in September 1983 highlighted four female members of New Mexico Wing who were featured in the 'Woman in Aviation' display at the Albuquerque International Airport. They were Capt. Margaret Kilgore, then Gallup Squadron Commander and Mission Pilot, Capt. Allene Lindstrom, a Los Alamos Mission Pilot and Mission Coordinator, 1stLt. Dawn Marino, a Mission Pilot also of the Los Alamos Squadron, 1stLt. JanDee Haag, a Mission Coordinator of Albuquerque, and Beverly Vito (not pictured). Ms. Vito was the second cadet in NM Wing to earn the coveted Spaatz award and became a Private Pilot at the age of 17.

Allene Lindstrom of Los Alamos was a CAP member for over 30 years before retiring from the organization. A CFI, she has held most of the positions at the squadron level and several at wing.

She recalls, *"My first position was Finance Officer when Tom Adams was squadron commander. However, Emergency Services was my primary focus over the years. I performed many roles that included Mission Pilot, Observer, and Mission Coordinator (MC). My efforts were often divided between flying the missions and the care and feeding of the airplanes. I 'mother henned' the airplanes!"*

100 Senior Members Capt Margaret Kilgore, Capt Allene Lindstrom, 1st lt. Dawn Moreno, and 1 Lt. JanDee Haag featured in the Cavalcade of Wings display at the Albuquerque International Airport

Allene was a Mission Check Pilot, Cadet Orientation pilot and the Standards and Evaluation Officer. She was eventually elevated to Chief Check Pilot—one of three in the Wing (and of course, the only female).

The Unit Commander usually made the recommendations for check pilots. Unit Instructors were nominated—they were first instructor pilots with the status of Mission/Observer Pilots. As the need justified, they were added to the list of Mission Check Pilots, Cadet Orientation pilots, and Squadron Check Pilots. Chief Check Pilots were designated by Wing.

Allene remembers that, *"For many years, Wing had only one Chief Check Pilot. If memory serves me correctly, under Jim Miller they decided to have three Chief Check pilots and put them in districts [Groups]. My district was Northern New Mexico."*

Check Pilots are required to attend a periodic National Check Pilot Conference presented locally. Allene's knowledge was considerable and she often called upon to provide it extemporaneously. *"At one of these, Jim asked me to give a 'lecture,'* Allene said, *"Being totally unprepared, I gulped and did some words about Cockpit Resource Management. Somehow, the attendees did not boo me out*"

"All Check pilots were required to fly with the Chief check pilot annually. This included giving checkouts in new aircraft. My favorite was the Cessna 206 that came from the Texas Wing—less all the paper work! So, we had to acquire a new Weight and Balance that was, at first, produced with an error as it was very late at night when the mechanic finished—bless his heart. That plane could be relied upon to offer an emergency at least once in the flight—or so it seemed. All pilots I flew with passed but I have flown with Wing Commanders who did not pass. Proficiency was the key!"

"On the squadron side," she relates, *"I also was Operations Officer, which basically said I had free rein and was supposed to know everything!"* At a Commanders call when she substituted for Clark Swannack on one occasion, Lloyd Sallee introduced her by saying: *"And this is Allene Lindstrom from Los Alamos; she runs the Squadron. She knows it and I know it, but no one else knows it!"* It remains one of her favorite compliments.

Pat Norvell was so afraid of flying that she never got into an airplane until 1979, when a family emergency required her to get to the east coast immediately. After that, her husband Jim told her about his orientation rides as a CAP cadet, and she joined CAP to help overcome her fear by flying in a small plane. Later, as the Wing Public Affairs Officer, she rode all over the state to perform her duties. Although she got used to flying, she was still not entirely comfortable in flight, and says, "*I would sit a little nervously in the back, holding on to my Bible, until one frequent pilot asked me not to bring it anymore, since it gave a false impression of his piloting skills.*"

101 Mary Livingston, Jan Dee Haag, Jane Korzan, Pat Norvell, all female staff at SAREVAL in 1983. Staff received an outstanding evaluation

Pat got into the Public Affairs (PA) function quite serendipitously. During a mission back in 1980, Pat and Jim went over to the old trailer at Alameda Airport that functioned as the Mobile Operations Center to unlock it for Bob Haulenbeek. Bob, who was the Mission Commander, was setting up for a search for a plane with some Mormon missionaries that was reported overdue. Bob said he need a PAO and asked Pat if should would perform the role.

Pat indicated that she had no experience with the function—that she was an administrator. Bob said he would coach her through the process and gave her first lesson as they continued setting up for the mission.

Pat recalls, "I *had no idea what I was getting into but I got a lot of good training out of that mission. On the next mission, for a helicopter, I accidentally discovered how the Air Force worked the*

PA function. I told a news reporter some information about the progress of the search. Shortly afterwards, I got a call from the Air Force PA admonishing me and letting me know that 'nobody releases information on an AF mission except the AF!' Of course, a part of the problem was that news reporters tend to add words to what the PA says."

After her rough start of learning PAO on-the-job, Pat decided that other PAOs in the wing should benefit from that experience. She enlisted senior members Ruth Roberts (who later followed Pat as the Wing PAO) and Madge Harrah (a professional author of children's books and biographies) to help her develop and conduct a training course for mission PAOs. They included role-play, with people carrying big TV cameras getting in the students' faces for stories. They also invited local TV stations to the training so the media could learn what the PAOs could provide to them.
As a result of the training course, Pat was asked by the State of NM to provide PA training to state ground teams working on missions.

Pat also relates she learned the value of training for CAP skills from former Gallup Squadron CO Margaret Kilgore, who was really big on training. Pat recalls, "*Margaret trained me that no one gets into the mission command center trailer without showing ID. Later, a hatless man wearing a trench coat wanted in, but I told him I'd have to see his ID first. He said that didn't apply to him, but I enforced the rule and wouldn't let him in. Turns out that under his trench coat, he was wearing his USAF colonel's uniform, but I couldn't see it. He was mad, of course, but later he told me I had done the right thing.*"

As the current Wing Administrative Officer, Pat conducts training for other administrative personnel, including a class in August, 2009. She also has volunteered to mentor new administrative staff.

When asked why she spent so much time and effort on CAP, Pat replied, "*CAP gave me so much I can never give it all back. It gave me a home where I could succeed on my own. Before the opportunities CAP gave me, I was totally dependent, and never made decisions on my own. CAP gave me the confidence to be my own person. I even went back to school.*"

In her years in the Wing, Pat has been PAO of the Year (1994) and Senior Member of the Year (1998). With her husband Jim, she was recognized as Family of the Year (1995) and for their Decade of Dedication (1998).

Wing Administrator LtCol **Corliss Grubert** is another person who has been a key member of the staff for more than 30 years. Her memory is replete with the names of people, places, events, and dates. She started attending CAP meetings (ABQ Squadron II) in 1974 with her husband Chuck, who would become an avid pilot. When the squadron needed someone to run the alerting roster, Corliss volunteered, and she has been a mainstay for CAP in New Mexico ever since. Her two focus areas have been administration and emergency services, and a combination of both. "*I really liked running missions, including the briefings/debriefings and getting the financial documents done right. I was helping people and making a difference.*" Corliss was a fully qualified Mission Observer, Mission Information Officer, Mission Operations Officer AND a Mission Coordinator with numerous missions to her credit.

In 1978, Wing Commander Earl Livingston wanted CAP to have someone in the wing office during the day, and hired Corliss to perform administrative duties for the wing. One of those duties included keeping an eye on the wing aircraft tied down on the flight line, right outside the office. She remembers, "*One time in 1980 there were high wind warnings on the base. When I checked on the airplanes, the Super Cub was flying—with no pilot. The wind was coming from exactly the right angle and was strong enough to keep the airplane in the air, even though chained to the ground. My husband reassured me it was okay since the tie-downs were secure. Then I was worried what would happen when the wind stopped, but it made a gentle touchdown on its own.*"

Another activity Corliss enjoyed was setting up wing conferences, "*but for the past ten years I gave that up, because I saw a need to train others and give them a chance to develop.*"

Corliss and Chuck have a CAP family, including children who were cadets, and they were recognized in 1987 as the Wing Family of the Year. Corliss was the Wing Senior Member of the Year in 1993, and she and Chuck were honored in 1995 for their Decade of Dedication.

Corliss recalls attending Pacific Region Staff College in 1980 "*to see how different regions did things. One CO from CA Wing wouldn't accept a new cadet unless at least one parent joined and took on at least one task, even if it was something as simple as aluminum can recycling. I've tried to pass that concept of parental involvement on to all the new Squadron CO's, because if a parent is involved, the cadet will be more likely to progress in the program; the kids will be happier and the squadron more productive.*"

Although Corliss retired as a state employee in 2005, she is still Wing Administrative Officer for corporate CAP, still serving CAP's vital missions. Some of her favorite memories are "*seeing young people develop, become more disciplined, learning teamwork, working toward a common goal.*"

Judy Licht has been a member of Las Cruces Composite Squadron since 1981. She was the commander of the Las Cruces Squadron in 1997-1998, and is now the Deputy CO.
Judy got involved in CAP as many do, because of family. Her son loved airplanes, so a friend recommended CAP to Judy as an organization for young people to get involved in aviation. Judy and her son both joined, and they "*had a great time together.*"

Judy is a pilot, and she was glad to find a way to continue flying. She remembers, "*I was flying on a mission near Silver City, and spotted a wrecked aircraft in a ravine close to an airstrip. After landing at the airstrip, we walked down to the crash and found a survivor. Knowing we were able to help save a life is one of my best memories in CAP.*"

When asked what kept her involved in CAP even after her son grew up, Judy replies, "*meeting good people, working on flying skills, being a mission pilot, working on team search and rescue and with cadets, and making a difference.*"

Although **Roberta Himebrook**'s husband is a long-time member of CAP, she didn't become a member until her son Les, who was a cadet in the Alamogordo Squadron, told her, "*Mom, we need you. You have to do some things in the squadron.*" She became the Squadron Aerospace Science Officer, and says, "*It was a wonderful family activity.*" At the time, Roberta was on the faculty of New Mexico State University-Alamogordo as a math professor. With her masters' degrees in mathematics and educational counseling and her teaching experience, she was able to enrich the cadets' aerospace learning in ways that made it seem like fun, not studying. She recalls, "*We drove the cadets to Colorado to visit NORAD and see the model rocketry museum in Colorado Springs. On the drive, we did educational activities like asking questions on aerospace topics on the radio. The cadets thought they were practicing radio skills, but they were really learning about the topics.*"

Roberta also learned to be a mission coordinator, and she remembers particularly one REDCAP mission in Roswell, where most of the mission base staff was cadets—doing briefings, debriefings, radio operators, etc. Roberta herself doesn't fly for physiological reasons: "*I go up, I throw up.*"

When Col. Haulenbeek recruited her to be the NM Wing Director of Cadet Programs, she focused on applying creativity to the wing cadet programs. She was not as interested in the military aspects of the organization (drill, rank, uniforms, etc.) as in the education and development of young people, the leadership and scientific learning.

In fact, she wasn't very conscious of rank at all. As an Air Force officer's wife, she was used to driving onto the base and being saluted by the guards because of the officer's sticker on the car. When she became a CAP officer and drove onto the base, she recalls, "*My son Les kept reminding me, 'Mom, you've got to salute back.*'"

Roberta combined Cadet Advisory Council meetings with leadership events. She said she arranged guest speakers from different disciplines because "*I wanted the cadets exposed to leadership in many fields, not just the military.*"

She also wrote and sent to CAP HQ a program on how to do training for senior member leaders of cadet programs.
Roberta remembers during that time, "*We didn't have enough cadets for drill team competitions, so we had Color Guard competitions. We wrote up rules for the competitions and forwarded them to Region. Our rules were adopted by the region and included as part of the national Color Guard rules.*"

When Roberta became the head of the Math and Science Department at NMSU-Alamogordo, she was so busy she stepped down from the Cadet Programs Director position. Later, when Ric was the Wing Emergency Services Director, she spent more time working on missions, although they had worked on missions as a family earlier and was already a mission coordinator (Old term for incident commander)

Then, when Ric became the Deputy for Cadets, she helped him. Later, when their son Les was stationed at KAFB as an Air Force officer, he served as NM Wing Deputy for Cadets, making them the only family where every member held that position.

After Ric became the wing Vice Commander, and they traveled to Albuquerque frequently, the Wing Commander, COL. Norvell, needed someone to step in at the last minute as the Wing Personnel Officer to help get ready for an evaluation. Roberta stepped in, they passed the evaluation just fine, and she stayed Personnel Officer for seven or eight years. After leaving the position, she explains, "*Ric had a lot of time to help me when I was Personnel Officer, so when he became the Wing Commander, I told everyone I stepped down because my assistant (Ric) had abandoned me.*"

Roberta also served at the Encampment Deputy Commander one year when Ruth Roberts was the Encampment Commander.

Her current position is Advisor to the Wing Commander, and Ric emphasizes, "*She's a very* <u>*active*</u> *advisor.*"

Roberta joined CAP because her son asked her. Her reasons for staying are: "*Family, enjoyment, friendships, helping people, a mission to help beyond, aerospace education, cadets, emergency missions, and lots of personal fun.*"

Sharon Lane joined CAP in 1993, even though she says, "*I had no intention of being anything more than a 'mom' in my son's Farmington Composite Squadron's Cadet Program. He had asked me to volunteer to be the Deputy Commander of Cadets because the man who had been the DCC was stepping down and, in my son's opinion, 'there was no one else to take it.' And so it began.*"

She attended her first New Mexico Wing Conference which was held in Taos, NM in the spring of 1994. During that conference, one of the NM Wing members had their Lt Col rank pinned on and another member received their Gill Robb Wilson Award. She remembered saying to herself, *I want to have those things happen to me some day.* She added, "*I had no idea of what lofty goals I set for myself that day and no idea there was to be a love affair that would last the rest of my life. That love affair was Civil Air Patrol.*"

102 Lt Col Beverly (Pepe) Vito (right) listens to Lt Col Sharon Lane describe a prairie dog she saw at the 2009 SWR Staff College Picnic. (Photo by Maj Russell Davis, OK Wing)

As her exposure to wing activities increased, Sharon recognized areas where she wanted to participate beyond the squadron level. She jumped into Emergency Services and became a mission qualified Public Affairs Officer. Sharon recalls, "As *fate would have it, New Mexico Wing was part of the largest search ever tasked to the wing. Because the Mission Coordinator was from Farmington and because the MC knew I was qualified for the position, I participated as part of the Mission Base personnel during that high-profile search. The intensity of the mission again opened doors in my mind about where I wanted to go in CAP."*

In 1995, Sharon attended the SWR Staff College held at Kirtland AFB in Albuquerque and she said, "*I fell in love with the college and its objective to train good CAP leaders."* She was invited back the following year to be a Seminar Advisor then was invited back every year after that as a staffer at the college. In 2007 and 2008, she served as the Director of the college and for her dedication to the college she was awarded the Meritorious Service Award.

Her loyalties to her beloved Farmington Composite Squadron became evident when she saw a need for a more modern meeting and hangar facility. Sharon went to work setting in motion funding for a stand-alone Civil Air Patrol facility at the Four Corners Regional Airport in Farmington. She lobbied and won approval of then Representative Nick Tinnen, who incidentally was a childhood friend, and CAP was awarded the initial request of funding. Due to unforeseen glitches, the squadron needed to obtain more funding to finish the project. Sharon again called upon the local Senator William Sharer to petition the NM Legislature for the funds. They were granted and the state-of-the-art facility was finished. By the time the facility was completed, she and her husband Harry had moved from Farmington and she never got to enjoy the new facility as a squadron member.

Sharon was willing to do what was asked of her at the squadron level, the wing level and at the Region level. She chaired and did the logistics for three Wing Conferences and, as the NM Wing Cadet Programs Director, organized and implemented two NM Wing Cadet Conferences. At the squadron level she served in the role of Squadron Commander and at the Wing level she served as the NM Wing Public Affairs Officer, NM Wing Inspector General, NM Wing Legislative Liaison and NM Wing Vice-Commander. Because of her dedicated contributions to the Wing, Sharon was recognized as Wing PAO of the year in 1998, and with her daughter Griffyn was named as Family of the Year in 2000. Sharon was honored as the Wing Senior Member of the Year in 2002-2003 and was recognized for her Decade of Dedication in 2007. She became the SWR Inspector General in 2008.

In spite of these rewards, what meant the most to her was meeting the goals she set for herself. As she recalls, "*While living by my personal philosophy of 'Do not pursue glory, pursue excellence – never grow weary of* 'Well Done'*, in 1999 I was presented my Gill*

Robb Wilson award and in 2003 I was pinned on as a Lt Col. I had met the goals I set for myself so many years ago and I felt like every minute of the 'blood, sweat and tears' to achieve those goals was worth it!"

Shirley Kay joined CAP in 1998, a few months after the death of her husband, who was very involved with the Alamogordo Squadron. She was looking for something to focus on, and chose CAP because, "*the idea of service and working with cadets was attractive to me."*

Shirley recalled a mission in May 2001 searching for a missing glider in the mountains east of Alamogordo. *"That's when I got into Emergency Services. I saw the teamwork that happened. I worked as a radio operator for 2 days, then as the logistics person to support the mission."* Since then she has been very involved in Emergency Services, and is a Level 2 Incident Commander.

Shirley served as Squadron Commander from 2002 to 2009, and was Wing Senior Member of the Year in 2007. She currently serves as the Wing Director of Logistics and Wing Operations Assistant for the Web Mission Information Reporting System (mission tracking).

Shirley cites several things when asked why she has worked so hard in CAP. "*The skills I have gained from CAP have helped me in my document control position at White Sands Missile Range, and the job has helped me in CAP. In working with cadets and seniors, I've had a chance to mentor and be mentored, and been able to see the results of my efforts. I view CAP as 'taking care of extended family', and I've been lucky to increase that extended family by making friends not just in the wing, but also in the region and even at national conferences."*

Donna Bracken is the Wing Supply Officer and Summer Encampment Director. She joined CAP in 2003 after seeing a need for help in the squadron her sons had joined as cadets. Donna recalls, "*There were only a couple of adult senior members working* *with the cadets. I knew one of them because we were both home-schooling moms, so I asked her if she needed help. She told me she'd love it, but I've have to join. So I joined CAP to help with paperwork. I was the Admin. Officer for four months, and then the commander had to leave because of a schedule conflict, so I became the Squadron Commander. That was only four months before a Subordinate Unit Inspection. We all worked very hard to get ready for it, and received an Outstanding rating.*"

"*After three years as Sqdn CO, I received some excellent advice from a young senior member, Lt. Joe Friel, that I should move on to avoid burning out. I knew he was right, so I went back to administrative and training positions.*" One of those duties was writing grant applications to the Boeing Aircraft Company for funds to support projects such as the Teacher Workshops and the 'Fly a Teacher' program. NM Wing paid for the first day of a grant-writers' course, and Donna was so impressed she paid for the second day, the practice workshop, on her own. She wrote the grants for the first three years, and succeeded in getting funds every time.

Donna participates in Emergency Services on the ground, since she claims she's "*not a flyer in a little plane.*" Her skills and training as a nurse are particularly affective in Critical Incident Stress Management.

In Donna's role as Summer Encampment Director, she was part of the team that established a relationship with the Army National Guard, which works very well for the Wing as a place to conduct encampments. Donna explains, "*The Guard housing facilities are open bay, which means they only have to charge us four dollars a night per person instead of the fifty dollars per night at KAFB. That way more cadets can afford to attend. Besides, the people at the Guard have been just wonderful to us.*"

Donna took over the Supply Officer position in the fall of 2008, when the Wing was in a Level 1 freeze because of incomplete records, with one month to prepare for an inspection to clear the freeze. Fortunately, she claims, "*I love a challenge. It took about nine hours a day for three weeks, with paper spread all over. I warned everyone, 'Nobody sneeze, and nobody turn on a fan.' With help from friends to locate missing items, we passed the inspection with no write-ups and four 'Commendable's.*"

Donna also has a "*wonderful, supportive husband. I've taken a cadet Color Guard team to regional competition for many years. My husband does a thorough check on the CAP van to make sure everything is in good working order before I drive the cadets. He also knows about computers, and helps me take care of the ones in Supply.*"

Other CAPers have described Donna as energetic, upbeat, and a good example of someone living well with an inner, positive drive.

Why does she do all this work? "*I love kids. I taught middle school in Hawaii before we transferred to Albuquerque. I want kids to do their best to succeed, to be able to do well in the competitions in life (football team, speech competition, job applications). I try to help them get scholarships; give them every chance to be successful to the highest degree they can. I also love my country and love teaching patriotism.*"

Readers can see some of the recurring themes for these women: family, friendships, service to country and community, helping others, gratitude for what they received, and fun!

There are many more women who have made an impact on New Mexico Wing, but whose stories were not available. Some of those include the following brief lines.

Pat Chochrell Balok, a cadet in the late 1950s through early 1960s. Later, as a senior member, Pat was instrumental in the SEP in Gallup, before retiring to Roswell.

Debbie Martin, former Squadron CO of the Sierra Middle School Squadron in Las Cruces, as well as Incident Commander and volunteer staff for interacting with National Guard.

Pamela Sever, Spaatz Award #1274, who implemented the SEP program in Monroe Middle School to high success. After transferring out of state, Pam returns every year as Commander of the PJOC course, in order to ensure it remains in New Mexico.

Ruth Roberts, long-time (now retired) member in Farmington, who not only worked many missions as Mission Coordinator, but was Squadron CO, Wing PAO, Senior Member of the Year in 1988, Family of the Year in 1990, and (with her husband) honored for Decade of Dedication in 1996.

103 Albuquerque Sdqn 1 building KAFB, circa mid-1950's. (Front L to R) LtCol Bayne Spring, Wing Dir of Admin, (unk), Col J. Gibbs Spring, Wing CO, Maj Juanda Sawyer, Wing Coord for Women, (unk), Capt. Frank McLaughlin, Sqdn I CO, (un), Lt. Roma Coats, Sqdn 1 Adjutant. (Back center (under sign): Capt. Ira Kessler, Sqdn 1 Commandant of Cadets. Behind McLaughlin is Erwin (Bud) Bartow, beloved of cadets for all the bus trips he drove, and later Sqdn CO.

In-Touch Across the Wing

Newsletters—In the early days, keeping the Wing membership informed about newsworthy events typically took the form of mimeographed copies of a few pages being mailed or handed out at squadron meetings on a monthly basis.

The Enchanted Wing News was a Quarterly Wing Newsletter that began with the Spring 1982 issue. It was a very professional looking with high quality photos and bound. Over the years, the level of effort was related often to the available people and the funding.

The 1992 Summer Edition was very well done—a 26-page bound publication with good quality photos and advertising. It was the effort of Maj Ruth Roberts, the Public Affairs Officer.

By the turn of the millennium, the Enchanted Wing newsletter had given way to the Cactus Courier which was produced by Lt Col Sharon Lane and then 1Lt Gretta Christensen.

Many squadrons periodically published their own newsletters. These efforts are important for several reasons. First, they make each member of the squadron aware of what is going on. This assures that members who may not be inclined to make every meeting are still 'in the loop'. It is also very important that parents of cadets receive copies so that they can see promotions and activities. There are few events in life that will perk-up a parent than seeing the name of their son or daughter in print! Finally, some of the newsletters are written and produced by the cadets themselves, giving them an opportunity to develop many new skills.

In 1988, 44 stories were sent to the CAP News of which 59% were printed.

Web Sites—With the advent of the Internet, NM Wing entered Cyberspace. Most written communications were put onto the web pages of the NM Wings site and this reduced the paperwork burden and the cost of mailing each issue. In 1998, The NM Wing website was awarded the 'Digital Government Award of Excellence' for its efforts.

The problem with moving the communications to the web was that apparently few bothered to keep hardcopy and when files were deleted, so was the history. Another problem is that often the person who originates the site leaves and no one is available to maintain it. Old information is sometimes more deadly than no information.

In 2007, Eagle Cadet Squadron not only got its own website but also appointed its first Information Technology (IT) Officer—Philip R. Keay. In 2009, Eagle had its own My Space account (myspace.com/eagle012) which is administered by C/Lt Col. Dustin T. Wittman.

Yearbooks—Several yearbooks were periodically created within the wing. One in particular, the 1969-1970 edition, was put together under the direction of Cadet Beverly (Pepe) Vito. A few copies have survived the test of time and several excerpts are included in this book. Perhaps it would be well for the cadets to consider taking on the challenge of producing at least a biennial yearbook to capture the events that made their time in CAP a memorable experience.

Wing Staff Meetings go Virtual — In July 2008, wing commander Col Richard F. Himebrook announced that the September Wing Commanders' Staff Meeting would held by conference call, in a move to save costs within the wing. *"It doesn't make any sense for someone to drive four hours from Farmington, and four hours back. That's a full day of driving just for one meeting,"* Col Himebrook said.

As web video conferencing becomes more prolific, it is the next step to providing virtual meetings to improve the sharing of information while reducing costs.

Snapshot in Time

Then there was the move to the present headquarters building back in 1996. The Wing Commander (Dennis Manzanares) got a call that Wing HQ had to be moved within a few weeks. Apparently, the building they were in was to be demolished to remove asbestos. At first, more than a few of the HQ people were a bit skeptical that a quick move like that could be expected or completed. Apparently, the base had a contractor who would do the job for a good price if CAP could be out of the building by the short deadline.

Claude Luisada (Chief of Staff) volunteered to make it happen. The 'new' building was cleaned; its many broken windows repaired, and new carpet was put down. Luisada was on site almost continually for the duration and the move came off on schedule.

The old building… languished for almost a year before it was finally removed.

NM Wing Census Over the Years							
Year	**Units**	**Seniors**	**Cadets**	**Pilots**	**Corp A/C**	**Member A/C**	**Total**
1966		426	363	155		45	
1967		376	313			35	
1968		320	289	150		32	
1969		*280*	319	190			
1982	21	514	456		(9)		970
1990	15						
2002					(6) C172 (5) C182 (2) U206 (1) T-34		
2009	15	492	409	57	(13)		901

CAP National in 2008 had 1700 units with 53,000 members and 535 Aircraft.

104 Certificate of Appreciation Spring 1982 (L to R) Chief Jim Knowles (senior enlisted advisor Nation HQ), Chief John Toby, T/Sgt Martin Aloarey, LtCol Thomas Doughty, Col Lloyd Sallee

105 NM Wing hosted the National Inspector General College in 1998 at Kirtland AFB.

106 NM CAP signing Memo of Understanding with State of New Mexico Jun 2009. Sitting (l to r) Mr. George Jeantete (Director NM Dept of Military Affairs) and Col Richard Himebrook, NM Wing Commander. Back row (l-r) BGen Jack Fox, Capt John Gravel NMCAP Operations Officer, Col Joy Nelson NM Wing Vice Commander.

John H Gravel

107 T-34 N422NM over Rio Rancho (what there was of it) circa late 1960s. The old Alameda Airport (also called 7-Bar) is in the 10:30 position 3/8" from the vertical stabilizer.

108 Gil Day (former AZ Wing CO), Col. Dorothy Warren (SW Region vice), Joe Gold NM Wing CO, Don Jakusz NM former Wing Commander, unnamed (circa 1993)

9. Aerospace Education Program

One of the early advocates of aerospace education in the New Mexico Wing was LtCol Eldred R. Harrington who served as the Deputy for Aerospace Education in the 1950s and 60s. The following is an excerpt from the Aerospace Training Manual for NM Wing (1966).

> Every organization is likely to have some character who is interesting because of unusual eccentricity. Harrington was a candidate for this doubtful distinction in the New Mexico Wing when he joined in 1952. On two separate occasions he and Captain Joe Bridges conducted workshops for aerospace education in Albuquerque in 1952 and 1953.
>
> Harrington had started formal courses in aviation as early as 1935 when he was the Director of Secondary Education for the Albuquerque schools.. Some years before he was a member of the CAP, he was called to Washington to meet with CAP and U.S. Air Force educators on planning conferences. In 1957 he was engaged by the Special Weapons Command of the air force to write an educational brochure for circulation throughout the command. This brochure went through several editions with an emphasis on interesting students in science and mathematics and on aerospace topics. With Lieutenant Colonel Harry Crosby he wrote manuals for senior aerospace training in CAP and one on search and rescue. Crosby and other members of the staff of the New Mexico Wing furnished most of the technical data while it had to pass Harrington for simplicity.

Harrington described himself as being something of a "nut" on attending colleges and universities—23 in all. From these institutions, he acquired a total of 675 semester hours of credit, more than 350 hours since he received a Ph.D. degree in physical chemistry in 1940. He has never taken time off to go to school—always the schooling has been done while he was holding down a full time job. In the early days it was often at night as when he was employed as a journeyman machinist. His major educational fields included chemistry, civil engineering, and geology—though he has also satisfied the requirements for degrees in mathematics and physics. He has seven earned degrees and could have received four others if he paid the diploma fees. He was chosen as the Engineer of the Year for New Mexico in 1963. He has taught at each one of the six state colleges and universities in New Mexico and has been a faculty member at Howard Payne College in Texas. He authored four text books and 280 magazine articles.

The legacy that Harrington and Crosby left, because of their efforts to provide a Senior Training Program, were significant. One only has to leaf through the few remaining examples of the manuals that were produced by these and others during the 1950s and 60s to get some sense of the effort that was made to disseminate information about a wide range of topics from aerospace education to communications and search and rescue operations.

In the 1980s, Ernie Inmon pursued a vigorous campaign to open up the public schools around the state to the CAP aerospace education program. He met with only limited success however. While aerospace topics may be exciting and motivating, the level of knowledge of the classroom teacher, and their ability to weave the topics into the curriculum, is often a limiting factor. Suki Harada took over from Inmon in 1989.

In the early 1990s, Major Dave Adams, then a recent AF retiree joined Squadron II and accepted the Wing Staff position of Aerospace Education Officer under Wing Commander Col. Jakusz. Adams sought out opportunities for the Aerospace Youth programs and recommended that the CAP Aerospace Education (AE) and the FAA program for “Aerospace Opportunities” be integrated (jointly presented). Again new ground was going to be the base for a program.

The Native American school system in Western New Mexico was the primary area addressed and, with the concurrence of Region and National Aerospace offices, NM Wing took the program to the Pueblos. This joining of resources proved highly successful and resulted in National HQ Commendations to the Wing and to Dave Adams.

In 2004, Dan Morgan became Director of Aerospace Education, Dan and his predecessors set some high standards. Dan lived in Santa Fe and had a job in Nevada working on the Globalhawk (unmanned surveillance aircraft). He would fly his C182 back to New Mexico on the weekends to keep his commitments for Aerospace Education. He received an Outstanding (now called Highly Successful) rating in his CI inspection in 2005.

Unfortunately, in 2006 he moved to Washington State to take a job for the Boeing Aircraft Company. LTC Roland Dewing, who was the wing Internal Aerospace Officer, then became the Director. With the help of his staff, Internal AEO 1Lt Judy Candelaria, and External AEO Maj Ted Spitzmiller, they have worked hard to meet the standards set by Dan and his predecessors. They received a Highly Successful rating in the recent CI inspection in May 09.

In 2008 New Mexico wing received the Region Brewer nomination for Cadet and Senior Member.

- *Category 1:* C/Lt Col Dustin Wittman, NM 012
- *Category 2*: Major Joseph R Perea NM 012

At the 2008 Annual Wing Conference Mary Feik was the special guest. She gave a talk about her experiences and met with Cadets.

In 2006 through the efforts of then wing commander Colonel Buethe, and LO Fred Harsany, NM Wing applied for and received a local grant from Boeing Aircraft Company for $7500. With help from Major Donna Bracken, the wing continued receiving the grant; $10,000 in 2007, $7500 in 2008 and $12000 for 2009. Among projects supported are the 'Teacher Workshops' and the 'Fly a Teacher' program where more than 80 teachers have received a session of flight instruction.

The goal of 'Fly a Teacher' is twofold:

- to increase the number of teachers in New Mexico with an understanding of aerospace subjects and
- connecting classrooms from kindergarten to grade twelve to the math and science in the aerospace industry.

This program provides the excitement, knowledge, and the tools teachers need to make that connection. Teachers that attend the program are given a one-hour flight in a CAP aircraft. In addition to our national program syllabus, the teachers are provided up to 4 hours of classroom instruction that includes CAP aerospace programs, jobs and opportunities in Aerospace, Bernoulli's Principle, four forces of flight, aviation navigation, and many hands on activities. They leave with lots of tools that they can use in their classrooms to promote learning math and science with Aerospace, including CAP textbooks 'Aerospace Dimensions' and 'Aerospace the Journey of Flight.' They also receive lesson plans using New Mexico and national standards relating to teaching aerospace subjects.

Teacher Training is conducted in partnership with the Air Force Research Laboratory's La Luz Academy. NM Wing has developed an excellent working relationship with Star Base La Luz Director Ronda Cole. Not only does she and her staff make presentations for our Teacher workshops, but CAP Pilots and instructors make periodic visits to Star Base classes of sixth graders to make presentations about their flight experiences.

10. NM Wing Aircraft

With aviation being the focus of the Civil Air Patrol, airplanes play a prominent role in New Mexico Wing's history. Although the initial intent of CAP's formation was to provide an organized use of civilian aircraft for the war effort, within a short time, the government began to provide surplus aircraft. The majority of these were known as *liaison* types (with L prefix designations), such as the Taylorcraft L-2, the Piper L-4 and the Stinson L-5. These single engine planes were used by the military for "observation" as well as short distance transport of key personal.

Taylorcraft L-2 Grasshopper — This was the first aircraft to be mentioned in a newspaper article (November 1943), when three were allocated to NM Wing. Originally built under the designation YO-57 prior to World War II, for light transport and courier duties, they were redesignated the L-2 1942.

With a crew of two in a tandem cockpit, the L-2 had an empty weight of 680 pounds and a gross weight of 1200 pounds. A Continental O-170 air-cooled engine that developed 65 hp powered it. With a cruise speed of 83 mph, it had a maximum range of only 230 miles and a ceiling of 10,400 feet.

109 Taylorcraft L-2 "Grasshopper"

Aeronca L-3 — Another 2-place observation aircraft, the L-3, was formerly known as the O-58, until its designation was changed. Neither the L-2 nor the L-3 saw service overseas because they had poor flying qualities. They were used stateside as trainers. The L-3 was powered by a 65 hp YO-170 engine that gave it performance comparable to the L-2.

110 Aeronca L-3

Piper L-4 — The L-4 shared the same moniker as the L-2; 'Grasshopper' and was an application of the famous civilian J-3 Cub to the military requirement. Originally designated as the O-59, it was powered by a Continental 65 hp horizontally opposed engine that gave it a cruise speed of 85 mph, a range of 190 miles and a service ceiling of 9,300 feet. Later versions saw an upgrade to 75 and then 100 hp causing slight increases to the L-4's original gross weight of 1,100 pounds.

111 Piper L-4 "Grasshopper"

Stinson L-5 Sentinel — Was an outgrowth of the civilian Model 105 Voyager and was first designated at the O-62. Like most of the other early L series, it was constructed of steel tubing, plywood and doped cotton fabric. Sporting a Lycoming O-435, it weighed in at 1550 pounds empty and 2050 pounds at gross weight. Its 185 hp and 15,800 foot service ceiling made it one of the more useful aircraft for SAR missions in the mountains of New Mexico through the 1950s. These sold 'brand new' for about $3,000 dollars just before the war.

112 Stinson L-5 "Flying Jeep"

Fairchild AT-13? —"*...Fairchild multi-engine aircraft have been acquired by NM Wing*" was the subject of an article in the Albuquerque Journal of 1944. As Fairchild built relatively few multi-engine planes, these would almost have to be the AT-13, an advanced multi-engine trainer of limited production. These were 'big' planes by CAP standards of the day with engines ranging from 310 hp in-line to 600 hp radials and a gross weight around 10,000 pounds. One wonders if the article really meant "multi-engine." More likely, the single engine Fairchild C-61, better known in the civilian world as the F-24 Forwarder, may have been the plane referenced. These were powered by a single 145 hp or 165 hp engine. However, until further information is unearthed, we must assume the report is accurate.

113 "Multi-engine Fairchild aircraft" was allegedly assigned to the New Mexico Wing in 1945. This AT-13 is one of the few that Fairchild ever built. How would you like to take a Form 5 in this?

114 Fairchild C-61 (F24 Forwarder)

Stearman PT-17 Kaydet — Was an outgrowth of the PT-13. Boeing bought the Stearman Company in 1934 and so the designation may be reported as a Boeing PT-17 or Model 75. Four PT-17 Stearman biplanes arrived in New Mexico on May 28, 1945. This two-place bi-plane was the standard primary trainer before and during much of World War II. The PT-17 was of mixed construction with wings of wood covered with fabric and a fuselage of fabric covered welded steel framework. The 220 hp Continental R-670 five-cylinder engine powered most models, and provided a top speed of 124 mph with a 500-mile range and a ceiling of 11,000 feet.

The designation 'PT' defined the 'primary trainer.' The Canadians affixed the moniker 'Kaydet', and the U.S. Army universally adopted the name. It had an empty 1,936 lbs., and a gross weight of 2,717 lbs.

115 Boeing PT-17 Kaydet. Probably the only biplane to actually serve in the New Mexico Wing although several CAP members owned biplanes and had the CAP emblem affixed.

Fairchild PT-19 Cornell — The PT-19 was a bit more challenging aircraft to fly than the PT-17 with a higher stalling speed. With two open cockpits, the PT-19 was powered by the Ranger L-440 six-cylinder, inverted, air-cooled inline engine of 175 horsepower. This was later increased to 200 hp in the PT-19A. It was essentially the same weight, both empty and at gross, as the PT-17.

The final version of the PT-19 had an enclosed-cockpit and was designated the PT-26 equipped with the 200 hp Ranger engine. The New Mexico Wing reportedly used both versions as early as 1946.

116 Fairchild PT-19 Cornell was one of the few open cockpit airplanes assigned to the CAP in New Mexico during and immediately after the war.

Aeronca L-16A — The L-16 figured prominently in many CAP dispatches for the 30 years that followed the end of World War II, when many surplus planes became available to CAP. The L-16 was developed from the Aeronca Model 7 Champion (L-3) of which more than 10,000 were built between 1946 and 1950 during the post-war expansion of General Aviation.

117 Aeronca L-16

The Continental C-85 powered over 500 of these tandem placed aircraft acquired by the military during the Korean War—with most of the survivors finding their way to CAP units across the country by the late 1950s. The L-16A had an empty weight of 870 pounds with a gross of 1300 pounds while the L-19B used the 90 hp Continental O-205 and had a gross of 1450 pounds. NM Wing operated at least five L-16s—a few for over 30 years.

Piper L-21 (PA-18) Super Cub — Was a logical progression of the J-3 and was used by the US Army and Air Force beginning in 1951. It was a tandem two-seater with excellent short field performance. Powered by an O-235 Continental producing either a 90 hp (without flaps) or a 115 hp (equipped with flaps) the latter Super Cub could become airborne in 300 feet at sea level with some flap extended. Although New Mexico's high altitude increased these numbers, the PA-18 was a superb airplane for its time.

118 Preparing the L-21 for flight on a cold day. Note the boy and his dog.

The empty weight was about 900 pounds with a gross weight of 1,500 pounds, while later versions sported the O-290 Lycoming of 135 hp. Yet more power was available with later models using the Lycoming O-320 at 150-160 hp, while the gross weight increased to 1,750 pounds. These high performance models cruised at 120 mph and had a 400 miles range. The service ceiling was an amazing 19,000 feet.

Beechcraft D-18 (C-45) — Used by USAF/CAP Liaison Officers in the 1950s to transport personnel and equipment. Designed in the late 1930 they performed a variety of roles during WWII such as navigation training. They were powered by a variety of engines, the most common being the 450 hp Pratt & Whitney R-985.

With a gross weight of 8700 pounds, they cruised at 160 kts and were noted for converting avgas into lots of noise. They were easy to fly and typically seated 6-8 passengers.

119 Beech D-18 (UC-45) Expeditor

Demise of the Tail Wheel — While taildraggers (conventional gear) have always been considered what "real aviators fly," there are pilots who may not have had the opportunity or the skill set to complete a checkout. As the newer generation of pilots came on the scene who had not cut their teeth on the taildragger, problems result. The PA-18 N267T managed a ground loop in May of 1966 and again in 1970. The L-16s had their share of problems when N75067 failed to "obtain/maintain flying speed" departing from Pena Blanca airport on April 26, 1974 and was destroyed. N6478C ground looped while landing at Coronado on April 15, 1974 and was substantially damaged. Fortunately, none of these accidents resulted in any serious injuries. By the late 1970s, National HQ had decided to remove all tailwheel aircraft from the CAP inventory.

Ryan Navion L-17— Originally designed at the end of World War II by North American Aviation for the civilian market, 83 Navions were ordered by the Army Air Force and designated them L-17A. Ryan Aeronautical Company acquired the design in 1948, and built approximately 1,200 examples over the following three years. The Navion A had a 205 hp engine and the Navion B had 260 hp with either the Lycoming GO-435-C2, or Continental IO-470 engine. The Navion A became the military L-17B.

120 Navion was a popular four place aircraft produced after WWII.

The four-place Navion A had a gross weight of 2750 pounds and a cruise speed of 130 kts, while the Navion B had the 260 hp engine and a gross of 2950 pounds, and 140 kts cruise.

Considered easy to fly, it was the plane the author received his first hour of dual in October of 1963 at the Sandia Base Flying Club. Two Navions were reported flying with the New Mexico wing by Pat Patterson. Little information has surfaced as to the period when the Navion served with the NM Wing.

Beech T-34 Mentor — Perhaps no aircraft operated by the CAP has evoked as much enthusiasm as the T-34. Used by the Air Force as a primary trainer in the 1950's, they started becoming available to CAP by the mid-1960s. The T-34 was developed in 1948 as the Beechcraft Model 45 in a private venture to influence the Air Force to purchase a 'modern' and more economical primary trainer. As an outgrowth of the highly successful Beech Bonanza, the fuselage was completely redesigned as a narrower tandem two-place with a bubble canopy.

121 NM Wing flew several of these T-34As beginning with AF Serial 55-276A, registered as N422NM.

The T-34 was stressed for +10g and -4.5g, while the 185 hp Continental E-185 engine had only a third of the power of the T-6's and was the same as that fitted to contemporary Bonanzas. With an empty weight of 2055 and a gross weight of 2,900 pounds, the T-34 could achieve a maximum speed of 188 mph.

The engine was upgraded to the Continental E-225 and production began in 1953, when Beechcraft began delivering T-34As to the USAF. In 1955, production of the Navy T-34B began which had only differential braking instead of nosewheel steering and more wing dihedral. T-34A production was completed in 1956, with T-34Bs being built until 1957. Total production of the Continental-engine versions in the US and abroad was 1,904 aircraft.

NM Wing flew several of these T-34As beginning with AF Serial 55-276A, registered as N422NM. Accepted by USAF on July 18, 1956, it was stationed at Spence AFB in Moultrie Georgia from Aug 1958 until July 1960. It was delivered to CAP on August 13, 1964 and transferred to NM Wing by CWO Dallis Copeland in February1965.

T-34A (Serial 55-276A) was accepted by USAF in June 1955 at Sawyer AFB MI, and then assigned to Kincheloe AFB 507th Fighter Wing where it was flown by the Kincheloe Aero club until April 1964. It became N421NM and was equipped with a Narco Mk II radio.

Two other T-34As were acquired shortly thereafter being assigned the registrations N423NM and N424NM. Over the course of several decades, most were involved in accidents.

N421NM made a wheels-up landing at the old Alameda Airport on August 12, 1967 following a power failure on take-off and was repaired. It was later lost in 1980 during a SAREX.

N422NM was entering the traffic pattern at the Alameda airport on November 15, 1985 when the pilot experienced severe vibrations. The pilot Reed Mulkey (a 10,000-hour former military pilot) and crewmember Anna Mulkey were seriously injured when the plane stalled about 10 feet above the terrain while attempting and off-airport landing. An investigation revealed an improper overhaul caused one of the propeller–pitch activating pins to fracture.

N424NM was damaged beyond repair in a fatal landing accident at ABQ. Harold Roberts reports that this aircraft was N12269 which became N424NM. The date was June 19, 1965 and the cause was extreme wind shear from a nearby thunderstorm.

After the crash of N421NM on the mountain east of Taos in 1980, the Wing purchased another T-34 N5357G from Mississippi Wing in 1981. This was a T-34B (US Navy model) and was reregistered as N424NM.

In 2004, a series of crashes involving in-flight structural failures grounded the entire US civilian fleet of T-34s. The edict was eventually lifted but the performance envelope of the plane was restricted. The last T-34, the subject of much debate because of airworthiness issues, was eventually sold at a CAP auction to a private owner in 2006. What made this sale particularly painful was that it was the last T-34 in service with the Civil Air Patrol.

One year later that same aircraft had been upgraded with new wing spars and a new carry-thru assembly that removed ALL restrictions from it and returned it to fully acrobatic status.

Helio HT-295 Tri-Gear Courier — The HT-295 was one of the more unique aircraft operated by the New Mexico Wing in the late 1970s. The manufacturer added the 'T' to the H-295 designation when the aircraft was converted to tricycle gear. Built by the Helio Aircraft Company of Pittsburg, Kansas during the 1950s, this aircraft was a replacement for the PA-18 Super Cub—CAP NHQ decreed no more tailwheel aircraft because of accident statistics. Only 19 Tri-Gears were built of this variant, which was known as the L-28A (U-10D when flown by the CIA in Southeast Asia). It was powered by a Lycoming GO-480 of 295 hp (hence the designation 295) and had a 3600-pound gross weight. Using leading edge slats, the plane had exceptional short field performance. Maintenance problems with the geared engine made for a short life in the CAP inventory.

122 Helio Courier L-29 secured at the 'old' tie-down area east of the Operations hanger

Piper PA-28 Cherokee — The Cherokee was a series of all-metal, four-seat, single-engine piston-powered airplanes with low-mounted wings and tricycle landing gear. Sporting a single door on the co-pilot side, PA-28 received its type certificate 1960 and the series remains in production in 2009.

Piper has created variations within the Cherokee family by installing engines ranging from 140 to 300 hp (105-220 kW), providing turbocharging, offering fixed or retractable landing gear, fixed-pitch or constant speed propellers, and stretching the fuselage to accommodate 6 people.

The three-digit number that follows the basic type designation specifies the horsepower. Begining with the PA-28-140 the engine power has steadily increased through -150, -160 (Lycoming O-320) and -180 (Lycoming O-360). The -161 and -181 represented a slight change in wing configuration in the 1970s.

With an Empty weight of 1660 lb and a Gross weight: 2550 lb , the PA-28-180 was the model used by the Wing during the 1970s. Because of the low wing, they were not favored for search operations. PA-28-140 N6122W was substantially damaged during a solo flight on November 27, 1968 when the 16-hour student failed to maintain directional control during the landing.

123 Piper Cherokee 180

Cessna 150 Commuter — The C150 was a two place side-by-side aircraft built in large numbers between 1958 and 1982. Early models had a gross weight of 1500 pounds, which significantly limited the useful load. Later versions were increased to 1600 pounds, but with only 22.5 gallons of fuel, this limited the effective mission duration to 3.0 hours.

With a crew of two, its usefulness was limited. However, NM Wing used its C150s very effectively over the more than 20 years of service. Because of their low power (100 HP), density altitude played a role in defining the operating environment.

124 The Cessna 150 was woefully underpowered for the density altitudes found in New Mexico. When flown conservatively, it had a long and useful life.

Cessna 172 Skyhawk — This plane is a favorite of pilots because of its honest handling qualities and its ability to serve effectively in many roles. In its early configuration in 1956, it was powered by a Continental O-300 with 145 HP. This was upgraded by Cessna through the years to 150 HP (1964) and then 160 HP (1977). The 1980s saw the XP model with 195 HP. Other iterations included the Air Force 205 HP T-41B with a constant speed propeller.

It has the ability to carry four passengers, although on most missions this is reduced to three because of gross weight limitations and density altitude considerations. Most of the C-172s in the New Mexico Wing have been upgraded with the 180 HP Supplemental Type Certificate to increase the GW to 2550 pounds. However, with the larger engine comes a higher fuel consumption and reduced endurance. It has a typical mission time of 3.5 hours with one hour of fuel reserve.

125 The C172 is one of the most versatile airplanes in the CAP fleet.

Cessna 182 Skylane — One of the most useful aircraft is the C182 because of its ability to carry four persons, a large fuel capacity, and its high wing position. With a 230 hp Lycoming, the Skylane may have up to 88 gallons of fuel. This allows for extended endurance (6+ hours), or flexible mission support for high altitude operations with reduced fuel loads.

NM Wing's first Cessna 182 was N3311F which was leased from LTC Larry Harrah to help improve the Wing's high altitude search capability. Although this aircraft was never owned by CAP, it showed the way to the future in NM Wing and National HQ became more interested in using Cessna 182s.

With CAP's expanding role in emergency services more fully recognized at the congressional level, funding for a new generation of Technically Advanced Aircraft (TAA) with enhanced avionics allowed the Wing to take possession of a new C-182T (N780CP) with the Garmin G1000 'Glass Cockpit' in May of 1986. That plane transferred to Mississippi Wing in January of 2007 when New Mexico received N292CP and N374CP. The capabilities of these aircraft to employ state-of-the-art navigation systems, XM weather monitoring, and Traffic Information Systems, provides a high level of mission capability.

126 The C182 is now considered the minimal performance A/C for search operations in New Mexico's mountainous terrain

Cessna 206 Skywagon — With its Continental I0-520 fuel injected 285 HP engine and six seats, the 206 quickly became a mainstay and is used both for SAR and aircrew and staff transport around the state. This increase in capability opened up new mission profiles. Colonel Larry Harrah purchased the first of these aircraft (U206 N9375Z) for the Wing during his tenure as Wing Commander. N7360C flew for a number of years, but low utilization due to maintenance issues encouraged its transfer to another Wing.

127 The main difference between the C206 and the U206 is the location of the right side door. The U206 uses a double door that opens into the two rear seats for easy loading.

Gippsland GA8 Airvan — Manufactured by Gippsland Aeronautics of Victoria, Australia, the GA8 is the only aircraft in the CAP inventory that is not American made. Its very spacious interior can seat eight including one pilot. Although this aircraft is located with the NM Wing, it is a 'National' asset. Eighteen Airvans are operated nationwide of which 16 are equipped with the Airborne Real-time Cueing Hyperspectral Enhanced Reconnaissance (ARCHER) system. This system, which displaces two seats, can be used to search for aircraft wreckage based on its spectral signature.

128 GA-8 N612CP saw considerable service during Hurricane Katrina in September 1985 when LTC Jerry Burton flew it to Mississippi to aid in the rescue and recovery effort.

With an Empty weight of 2200 lb (997 kg) and a Gross weight: 4000 lb (1814 kg) it is the largest aircraft operated by the New Mexico Wing. Powered by a single Lycoming I0-540-K1A5 horizontally-opposed six-cylinder engine of 310 hp, its maximum speed is listed as 214 mph (343 km/h) with a range of 930 miles (1722 km).

Snapshot in Time

In the early years, CAP depended on the airplanes of its members; today the majority of the aircraft flown are corporate owned. High wing aircraft dominate because of the good viewing they provide as well as their relatively economical and easy to fly attributes.

A 1968 report indicated that NM Wing had 14 A/C with an average age of 17 years. Six were equipped with radios. These were allocated as shown below. Note that the Wing was divided into groups at that point. There were also eight member owned aircraft.

New Mexico Wing Aircraft as of 1968		
Central Group		
ABQ	N421NM	Beech T-34A
ABQ	N422NM	Beech T-34A
ABQ	N267T	PA-18
Socorro	N6476C	Aeronca L-16A
Northern Group		
Las Vegas	N75068	Aeronca L-16A
Los Alamos	N75060	Stinson L-5E
Santa Fe	N6478C	Aeronca L-16A
Southeastern Group		
Artesia	N75066	Piper L-4B
Carlsbad	N75069	Aeronca L-16A
Hobbs	N75067	Aeronca L-16A
Hobbs	N424NM	T-34A Narco Mk II
Hobbs	N5122G	Piper PA-28 Narco Mk XXII
Southwestern Group		
Alamogordo	N161T	Piper PA-18
Las Cruces	N5870	Cessna 150E Narco Mk II

11. Communications

One aspect of CAP that was heavily emphasized during its inception in WWII was the ability to use the facilities of amateur radio operators to enhance the communications capabilities for its coastal patrol as well as search and rescue. Known as "ham operators," these highly skilled and enthusiastic volunteers allowed CAP to provide the country with a nationwide network of portable low frequency stations.

129 No, those are not fishing poles, but radio antennas. Many an activity was 'planned in the dirt'.

Following the war, this communications network grew and enhanced CAPs ability to address its role in disaster relief. In these early days before cell phones and satellites, this capability was critical in helping state and federal agencies communicate. New Mexico was particularly in need of this form of radio infrastructure because of its size and inaccessible regions.

SAR Trailers and Mobile Operations Centers

Ric Himebrook recalls that in the late 1950s it was recognized that some form of mobile communications was needed to improve the command and control aspects of a mission. *"An old school bus was outfitted with communications gear. It was maintained by George Hankins (now deceased) of Squadron III. He took the vehicle (radio call Zuni 19) on many missions, often alone, he would have to set it up and man it. He developed a winch so he could get the generator out to be used on missions. He got an HF radio available for the driver—so he could get messages while mobile.*

Another mobile unit was developed in a discarded AF truck. What I remember about it was we could run all the radios – or coffee – not both." As a cadet, Himebrook operated out of both of them.

130 CAP Mobile Communications Unit 1957

Larry Zentner notes that management and location of command and control of SAREX's and REDCAP's usually took place at airports; they still do today in many cases. *"Some units enjoy the privilege of ownership of former military hangers or airport facilities, when the military scaled back the size of its forces after World War II, Korea, and then Viet Nam. However, not every mission would enjoy established CAP facilities at an airport. Some CAP units lacked a full complement of radios and mission support materials to manage the SAR or ES mission activity."*

In the spring of 1976, then wing commander, Colonel Earl Livingston, commissioned NM Wing ES staff to develop a mobile operations trailer that would complement a fixed base of operations and if necessary provide a standalone operations support center. To accomplish this assignment, Wing Logistics screened a 20 foot mobile home trailer through the Defense Reutilization and Marketing Office (DRMO). The trailer had been used by the US Army Missile Tracking Program in White Sand Missile Range, it was stripped down for office use and was perfect for CAP ES mission work. When the trailer arrived at Kirtland AFB, NM, Wing had the trailer painted white and new CAP seals attached to each of the four exterior walls and large black CAP letters painted on the roof.

To tow the trailer, a relatively new Ford ¾ quarter ton, 4-wheel drive pickup truck was found. It too received a new coat of paint, complements of Maaco Paint service in Albuquerque, NM. What was needed next was a plan to outfit the trailer and equip both the trailer and truck with radios and SAR materials. Wing ES SAR officer, 1Lt Larry Zentner drafted a plan. The plan included installing recently authorized VHF-FM radios (which were replacing the former VHF-AM capability), aircraft radio, an HF for state and region contacts (the antenna wire was 90 feet long), as well as permanently maintaining gridded sectional charts under plastic on the wall. The office would be stocked with a variety of office administration supplies, blank forms, a telephone (landline), and one desk and a few chairs.

By September 1976, the trailer was complete. The trailer and truck were parked in the Kirtland AFB east-side motor pool, along with all the other corporate vehicles. This was a convenient location, as CAP NMW headquarters and USAF Liaison Office was across the street in the 3-story office complex at the intersection of K St. and 1st St.

From 1976 into the 1980's, the trailer deployed to numerous SAREX's and REDCAP's throughout NMW. The most popular deployment site was to the 7-Bar (Alameda) airport just south of a new residential area known as Rio Rancho. While aircraft flew out of Albuquerque's Sunport, Santa Fe, Los Alamos, Grants, and many other locations, the 7-Bar airport offered uncluttered airspace, and quick landings and takeoffs. The fixed base operator was very supportive to CAP members, but would not permit permanent installation of antennas or an operation support office. Not a problem, the trailer filled the gap.

The trailer would continue service into the early 1980's until it was decommissioned and returned to DRMO. During its service tenure, it provided critical communications and resources required to accomplish the CAP mission. The USAF Rescue and Recovery Service came up with a motto that CAP and many other SAR organizations have lived up to; the trailer concept is alive today, "So that others may live".

In 2002, then NMW commander Colonel Jim Norvell, received a grant and supplementary funding to design and build a new Mobile Operations Center (MOC) for air operations command and control that would support the widely accepted Incident Command System (a fall-out from the 9-11 terrorist incidents). Then NMW director of communications, CAP Lt Colonel Larry Zentner, offered a plan to purchase a new trailer, design a state-of-the art communications package, and lead the construction crew of our newest MOC. Permission was granted.

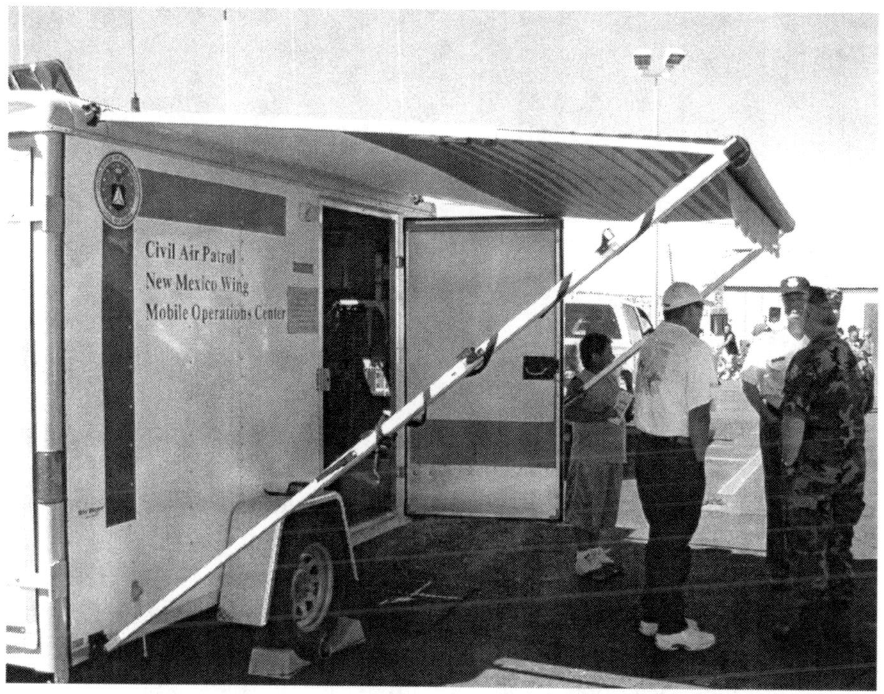

131 CAP Mobile Communications Trailer

In March 2003, the Albuquerque (ABQ) MOC was commissioned. NMW is grateful to the following CAP members who helped construct the ABQ MOC, Colonel Frank Buethe, Maj Bob Ross, Maj David Simonson, Capt John Choc, 1Lt John Grassham, 1Lt Jason Zentner, and 1Lt Kaycee Gilbert.

While the 1976 trailer had 3 radios, one map board, and some blank forms to support a SAR mission; the 2003 ABQ MOC supports ICS incidents with 7 radios (capable of communicating on frequencies ranging from HF, through VHF FM and AM, up into the UHF bands). It also has a cellular phone, slow-scan aerial imagery system, multiple map and status boards, computerized mapping, forms management and printer system, live weather station, and wire-less Internet local area network. While CAP NMW may have spent $1,000 to put the 1976 trailer on-line, the 2003 MOC invested over $25,000 in resource materials.

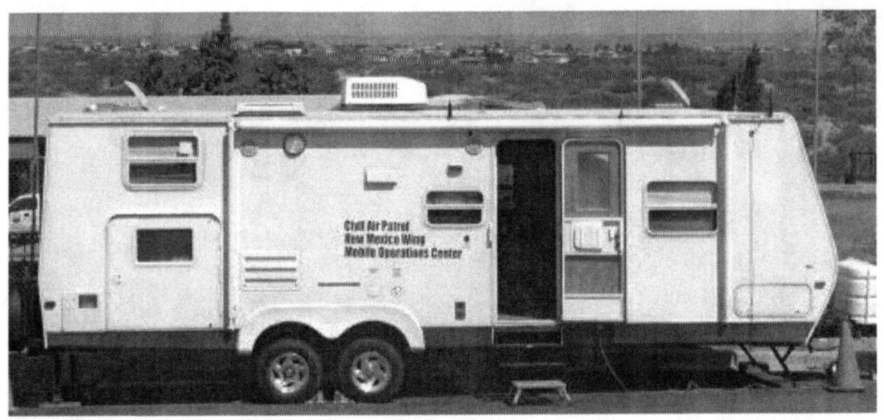

132 New Mexico's newest Mobile Communications Trailer

In the summer of 2007, FEMA released hundreds of mobile homes to CAP for future MOC services. NM Wing acquired two of these units, which are dispersed north and south, to complement the existing facility centrally located in Albuquerque. The van in Las Cruces is assigned to the Wing and is under the auspices of Cline as the Wing Com Officer. In Taos, Blair Bouchier provides the lead (Taos paid for the equipment. Both individuals guided their local unit to design and outfit their MOC with communications and ICS resources, similar to the MOC in Albuquerque.

All of these trailers or MOC's were designed and constructed for our primary mission objective, "So that others may live".

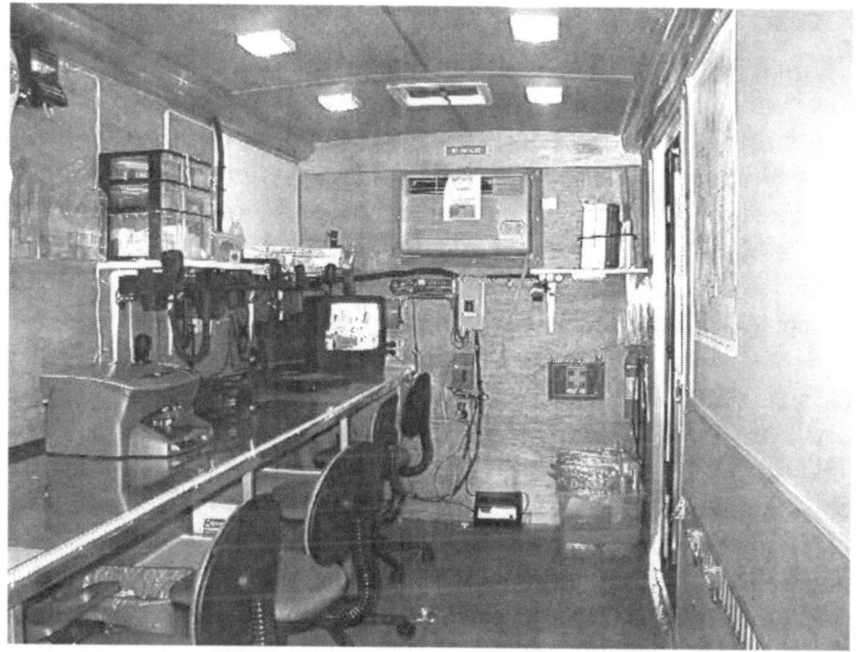

133 The 2003 ABQ MOC supports ICS incidents with seven radios capable of communicating on frequencies ranging from HF, through VHF FM and AM, up into the UHF bands.

Personal Reflections

Eugene McKim, who was a member of the Las Cruces Squadron in the early 1950s learned from an amateur radio manual and had earned a radio license. He had worked at the NMSU campus radio station when he was a student. Several members were interested in communications, including his boss at the station, the chief engineer. The squadron received a radio from Wing and, as McKim happened to be the only communications guy at the next meeting, so he was asked to set up the communications section. Much of the following description will be of interest primarily to old radio hams so hang on.

The transmitter was a Globe King, built by an amateur in Iowa, who apparently used whatever parts he could find. It had BMW coils - 160 meter and 80-meter coils. McKim used 80-meter coils because the required frequency was 2.37 Megacycles.

Unfortunately, at the first building near the tracks, they had communications set up in the middle of the barracks, and he needed to put up poles at each end, 200 feet apart. One member worked at the telephone company and they had many telephone poles lying around—so much for the first part of the problem. McKim put up a couple of two by fours at the top, bolted together, so that it could be rotated down towards insulators and antenna. He used very strong copper weld wire, about three hundred feet bought for 99 cents; and three insulators, which cost 12 cents apiece. He needed 50 feet of coaxial, which they did not have, so he used twisted lamp cord—a standard ham radio procedure.

The receiver was a WWII airborne type, with a 110-volt power supply. The transmitter was about 4 feet tall in three sections, power supplies on bottom, middle was the modulator, top was the RF section. Power output used V70Ds made by the Taylor Corp. It had two power levels, 400 watts, and 200 watts. The 866 mercury vapor rectifiers had to warm up, and could easily arc out. Also used were 866 'juniors' for the modulators, and different rectifiers for another part - a real mismatch.

There was a switch used on telephones, line 1 to line 2, to toggle from transmitter to receiver. 110VAC was used to turn on the transmitter—a hazard, a technique learned from the amateur radio manual. McKim claims not to have had any trouble with it. *"The first move to the college was a more handy site because they had a latrine,"* he recalls, but they had to put up the antenna again. Fortunately, there was a telephone pole nearby and they ran the antenna from that. The college asked them if they had permission, McKim is unclear on the answer but they did not have to take it down.

The move to new barracks in the extreme southern part of the campus required them to put up telephone poles again. *"No trouble there, because we were out in the boonies."* They had a WW II VHF CR522 transceiver, designed by British. It had four channels, with a crystal for each channel. Each time it was taken apart, the transmitter had to be tuned again. The power supply ran off 110 AC, instead of DC. Of course, they needed low voltage for the carbon microphones.

After putting up the antenna (yet again), some members went to a lookout up in the Black Range, and they were able to talk back to Las Cruces on the VHF. There were some dead spots however. On the HF there was a Wing net every Tuesday evening. Sometimes they were unable to hear anyone; other times they would hear people in Florida. The messages were formal—the same format at the Army Air Force and were not allowed to use radio "slang." McKim had to retune the radios each week.

During SAR missions, the ability to communicate with airborne assets is critical. As most search patterns are flown at low altitudes—and VHF communications is line-of-sight—there is a need for an airborne communications outpost that is called "High Bird." Col. Robert Haulenbeek initiated this function in New Mexico in the 1970s. The "High Bird" is often used to relay information between the search aircraft and the mission base.

As the Wing grew, repeater stations were installed across the state to aid in the ability to converse rapidly and reliably over long distances. At least one pilot however recalled of the repeater system; *"It mostly provides frustration and a distraction for aircrews from their primary mission."*

You can't make everybody happy!

12. New Mexico Wing in the 21st Century

Looking back over 70 years of CAP history, it is interesting to note the changes in technology. There has been virtually no change in aircraft form or function. Nor have new engine designs or types taken hold. The C182 we purchase today is essentially the same aircraft marketed 50 years ago. What has seen a revolutionary change is the electronics. The integrated circuit and the microcomputer industry it has spawned have provided a quantum leap in our communications, navigation and the overall realm of situational awareness. Thus, while we still fly at two miles per minute, our ability to perform that CAP mission has expanded dramatically.

The low frequency range of the 1940s gave way to the VOR network of the 1960s. The brief foray into LORAN in the 1980s was short-circuited by the advent of GPS. The ability to take airborne photos and send them 'in real time' to ground stations provides unprecedented movement of information. As we enter the 21st century and explore the new capabilities of the class cockpit and the ARCHER system, the future may hold still more surprises that we cannot predict.

The Glass Cockpit

With expanded emergency services roles entrusted to CAP, Technically Advanced Aircraft (TAA), such as the Garmin G1000 equipped Cessna C182T, provides a greatly enhanced capability. More than 500 aircraft of this type are expected to be delivered within the next decade to improve substantially, the potential of CAP to execute critical missions—whether search and rescue, disaster relief, or homeland security. These aircraft provide the ability to fly demanding flight profiles with extreme accuracy and transport critical assets to precise locations with exact timing— performing these tasks with a high degree of assurance.

The TAA moniker is applicable to these aircraft because of their use of high technology that greatly enhances flight planning, navigation, real-time XM weather displays, traffic avoidance, and terrain awareness. These graphical cockpit displays replace the traditional flight and navigation instruments, and the information they provide places increased demands on the pilot for improved flight management and decision making skills. Becoming proficient and remaining current with the wide variety of functions provided by the Global Positioning System and state-of-the-art autopilot is essential. This requires dedication and a significant effort for the pilot who seeks to master the capabilities of this high value CAP asset.

Because CAP is a volunteer organization, the ability of aircrews to train to high levels of proficiency in these high-tech aircraft is perhaps the greatest challenge. An ad hoc approach to providing training is no longer sufficient. Only the truly dedicated will master the skills necessary to become proficient with the G1000 as well as other assets such as ARCHER. Aerospace education must be integrated with the demanding emergency services expertise to achieve the required goals.

As each Wing has taken delivery of its new aircraft, two experienced C182 instructor pilots were trained by Cessna at their facility in Independence, Kansas. In May of 2006, Brian Morrison and Ted Spitzmiller were selected to attend the G1000 training and returned with a new C182T (N780CP). Over the next 18 months, 37 NM Wing pilots completed the transition-training program to the Glass Cockpit and the aircraft flew more than 600 hours. In December of 2007, two new C182Ts (N292CP and N374CP) were acquired by the Wing and N780CP was sent to the Louisiana Wing.

134 Training is the key to effective use of assets such as the G1000 Glass Cockpit. Ted Spitzmiller presents a G1000 session at a SQII monthly safety meeting (2008).

Because the G1000 systems provide so many capabilities, much of the flight operation can be accomplished with the autopilot to reduce the cockpit workload. This addition of a high degree of automation requires a new approach to training to assure automation competence—the demonstrated ability to understand and operate the automated systems installed in the aircraft.

Because automated systems may provide cues to pilots that are different from the traditional instruments they replace, it is vital that the pilot avoid automation surprise. Likewise, the pilot must learn to trust and use automated systems to overcome automation bias. Of particular importance is the concept of Proficiency Based Qualification—the foundation of the Form 5 sign-off that is based on demonstrated performance rather than other flight time or experience qualifiers.

Hyperspectral Imaging System

This article, excerpted from the CAP National Website, describes the HyperSpectral Imaging system:

> CAP's custom-designed system is the first fully operational large-scale HSI system in the nation. The new system, dubbed ARCHER (Airborne Real-Time Cueing Hyperspectral Enhanced Reconnaissance), is installed in CAP aircraft for aerial reconnaissance. This technology will increase CAP's effectiveness in search and rescue, disaster relief, and homeland security mission. Hyperspectral imaging allows CAP aircraft to identify an object on the ground as small as one meter in size from half a mile in the air, even if it's partially hidden from view by trees or bushes. With this new capability, CAP has positioning itself to become a leader in low-cost, on-demand aerial imaging technology for homeland security and emergency management."
>
> Hyperspectral imaging allows an operator in a CAP plane to program into an onboard computer the "spectral signature" of the object under search. A sensitive HSI camera onboard can then detect and pinpoint any object(s) on the ground that matches the signature. The HSI sensor is also capable of detecting anomalies, objects significantly different from the background in which they are located. Data on possible "targets" that match the spectral signature or anomalies can be processed in real time, stored and analyzed, and transmitted to ground teams. HSI works by analyzing an object's reflected light. Thus, it cannot detect objects at night, underwater, under dense cover, underground, under snow or inside buildings.
>
> HSI can be used in conjunction with CAP's existing satellite-transmitted digital imaging system (SDIS) to send images from the aircraft to the ground via e-mail and a satellite phone. CAP's SDIS system can send such transmissions in two minutes or less, allowing ground operators to redirect the aircraft or deploy ground search teams.
>
> Since 2003, CAP has invested almost $5 million in the ARCHER system, along with additional funds for Gippsland GA8 Airvans to serve as the system platform. Funding for ARCHER was provided to CAP by Congress under the 2002 Defense Appropriations Act.

> As an organization, continuous training of our volunteer members on the newest technologies in their areas of expertise is critical because the technology of aerial reconnaissance is constantly changing and improving.

One of the first uses of the GA-8 with ARCHER was REDCAP mission 07-M-288 (the first week of March 2007). Centered out of Carlsbad, the search was looking for a doctor in a red Ingraham RV-6 homebuilt, high performance plane that had left California on February 28, 2007, on a flight to Texas. The ATP rated pilot, with 24,000 hours and 370 in the past six months, had not filed a flight plan but radar plots directed the search to the Guadalupe Mountains between NM and TX. Both wings worked the mission; Texas even sent ground teams and their GA8.

Although VFR conditions were forecast for the area on the day of the flight, several In-Flight Advisories (AIRMETs) were in effect for the airplane's route of flight for low visibility conditions, moderated turbulence.

The New Mexico crew consisted of mission pilot Joe Friel; observer Anthony Torres; ARCHER operator David Kuntz; and Andrew Selph on ARCHER TRAC. Selph noted that, *"We spend two days with ARCHER without any results. The lost plane was eventually discovered in July by NM State Police 40 miles southwest of Carlsbad, on the North side of the mountain range. We learned a lot about real world use of ARCHER."*

While we may have these high technology assets, learning to use them effectively may be the greatest challenge.

NM Wing's Role as UAV Simulators

In the fall of 2009, a new aircraft appeared on the NM Wing flight line. While it looks like a standard C182, the Air Force has installed a 'Predator Ball' under the left wing. In this unique program, the CAP aircraft will simulate the Air Force's deadly MQ-1 Predator or MQ-9 Reaper Unmanned Airborne Vehicles (UAV) in yet another role for CAP in Homeland Security.

CAP-U.S. Air Force spokesperson Col. Bill Ward said that the C182 will *"emulate the role of the UAV to allow Army and Marine personnel on the ground to train in the use of this effective drone that has had much success in Iraq and Afghanistan."* Because of the cost and limited availability of the drones, modifying the C182 and having it flown by CAP volunteers will reduce the cost and enhance the training scenario. The under-wing unit has the capability of locking onto a target and tracking it, just the way the UAV does. The primary difference is that a CAP pilot will respond to flight directives rather than the autopilot of the UAV.

Although the C182 has been upgraded to a 260 hp engine and sports a counter weight on the right wing, there are no other Predator accoutrements. Its role as a camera platform, is to use the pod to stream live video to the trainees as they evaluate the video and define their battlefield priorities.

Several NM Wing pilots have been trained to fly the Surrogate Predator (as the CAP 182 is known) to emulate the UAV.

135 C182 modified to perform as a Surrogate Predator

Epilogue

The mission of CAP has changed little over the years, but the supporting activities of those missions have. CAP does not do as much search and rescue as in the early years. The availability of radar to cover the contiguous 48 states, coupled with the ELT and the spread of habitation across the vast expanses of the continent have greatly reduced the need for the traditional search for a lost plane. The most recent hunt for Steve Fossett was a notable exception. But the expanded role of CAP in disaster relief such as occurred during hurricane Katrina and the Homeland Defense effort are strong indicators that the basic mission of CAP is a critical asset to America.

As with any organization, there have been times of strife within. More than a few have left with bitterness. Nevertheless, those who can see past the human frailties perceive the needs of our neighbors—our young people in particular, as a light in the occasional shadows of frustration. And, of course, the axiom of *'you can only get out of an organization what you are willing to put in,'* is a vital observation.

Bringing together almost 70 years of CAP activity in New Mexico from the dusty archives that have lain dormant for that period has been an interesting and challenging task. As I looked over the efforts of past members, it is a sobering reflection. Many have contributed so much, yet numerous projects and even entire squadrons have fallen by the wayside.

Perhaps it is the change in culture and the lack of a more cohesive community spirit, but CAP today does not seem to hold the same camaraderie of years past. We have not been able to draw-in the number of young people to fill squadrons around the state. Nevertheless, the future of CAP is at the squadron level!

In a 2007 article in the Eagle Squadron Newsletter, that celebrated the 50 year anniversary of that squadron, LtCol Paul Ballmer recalled, *"when over 100 members would show up for a meeting. Some of these past members currently serve as the New Mexico Wing Vice-Commander (Col Ric Himebrook), and the Deputy Commander for Cadets of the Northeast Heights Composite Squadron (LtCol Beverly (Pepe) Vito). As cadet members back then, they have seen many changes in the Civil Air Patrol and the New Mexico Wing during the past fifty years."*

He continued, *"The only thing that has stayed the same in the last fifty years is change. What about our future? Where will the Eagle Cadet Squadron be in 2032 or 2057, when we will be celebrating 75 or 100 years as a squadron? Many of you cadets will be the ones the squadron will remember 25 or 50 years from now. You are the ones who will make things happen and implement changes that are bound to come your way. As change dictated the past and allowed the squadron to improve and prosper for the last fifty years, change will dictate the future. You are the future decision makers and will shape things for years to come. Be prepared to take those changes in stride and run with them to make the CAP a better organization for the future. The next fifty years depends upon you."*

The Civil Air Patrol, like most volunteer organizations, takes on the persona of its people to create a distinct culture. While the cast of characters changes over the years, the enduring qualities of those who have gone before remains a legacy for those who follow.

The New Mexico Wing has been fortunate to have had people from many walks of life who have contributed to the organization. This is their story.

Addendum 1 — NM Wing Award Winners

Honored Member of the Year			
	Family of The Year	Cadet of The Year	Senior Member of the Year
1981			Don Cooper
1982	Looney	Andrew F. Selph	Lynn Looney/Lloyd Sallee
1983		Michael J. Moore	Allan Korzan
1984		Greg Matweyoff	Dennis Manzanares
1985		Timothy F. Selph	Ted Price
1986	Herb Traulsen	Darrell LaRoche	
1987	Grubert	Leslie Himebrook	
1988	Himebrook	Matthias Girardi	Mattie Ruth Roberts
1989	Abbott	Scott McCarty	Gary Williams
1990	Roberts	Gordon Weimer	Roberta Himebrook
1991	Romero	Brain MacFarlane	Beverly (Pepe) Vito
1992	Pfau	Emarae Garcia	Reed Mulkey
1993	Selph	James Romero	Corliss Grubert
1994	Jakusz	Ray Bailey	Maria Traulsen
1995	Norvell	Zachary Lane	Richard Himebrook
1996	Crawford/Ruetz	Adan Fachan	Claude Luisada
1997	Ross	Bart Bowman	Bob Ross
1998	Bourne	John Grassham	Patricia Norvell
1999	Lawson	Jessica Block	Dannie R. Roberts
2000	S & G Lane	Kate Schifani	Herbert Traulsen
2001	J & B Gary	Jason Zentner	Dave Gottheimer
02-03	F,J,J Zentner	Kaycee Gilbert	Sharon Lane
2004	M, A, J Peters	David M. Bracken	Janet L. Andraka
2005	Tromblry	Ben Andraka	Joe Friel
2006	Reames	Daniel Bracken	Dean Trombley
2007	Bracken	Kenneth Keintz	Shirley Kay
2008	Walt Brown	Bradley McNicol	John Gravel

Honored Member of the Year

	NCO of Year	National Nominee	Squadron Cmdr	Comm Officer	Public Affairs Officer
1981					
1982					
1983					
1984					
1985					
1986				L. Looney	
1987					
1988					
1989				L. Plemons	M Harrah
1990				R. Herlocker	
1991					G French
1992				L. Plemons	L Henson
1993					D Falcon
1994				J. Romero	P Norvell
1995				Wm Leehan	R Pomeranz
1996			A Selph		B Grassham
1997		Luke Davis	Schumerth	D. Beckman	T Cornell
1998			B Ross	J. Choc	S Lane
1999			Mick Daly	J. Zentner	
2000			T Laney		R Ross
2001			D McClard	L. Zentner	
02-03		K Gilbert	P Ballmer	R. Ross	G Christensen
2004			D Bracken	R. Ross	T Fuller
2005			J Stephens	G. McComas	M Sanchez
2006			J Gravel/ D. Bracken		C Matthews
2007			R Austin	P. Cline	G Christensen
2008	A Brown			N. Brown	Norm Reames

Honored Member/Squadron of the Year

	Flight Scholar	SEP Squadron of Year	Most Improved Squadron
1996	I Block		
1997	J Frick		
1998			
1999	J Grassham		
2000	K Schifani		
2001	J Spain		
02-03			
2004			
2005	C DeMarco		
2006			
2007			
2008		Eagle Ridge	Clovis

Honored Member of the Year

	Emergency Services	Safety Officer	Chaplain	Aerospace Education
1993				
1994		K Hayes		
1995		K Hayes		
1996				
1997	J. Gary	O Bourne	R Coleman	Jan. Lamm
1998	R Ruetz	O Bourne	C Moore	A. Tauche
1999	G Martin		Larry Burns	Bill Jackson
2000	D McClard	L Harrah	T Jackson	C Lemanski
2001	MSgt Hart	R Gibson	J SR Franz	R Haulenbeek
02-03	D Simonson	none	none	J P Baker
2004	Odend'hal	J Quick	C Moore, III	
2005	D Simonson	L Knoell	J Doughty	E Brummett
2006	J Gravel	B Jones	Larry Burns	N Johnson
	P Zarnan			D Andraka
2007	L Zentner		J Hoy	
2008		J Perea	Ben Craver	T Spitzmiller

Honored Member of the Year

	COS-Haulenbeek	Decade of Dedication	Emergency Services
1981			
1982			
1983			ABQ Sq II
1984			ABQ Sq II
1985			Alamogordo
1986			Santa Fe
1987			
1988		B&L Abbott	Santa Fe
1989			Alamogordo
1990		M&L Harrah	Los Alamos/SAF
1991		E&V Livingston	Los Alamos
1992		H&M Traulsen	Alamogordo
1993		R&R Himebrook	Alamogordo
1994		P&D Cline	Las Cruces
1995		C&C Grubert	Alamogordo
1996		D&R Roberts	Farmington
1997	J Zentner	T&N Price	Alamogordo
1998	F. Lui	J&P Norvell	
1999	R. Fugal	Bob Haulenbeek	
2000		D Manzanares	
2001	K. Gilbert	J Green	
02-03		G&D Martin	
2004		Herbert Traulsen	
2005		Bob Ross	
2006		Don Underwood	
2007		Sharon Lane	
		Beverly (Pepe)	
2008		Vito	

Honored Squadron of the Year

Year	Squadron of Year	Cadet Squadron	Emergency Services Sq	Special Mission Sq
1981	Black Sheep			
1982	Farmington			
1983	Alamogordo	Falcon		
1984	Santa Fe	Alamogordo		
1985	Alamogordo	Farmington		
1986	Santa Fe	Thunderbird		
1987				
1988	Santa Fe	Farmington		
1989	Farmington	Thunderbird	Santa Fe	
1990	Squadron II	Eagle		
1991	Los Alamos	Thunderbird	Los Alamos/SAF	Los Alamos
1992	High Plains	Farmington	Los Alamos	ABQ Sq II
1993	Las Cruces	Falcon	Santa Fe	
1994		Thunderbird	Los Alamos	
1995	High Plains	Thunderbird		AQB Sq II
1996	Farmington	Eagle		
1997	Alamogordo	Thunderbird		Farmington
1998	Thunderbird	Alamogordo	Los Alamos	ABQ Sq II
1999	Farmington	Eagle	Las Cruces	Alamogordo
2000	Roswell	Gallup	ABQ Sq II	Las Cruces
2001	Los Alamos	Las Cruces	Los Alamos	ABQ Sq II
2002-03	Farmington	Los Alamos	Alamogordo	Farmington
2004		Falcon		
2005	Gallup	Thunderbird	ALM & LRU	
2006	SAF	Thunderbird	Santa Fe	ABQ Sq II
2007	Clovis	Thunderbird		
2008	Sprit		Santa Fe	

Addendum 2 — List of NM Wing Aircraft

Aircraft	N-No.	Service	Year	Disposition
Fairchild ?				
Stearman PT-17 (4)		Feb 1946		Artesia Roswell
Ryan PT-19				
Piper L-4	**AF43590**	Las Cruces	1943a	
Piper L-4B (J-3C?)	**N75066**	Left before 1967	1943	
Stinson L-5E	**N75060**		1944	
Aeronca L-16A (7BCM)	**N75067**	C-85	1946	
Aeronca L-16A	N75068	Left before 1973	1947	
Aeronca L-16A	N75069	Destroyed 4/26/74	1947	
Aeronca L-16A (7BCM)	**N6479C**		1947	
Aeronca L-16A (7BCM)	**N6478C**		1947	
Aeronca L-16A (7BCM)	**N6476C**		1947	
Piper L-21	AF-675	August 1956		
Piper L-21	6482C	1956		AF-15895G?
Champion 7GCAA	**N9561S**	O-200	1965	Gnd loop 8/16/76
Piper PA-18-125	N267T	sold 1979	1953	Gnd Lood 62-80
Piper PA-18	**N161T**	O-235 12-13-77	1952	Hard Landing
Piper PA-28-180	**N5122G**	NHQ 1968	1968	Crash LVS
Piper PA-28-140	**N6122W**	Don Shepan LRU	1964	
Piper PA-28-180	**N6479J**	1988	1968	
Beech T-34A (A-45)	**N421NM**	13 Aug 64 1980	1955	Crash Taos
Beech T-34A (A-45)	**N422NM**	13 Aug 64 1988	1956	Belen, Alameda
Beech T-34A (A-45)	N423NM	13 Aug 64-69 N10545		Crash Rio Grande
Beech T-34A (A-45)	**N424NM**	13 Aug 64 1988	1953	
Beech T-34B (D-45)	N5357G	Rec'd		424NM tail no
Cessna C150	N5870E	Destroyed 4-82?	1959	Crash — prop
Cessna C150J	N50929	1969 LAM 1982		
Cessna C150H	**N7222S**	77-78	1967	
Cessna 172	**N8820B**	O300 Donated SQ2	1957	by Overton LAM
Cessna C172N	**N4842G**	1981- 2007	1990	
Cessna C172	N9474L	180 hp 9/29/04		Crash
Cessna C172M	**N5098R**	180 hp 1979-1987		
Cessna C172H	N1769F	180 hp 1987		

Aircraft	N-No.	Service	Year	Disposition
Cessna C172N	**N737NM**	160 hp Present	1977	Was 737MC
Cessna C172P	**N9436L**	1991 - 2004	1986	Crash LRU
Cessna C172P	**N98502**	2008 - **Present**	1985	
Cessna C172P	**N98456**	**Present**	1988	
Cessna C172N	**N6198F**	Present?	1977	
Cessna C172M	**N9182H**	1980 – 1998	1975	180HP
Cessna C172	N7997G	LAM		TO snow 1/19/77
?	**N7469J**	1988		
Cessna C172XP	N6364H	Clayton		
Cessna C172XP	N736HU	1988		
Cessna T-41A (C-172F)	**N5265F**	1973 Clovis O-300	1965	
Cessna T-41B	**N242WS**	1972 - 1987		(R-172E)
Cessna T-41B	**N93216**	1979		
Cessna C182J	**N2813F**		1966	
Cessna C182J	**N3311F**	1977 – 1985	1966	Leased fm Harrah
Cessna C182L	**N3479R**		1968	
Cessna C182	N2676Q	6/9/84 crash CO		
Cessna C182	N6319H	198.. – 6/12/2003		Crash Hobbs
Cessna C182R	**N2939E**	**Present**		
Cessna C182R	**N9455X**	1991 - **present**	1985	
Cessna C182R	**N6205H**	1999 - **Present**	1981	
Cessna C182R	**N9472E**	1987 - **Present**	1984	FMN 1989
Cessna C182Q	**N96844**	1994 - **Present**	1979	
Cessna C182P	**N1431M**	1979 - **Present**	1975	
Cessna C182T	**N780CP**	Jun 2006 Dec 2007	2006	Xferred to MS Wing
Cessna C182T	**N292CP**	Dec 2007 - **Present**	2007	
Cessna C182T	**N734CP**	Jan 2006 - **Present**	2007	
Cessna U206F	**N9599G**	1996-2003	1972	
Cessna U206G	**N9375Z**	1987 - **Present**	1981	
Cessna U206G	**N7360C**	1996 - 2007	1980	
Cessna C210D	**N3817Y**		1964	
Cessna 172	N8820B	1988	1956	
Helio Courier HT 295	**N9383G**	1987		
Gipsland GA-8	**N612CP**	2005 - **present**	2005	
Maul MT-7-235	**N116CP**	Present?		
Maul MXT-7-180	**N9223F**	….- 2006		
Ryan Navion	**N333W**			
Aircraft Ind L23	**N471BA**	2006 - **present**	2006	
Aircraft Ind L23	**N361BA**	2000 - **present**	2000	

Aircraft	N-No.	Service	Year	Disposition
Schweizer SGS 2-33A	**N5765S**	1998	1968	
SGU 2-22E	**N2770Z**	1994	1965	
SGS 1-26				
Blanik L-23				
Schleicher ASK-21	**N221CP**	1998		

Bold **Aircraft** denotes still active in CAP registry
Bold **N-Number** denotes active in FAA registry

Addendum 3 — NM Aircraft Crash Sites

Seq	Lat	Long	Type	N-No.	Date	Location
1	36 53	105 21	B-24			Costilla Pk
2	36 47	105 31	B-17			Questa
3	36 39	108 55	Cessna 190	N9878A		Fruitland
4	36 24	105 04	C-47			Cimarron
5	36 10	107 44	Aero Commander		01/03/63	Lybrook
6	36 08	105 19	B-52		01/03/63	Mora
7	35 57	107 10	Cessna 170			Cabezon Pk
8	35 55	105 40	Piper Tri-Pacer	N1211C	08/20/62	Truches
9	35 55	105 32	Piper PA-22	N6179D	06/26/64	Cowles
10	35 45	106 29	Piper PA-140	N6437W	04/01/65	Cochiti
11	35 45	105 37	AT-11			El Porvenir
12	35 40	107 21	Martin Matador			Cabazon Pk
13	35 40	105 20	Cessna 180	N9047C		
14	35 34	104 57	SR-71			Las Vegas
15	35 20	105 26	Cessna 172	N559X	01/16/66	Placitas
16	35 17	108 23	F-51			Cont Divide
17	35 15	107 36	B-17			Mt. Taylor
18	35 15	107 20	B-52		04/08/61	Marquez
19	35 15	106 11	C-47			Golden
20	35 15	105 53	North Amer T-6			Stanley
21	35 14	105 26	Unknown			N Sandia Peak
22	35 13	106 35	Piper PA-24-180	N9728J	06/09/67	
23	35 12	106 27	Martin 202	TWA	12/01/55	
24	35 12	106 26	RB-57F		11/08/68	
25	35 09	106 24	JRF-NAVY	8414E		S Sandia Pk
26	35 12	105 35	Piper Tri-Pacer	N7652	06/22/58	Leyba
27	35 10	106 50	Cessna 210	N168D	01/23/65	ABQ
28	35 08	108 00	BUDD CONE			Grants
29	35 08	107 54	Globe Swift	N3239L	07/03/63	Grants
30	35 08	106 26	Piper Aztec		12/03/61	S Sandia Pk
31	35 08	105 05		N3824H		Anton Chico
32	35 07	107 50	T-33	AF29850	04/07/62	Grants
33	35 07	106 25	Navion	N8617H	10/01/54	S Sandia Pk
34	35 07	106 22	Cessna ANB		02/01/67	S Sandia Pk
35	35 07	104 15	Morrissey	N1134PA	11/07/59	Newkirk

Seq	Lat	Long	Type	N-No.	Date	Location
36	35 06	106 25	Piper PA-24	N8339R	07/12/64	Tijeras
37	35 06	105 40	F-80	AF7208	03/29/52	Clines Corners
38	35 05	106 20	AD-6	13538	09/14/61	Tijeras
39	35 04	105 30	Beech	N3081A	08/16/69	Clines Corners
40	35 03	107 58	Piper PA-18			Grants
41	35 03	106 11	Cessna 180	N9400C	09/22/63	Edgewood
42	35 02	107 06	C-96			Correo
43	35 02	105 38	Cessna 182	N4746D	05/03/63	Clines Corners
44	35 01	108 26	F-51	44-64233	07/19/64	El Moro
45	35 00	105 02	Bell H-13			Santa Rosa
46	34 57	108 11	F-51			El Moro
47	34 53	106 22	Navy F6-A	PINE-6		Los Lunas
48	34 5x	107 45	Cessna	N2761N	09/24/62	Acoma Pueblo
49	34 50	104 58	Bonanza	N5932C	11/22/62	Pastura
50	34 48	107 09	Twin Bonanza	N322V	02/23/65	Los Lunas
51	34 48	106 05	Cessna 210	N6846R	04/14/68	Estancia
52	34 46	106 26	AT-11			Bosque Pk
53	34 43	107 22	B-57			Acoma Pueblo
54	34 41	107 21	Unknown		03/24/68	
55	34 41	106 23	T-37		02/27/69	
56	34 38	106 41	USAF O-2		09/02/67	Kirtland
57	34 36	103 20	Navion	N4987W	04/22/64	Clovis
58	34 34	108 09	PBY			Quemado
59	34 22	105 42	Bonanza	N38668	11/10/56	Cedarvale
60	34 28	107 04	Piper PA-22	N4436A	01/24/65	Bernardo
61	34 26	104 17	Piper Tri-Pacer	N812A	12/28/60	Ft Sumner
62	34 23	108 30	T-33	AF-50359	02/15/57	Quemado
63	34 09	105 46	Piper PA-32	N3408W	12/16/67	
64	34 06	107 10	B-17			Socorro
65	33 40	108 30	unknown			Reserve
66	33 24	108 50	TBM (Civ)			Glemwood042
67	33 13	105 08	Stinson			Roswell
68	33 12	105 50	F-80F	47172A	03/03/60	
69	33 05	107 35	Mooney Mk 21	N79856	08/13/67	
70	33 04	108 30				Gila
71	32 46	105 49	Cessna 140	NC89148		Alamogordo
72	32 45	105 45	B-24			Alamogordo
73	32 45	104 30	Piper Tri-Pacer	NC1290	04/13/57	Carlsbad

Seq	Lat	Long	Type	N-No.	Date	Location
74	32 40	106 36	B-17			
75	32 32	107 44	unknown			Cooks Pk
76	31 31	106 28	BT-13			Alamogordo
77	32 30	108 58	Piper PA-23	N4200F	03/09/63	Lordsburg
78	32 35	105 58	unknown			Alamogordo
79	32 17	106 33	B-25			Las Cruces
80	32 12	106 33	AT-11			Las Cruces
81	32 11	104 58	B-25			Carlsbad
82	32 05	104 40	BT-13	2875		Carlsbad
83	32 03	108 48	F6F			Lordsburg
84	31 55	104 50	BE-95	N9959R	03/18/66	Carlsbad
85	31 50	106 30	Lockheed 12			El Paso
86	35 53	106 52	PA-24	N6961P	12/11/65	
87	36 54	106 15	Cessna 182	N2263G		
88	35 05	105 33	BE-55	N308AA	08/17/69	
89	32 12	104 50	PA-28		08/31/69	
90	33 21	105 00	PA-28	N8691J	9/1/1969	
91	34 37	105 09	BE35	N3151N	10/26/69	
92	33 34	105 16	Cessna 310	N3016L	07/24/70	
93	31 39	106 45	PA-30	N8825Y	09/28/70	
94	31 55	108 43	Cessna 210	N6913R	09/30/70	
95	31 47	107 11	PA-28	N7526N	02/26/71	
96	35 34	105 54	BE 35	N620Q	07/20/71	
97	32 46	105 58	PA-22	N8736C	09/06/71	
98	33 42	105 15	Cessna 172	N5552R	09/18/71	
99	34 34	107 18	SI8	N1114K	10/21/71	
100	34 10	105 45	PA-28	N4670J	06/08/72	
101	33 23	108 40	PA-32	N4278R	06/22/72	
102			Cessna 172	N9200V	10/26/69	Albuquerque
103	35 30	106 25	Cessna 172	N8559X	01/16/66	
104	32 43	103 25	Mooney Mk 21	N74784	09/18/66	
105	34 58	108 34	Piper Tri-Pacer	N3272B	07/13/67	
106	33 36	104 12	T-33		07/28/67	
107	34 09	105 46	PA-32	N3408W	12/15/67	
108	34 41	107 21	Citabria	N5101T	03/24/68	
109	35 49	105 30	Cessna 180	N9047C	04/14/68	
110	35 40	108 35	Cessna 182	N6348A	04/22/68	
111	34 43	107 47	PA-22	N27xxP	04/23/68	
112	34 38	106 xx		N6846R		

Seq	Lat	Long	Type	N-No.	Date	Location
113	34 40	106 25	T-37	AF572301	02/23/69	
114	35 04	103 25	Cessna 180	N3371D	03/10/69	
115	35 57	105 32	Cessna 172	N5062A	12/01/71	
116	31 15	107 16	Piper PA-28	N2187R	02/13/93	
117	31 24	108 38	Piper Cherokee	unk	01/16/83	16 E Cloverdale
118	31 47	107 11	Piper PA-28	N7926N	02/26/71	
119	31 48	104 42	Cessna 172	N7546T	02/21/73	
120	31 55	108 43	Cessna 210	N6913R	09/30/70	
121	32 01	104 49	Beech BE58	N2019V	03/05/91	Whites City
122	32 05	106 59	Bellanca 17	N14774	09/17/00	
123	32 06	107 35	Cessna 172	N54378	11/19/94	
124	32 10	107 14	Mooney M20	N7414V	05/15/85	
125	32 11	104 57	F-15	unk	01/15/86	
126	32 11	104 58	B-25	unk		
127	32 12	104 50	Piper PA-28	unk	08/31/69	
128	32 12	106 33	Beech AT-11	unk		
129	32 17	106 33	B-25	unk		
130	32 25	105 58	Unknown			
131	32 31	106 28	BT-13	unk		
132	32 32	107 03	Piper PA-28R-200	N47402	03/14/93	Radium Springs
133	32 35	104 55	Unknown	N83286		
134	32 43	103 25	Mooney M21	N74784	9/18/66	
135	32 46	105 44	Cessna 140	N8914B		
136	32 46	105 58	Piper PA-22	N8736C	09/06/71	
137	32 46	106 10	Cessna 150	XB-BIV	08/09/73	Alamogordo
138	32 49	105 53	MU-2	N108SC	06/25/92	
139	32 53	106 06	F-4	N4733K	10/24/95	
140	33 01	107 45	T-34	unk	08/04/81	
141	33 07	107 33	Unknown	unk		
142	33 13	105 08	Stinson	unk		
143	33 20	105 05	T-33	unk	05/26/81	25 W Roswell
144	33 20	105 48	Piper PA-28	N43981	11/28/81	Ruidoso

Addendum 4 — NM Wing Staff – Apr 2009

WING HEADQUARTERS	Phone: 505-268-5678 DSN: 246-5080
POSITION	NAME
NM Wing Commander	Col Ric Himebrook
NM Vice Commander	Col Joy Nelson
Chief of Staff	Lt Col David Gottheimer
NM Wing Administrator	Corliss Grubert
NM Wing Secretary	Judy Candelaria
Special Advisors to the Wing CC	Capt Roberta Himebrook
NMWG Administrative Officer	Lt Col Pat Norvell
Director of Aerospace Education	Lt Col Roland Dewing
Internal AE Officer External AE Officer	Lt. Judy Candelaria Maj. Ted Spitzmiller
Aircraft Maintenance Assistant	LtCol Charles Kreis Col Larry Harrah
Aircraft Maintenance Information Officer	Capt Paul Siniscal
Aircraft Maintenance Purchase Order Officer	1Lt Joe Holland
Air Force Liaison Office-State Director - NM CAP Wing	Mr. Fred Harsany
AF Reserve Coordinator	Maj Joy Hickman, USAF
AF Reserve Coordinator Asst. IMA to Liaison Office	Capt. Todd Hulsey Maj Joy Hickman, USAF
BLM Flight Coordinator	Lt Col Dannie Roberts
Cadet Programs Director	Lt Col Paul J. Ballmer
Cadet Advisory Council Advisor	Lt Col Paul J. Ballmer
Cadet Advisory Council Chair	C/LtCol Daniel R. Bracken
Cadet Program - Unit & School Program Coordinator	Lt Col Claude Luisada
Cadet Programs Development	Lt Col Jay T. Tourtel
Cadet Activities Officer	Maj Kaycee Gilbert
Cadet Recruiting Officer O-Ride Coordinator	C/Lt Col Dustin Wittman Maj. James W. Steele
Summer Encampment Director	Maj Donna Bracken
Winter Encampment Director	Lt Col Paul J. Ballmer
DDR Coordinator	1Lt Robert Hickey
Cadet DDR Assistant	C/2Lt Nicholas Quintero
IACE Liaison	Maj Joseph Perea, MD
Cadet Glider Programs	Lt Col Roland Dewing **
Assist Glider Program	Maj Stuart Maxon **
Chaplain	LtCol John R. Doughty **

Communications	LtCol Paul R. Cline
Training Officer	LtCol Larry Zentner
Communications Licensing Officer Engineering Officer	Lt Col David Simonson Capt. Stan Nelson
DEA	Capt. Leroy Mclaren
Emergency Services	Lt Col Dave MacLauchlan
ES SAR Officer	LtCol Jon E Hitchcock
ES Admin	2Lt. Angela MacLauchlan
ES Disaster Relief	Lt Col Larry Zentner
CISM Coordinator	Aida Reames
ES Ground Operations	Capt John Grassham
Finance	Lt Col William Brown
Finance Assistant	Lt Col David Gottheimer
Historian	Col James Norvell
Homeland Security	Dennis Manzanares
Inspector General	Lt Col John Green
Legal Officer	Maj Alvin Jones
Assistant Legal Officer	Col Dennis Manzanares
Medical Officer	Maj Joseph Perea, MD
Asst Medical Officer	1Lt Patricia Quick, RN
National Asset Director	Lt Col Jerry Burton
NM Wing Calendar	1Lt. Maria-Lisa Dilda
Operations Director	Capt John Gravel
Operations Assistant -WMIRS	Capt Shirley Kay
AFJROTC FLIGHT POC	Capt Anthony Torres
DEA	Capt Leroy Mclaren
Plans and Programs	Col Dennis Manzanares
Personnel	Col James Norvell
Professional Development Director	Col Dennis Manzanares
Public Affairs Officer	2Lt Norman Reames
Safety Safety Administration	Maj. Joseph Perea, MD Griffyn Lane
Stan/Eval Officer	LtCol Tony Sobol
Director Logistics Supply Officer Assistant	Capt. Shirley Kay Maj. Donna Bracken Zach Rodehaver
Transportation	Capt. Richard Austin
Licensing Officer	Lt Col David Simonson
Asst Transportation Officer	Col Bob Haulenbeek
Web Security Administrator	Lt Col David Simonson
Webmaster	Capt John Gravel

Addendum 5 — NM Wing Squadrons – 2009

SQUADRON NAME- SWR-NM	COMMANDER	Pilots
Alamogordo Composite Squad **SWR-NM 073 Meets:** Monday 1815 to 2015	Capt. Clay Blevins	**2**
Albuquerque Heights Composite Squad **SWR-NM 083 Meets:** Thursday **Time:** 06:45pm	Lt Col Beverly (Pepe) Vito	1
Albuquerque Senior Squadron II **SWR-NM 030 Meets:** Safety: 2nd Wed 7:00 PM Maint: 4th Tues 6:30 pm	1st Lt. Walt Brown	19
Clovis High Plains Composite Squadron **SWR-NM 060 Meets:** 1st Tues. La Quinta Suites, 4521 N. Prince St. **Time: 7:00 pm**	Capt E. Richard Austin	3
Eagle Cadet Squadron ABQ **SWR-NM 012** (**Meets:** Thursday 7 - 9:15 pm	Lt Col Paul J. Ballmer	0
Eagle Deputy Commander of Seniors	Maj Joseph Perea	
Farmington Composite Squad. **SWR-NM 068 Meets:** 1st and 3rd Mond 7- 9:00 pm	Capt. Scott Zenonian **	**4**
Gallup Raptor Composite Squad **SWR-NM 065 Meets:** Thursday 6:30 pm	1Lt Phillip Overgaard	**0**
High Desert Composite Squadron **SWR-NM 085 Meets**: Monday– **6:30 - 9:00** Edgewood Fire Station #1Hwy 344 east of DQ	Capt. Chris Branan	**0**
Las Cruces Composite Squad. **SWR-NM 024 Meets:** 1st & 3rd Thursdays 1900 **Cadets: Every Tuesday - 1830-2030**	Capt. Walter Dutton Deputy Lt Col Judy Licht	3
Los Alamos Composite Squad **SWR-NM 016 Meets:** 3rd Tues 6:00 pm to 7:30 pm	Capt. Annette R. Peters *Annette R. Peters*	**8**
Rio Rancho Composite Squad **SWR-NM 077 Meets:** Every Thursday 7:00 pm	Lt Col David Simonson	**5**
Roswell Composite Squad **SWR-NM 082 Meets:** 1st. Mon at 7-9 pm Hanger 3rd. Sat at 9-12 am	Capt. Stanley A. Nelson	**4**
Santa Fe Composite Squadron **SWR-NM 018** (Senior)**Meets:** 2nd Monday 6:30pm (Cadet)**Meets:** Thursday 6:30	Capt. Pete Manos	**3**
Socorro Composite Squadron **SWR-NM 084 Meets:** Thursday 1830 County Annex Building, 198 Neel Ave	Capt David G. Finley	**0**
Taos Composite Squadron **SWR-NM 06 Meets:** 1st 3rd Sat Taos Airport CAP fac	1Lt Blair Bouchier	3

SQUADRON NAME- SWR-NM	**COMMANDER**	**Pilots**
Thunderbird Composite Squad ABQ **SWR-NM 033 Meets:** Tuesday **Time:** 6:45 -9:15 pm	Capt. Charles Mathews Sr.	1
Group 800 Commander	Lt Col Claude Luisada	
- Group 800 staff member	Lt Col Charles Kreis	1
- Group 800 staff member	Beatrice Chavez	
Eagle Ridge Mid School Cadet Sq **SWR-NM 805 Meets:** During Class Day	Capt Robert L. Will	
Espanola Military Academy Sq **SWR-NM 809 Meets:** During Class Day	Maj. Mark Gonzalez	
St. Therese Middle School Albq **SWR-NM 811 Meets: Thurs. 1730 hours** **Horizon Academy West** **SWR-NM 812 Meets Mon. & Wed.** **Rio Rancho H. S. Cadet Squadron** **SWR-NM 813 Meets: Mon, Tue ,Fri @2:27p** **Garfield Middle School Cadet Squadron SWR-NM 814 Meets: Daily 0930 to 1030** **Kennedy MS in Gallup** **SWR-NM 815**	SM Benjamin Noyce Capt. John Wehner SM Miroslav Jencik SM Randolph A Burton Thomas Payton	

About the Authors

Ted Spitzmiller first joined Civil Air Patrol on Jan. 31, 1958. He attended summer encampment in 1959 at McGuire AFB and had his first orientation flight that year in an Aeronca. He became cadet commander by 1960, and kept his CAP affiliation until joining the Army in 1963.

After his discharge in 1966, he worked for IBM and later at Los Alamos National Laboratory in New Mexico, attaining his commercial pilot's license and flight instructor rating. He rejoined CAP in 1973 and for 20 years was an instructor and check pilot for the Los Alamos Composite Squadron. He took a break from CAP while earning his master's degree in computer information systems, then renewed his membership in 2002 after his retirement. He served the Rio Rancho Falcon Composite Squadron as deputy commander for cadets and as the aerospace education officer. He is a wing check pilot with over 4300 hours of flight time in more than 62 different types of aircraft.

Spitzmiller has also contributed to CAP's School Enrichment Program. As the aerospace external officer for the wing; he makes presentations at schools and organizations in the Albuquerque area.

Gwen D. Sawyer grew up in a CAP family in New Mexico. She became a cadet the first day she was eligible and stayed in the program until the last day she could. After rising through the ranks, she had the honor of being the first cadet in New Mexico Wing to earn the Carl A. Spaatz Award. She credits her time in CAP with helping her be successful in her career as an FAA air traffic controller and manager.

Now retired from the FAA after many years in Oklahoma City, Gwen and her husband, George Bakula, live in Albuquerque, where they are active in church work, enjoy traveling the country and make frequent visits to Texas to see their daughter and grandchildren.

INDEX

A

B

G

H

I

J

K

L

M

N

S

LaVergne, TN USA
25 November 2009

165225LV00003B/23/P

9 781440 181269